D0712298

THE KANTIAN AESTHETIC

The Kantian Aesthetic

From Knowledge to the Avant-Garde

PAUL CROWTHER

OXFORD
UNIVERSITY PRESS

OXFORD
UNIVERSITY PRESS

Great Clarendon Street, Oxford OX2 6DP

Oxford University Press is a department of the University of Oxford.
It furthers the University's objective of excellence in research, scholarship,
and education by publishing worldwide in

Oxford New York

Auckland Cape Town Dar es Salaam Hong Kong Karachi
Kuala Lumpur Madrid Melbourne Mexico City Nairobi
New Delhi Shanghai Taipei Toronto

With offices in

Argentina Austria Brazil Chile Czech Republic France Greece
Guatemala Hungary Italy Japan Poland Portugal Singapore
South Korea Switzerland Thailand Turkey Ukraine Vietnam

Oxford is a registered trade mark of Oxford University Press
in the UK and in certain other countries

Published in the United States
by Oxford University Press Inc., New York

British Library Cataloguing in Publication Data

Data available

Library of Congress Cataloging in Publication Data

Data available

Typeset by Laserwords Private Limited, Chennai, India
Printed in Great Britain
on acid-free paper by
MPG Books Group, Bodmin and King's Lynn, Norfolk

ISBN 978-0-19-957997-6

Contents

Introduction

It is generally recognized that, since the 1970s, work on Kant's aesthetics has at last reached a level of intensity and excellence which approaches that of work done on his epistemology and moral philosophy. Major books and/or papers by Donald Crawford, Paul Guyer, Malcolm Budd, Gary Banham, Henry Allison, Béatrice Longuenesse, Eva Schaper, Salim Kemal, Rudolf Makkreel, Hannah Ginsborg, Antony Savile, Mary McCloskey, Douglas Burnham, Robert Wicks, Rachel Zuckert, and many others, have added inestimably to our understanding of Kant's aesthetics. Amongst these, Guyer's and Allison's works merit particular praise through their quite extraordinary depth of engagement with Kant's thought.

However, this great upsurge of scholarship has come at a price. The price is a widespread *interminablist* tendency in the interpretation of Kant. Interminablist is not at all a peevish characterization. One of the great problems of the *Critique of the Power of Judgment* (hereafter referred to as the 'third *Critique*') is that for every formulation of one of Kant's major ideas, alternative—sometimes contradictory—presentations of the same notion can be often found elsewhere in the text. Kant's major Anglo-American and German commentators then tend to expend a massive amount of interpretative energy in searching out ways to make him read consistently—often by relating his ideas to those found in other works from the Critical corpus. If a possible ground for consistency emerges, then the battle is taken to have been won.

The upshot of this is that Kant's aesthetic is often reduced to interminable toings and froings between his texts without, as it were, the theory being cashed out in terms of what it has the real potential to do—namely, solve general aesthetic problems. Put in a nutshell, interminablism is *the tendency to see Kant's aesthetic theory as the problem to be solved rather than a basis for problem solving*.

This creates two wide-ranging difficulties. On the one hand, the energy expended on making Kant's aesthetics internally consistent distracts from a proper degree of *critical scrutiny and revision* of his key concepts and arguments—i.e., a level of critique which would *maximize* their efficiency in solving problems in general aesthetics. On the other hand, interminablist approaches tend to avoid a sustained use of concrete examples which would show how the aforementioned concepts and arguments both illuminate, and are illuminated by, our living experience of aesthetic phenomena.

Embedded in these difficulties is a more specific worry. Béatrice Longuenesse argues that

The predicate 'beautiful' does not express a reality—namely the positive determination of a thing, known through our senses. Rather it expresses a feeling of pleasure brought about in the judging subject by his own mental activity in apprehending the object. This pleasure, albeit occasioned by the object, is elicited more directly by the receptivity of the judging subject to her own activity.[1]

Rachel Zuckert has drawn attention to similar approaches in other distinguished interpreters of Kant's aesthetics (namely, Henry Allison and Hannah Ginsborg). She then raises a problem that can be taken to apply to Longuenesse, also:

though they are textually grounded, they render Kant's account unsatisfactory as a description of aesthetic experience: [They hold, in effect, that] aesthetic judgment and pleasure are purely self-referential (about themselves/each other/their own universal communicability) and thus peculiarly empty. It is difficult to see why we should believe that this *is* what we're experiencing, claiming, or feeling in aesthetic experience.[2]

The point is, then, that interminablist approaches are unacceptably self-referential. Amplifying Zuckert's points, one might claim that they not only fail to engage with aesthetic phenomena *in concreto* (as noted earlier), but tend, indeed, to *shrink* (and thence distort)

---

[1] Béatrice Longuenesse, 'Kant's Leading Thread in the Analytic of the Beautiful', in Rebecca Kukla (ed.), *Aesthetics and Cognition in Kant's Critical Philosophy* (Cambridge: Cambridge University Press, 2006), 196–7. The mental state that she describes is one of the major Kantian *interminabilia*. Sometimes Kant emphasizes it as the subjective aspect of aesthetic judgement (as in Longuenesse's own characterization), but at other times he focuses on that structure of purposiveness without purpose in the phenomenal manifold which is responsible for stimulating the mental state in question.

[2] Rachel Zuckert, *Kant on Beauty and Biology* (Cambridge: Cambridge University Press, 2007), 189. This is one of the most original and provocative studies of Kant's aesthetics to have appeared in recent years. In particular, Zuckert shows an admirable willingness to illustrate her points with concrete examples.

them so as to fit the—at times profoundly strained—Kantian architectonic.

Interminablist approaches have a further unfortunate consequence.
They tend to be constrained by a narrow concentration on Kant's own
main interest—the theory of taste. His theories of fine art, and the
sublime, in consequence, receive less attention because it is felt that they
are marginal to this main concern.[3]

Now, it is right and proper that Kant's account of taste should occupy
centre-stage in one's *initial* orientation towards his aesthetic theory. This
is because the logical basics of his approach are set out there. However,
in terms of general problems in contemporary aesthetics, the question
of taste and beauty seem rather less central than they once were. Hence,
the energy expended on interpretation within the strict terms of Kant's
Critical aesthetics is problematic in a further sense, in so far as it is
focused on the area of his theory that is no longer of the most pressing
contemporary concern.

It is vital that the points I am making should not be taken as some
sort of blanket dismissal of scholarly exegesis. Rather, I am arguing that,
through interminablism, an opportunity is lost. For it seems a shame
that when so much valuable work is, at last, being done, it tends to
focus on the internal intricacies of Kant's theory, rather than engaging
more directly with more general problems in aesthetics and questions of
method in the understanding of the arts.

These worries might invite the following response. The alternative to
interminablism amounts to little more than a willingness to *revise* Kant.
But why should such revisionism be regarded as a *Kantian* aesthetic?
Professor Allison has observed, judiciously, that the great factors in
the formation of Kant's Critical philosophy are his doctrine of the
transcendental ideality of space and time, the primacy of freedom, and
the purposiveness of nature.[4] However, my own feeling is that whilst
these factors are of the greatest moment in explaining the genesis and
structure of Kant's Critical philosophy per se, they are not decisive for
its general viability—or at least not in relation to aesthetics.

There is, however, a further factor which is *distinctively* Kantian and
which, indeed, could be argued as giving his philosophy its greatest and

---

[3] This is, for example, the position taken by Henry Allison in his book *Kant's Theory of Taste* (Cambridge: Cambridge University Press, 2001), 8.

[4] Ibid. 6. Interestingly, on this same page, Allison notes the difficulties which Kant's own interminable characterizations of 'purposiveness' presented for the writing of *Kant's Theory of Taste*.

most enduring strength—namely, the insight that objective knowledge and the unity of the self are reciprocally correlated—one cannot have the one without the other. And, at the heart of this correlation are judgements which apply fundamental categorial 'pure concepts of the understanding' through the mediation of imagination. This (as I shall show at length in Chapter 1) is the basis of Kant's most sustained and important philosophical argument—the Transcendental Deduction of the Categories.

For Kant, an interplay of understanding and imagination achieved through certain phenomenal forms is also the basis of the pure aesthetic judgement. Indeed, I will go beyond Kant in suggesting that aesthetic judgements of a crude and basic kind are involved in infants' play and have an *enabling* role in the emergence of the categories and empirical concepts as fully achieved cognitive competences.

My own approach, therefore, is Kantian in so far as it centres on the key epistemological factors involved in the Transcendental Deduction. Indeed—and ironic though it may seem—I will take a *cognitivist* approach to Kant's aesthetics.[5] This approach emphasizes the importance of the categories and transcendental schemata in mediating the pure aesthetic judgement. Such judgements will be shown to constellate around cognitive exploration based on factors that are key conditions of objective knowledge, and of the unity of the self. This linkage is deeply resisted by most commentators.[6] But, through it, the meta-aesthetic and normative scope of Kant's theory can be established in compelling terms.

This being said, Kantian epistemology cannot provide a sufficient basis for aesthetic judgements. In particular, it cannot provide adequate grounds for Kant's claims concerning the universal validity of taste, nor for his theory of fine art. We need, therefore, an additional component in order to give his theory viability. Fortunately, as we shall see, at certain

---

[5] In this study, I give substance to the deep structures of the pure aesthetic judgement's general harmonizing of imagination and understanding per se, and explain why Kant takes this to be recognizable through the feeling of pleasure that it embodies.

[6] One important exception is Rudolph A. Makkreel in his *Imagination and Interpretation in Kant: The Hermeneutic Import of Kant's Critique of Judgment* (Chicago and London: University of Chicago Press, 1990). However, Makkreel does not give much significant illustration of what the role of the categories might amount to, *in concreto*. Malcolm Budd—whose incisive analyses are admirably free of interminablism—also recognizes that the categories must be involved in the pure aesthetic judgement, but again does not elaborate on this in any detail. See esp. p. 6 of the first instalment of his 'Delight in the Natural World: Kant on the Aesthetic Appreciation of Nature', *British Journal of Aesthetics*, 38 (1998), 1–18.

points in Kant's conception of taste, and in his linkage of genius and fine art, the importance of *a horizon of critical comparison* becomes apparent. By linking Kant's epistemological criteria to this critical horizon it is possible to establish his aesthetic in viable and comprehensive terms.

To show this, I will adopt a relatively *open* exegetical approach. This is one which favours economy in how Kant's broad outlines of argument are interpreted, and the maximization of their potential for solving general problems in aesthetics. A significant level of critique and/or willingness to revise concepts and arguments which diminish this viability are unavoidable consequences of this.

A Kantian aesthetic on these lines has great potential in the contemporary context. It is an approach which sees aesthetic phenomena not as culturally relative, pleasing marginalia to the main areas of human experience, but as profound *expressions of factors which are basic to our knowledge of world and self*. Indeed, Kant's emphasis on imagination and understanding in knowledge is not some hangover from eighteenth-century faculty psychology but one that provides an effective working basis for an account of cognition in general.

As noted earlier, the cognitive concepts involved here are central equally to aesthetic judgement. This continuity between the conditions of knowledge and the aesthetic is of the utmost worth. For, when linked to the aforementioned horizon of critical comparison, it enables a robust refutation of widespread contemporary relativism in questions of aesthetics. It can even negotiate many of those avant-garde works which are commonly supposed to have destroyed the significance of aesthetic criteria in the experience and definition of art.

In the present work, then, the Kantian aesthetic is expounded and revised so that it engages with and, I hope, solves general problems in the relation between epistemology and aesthetics. In particular, I will highlight the importance of his theories of adherent beauty, fine art, and the sublime in terms of their contemporary relevance.

The book is organized, more specifically, as follows. Chapter 1 is a detailed account and revision into effective working order of Kant's second version of the Transcendental Deduction from the *Critique of Pure Reason*. This complex argument is where he attempts to establish that basic correlation of objective knowledge and the unity of the self, which is achieved through the use of categorial concepts. It is the place, also, where Kant makes vital connections between understanding and imagination which are basic to cognition, and decisive for aesthetic judgement. I develop the argument by using insights from Gareth

Evans, and by thinking through how Kant's approach might be framed in ontogenetic terms.

In Chapter 2, a detailed analysis of Kant's doctrine of the 'schematism' from the *Critique of Pure Reason* is offered. This doctrine is where Kant gives a richer and deeper account of the cognitive role of imagination. I consider the significance of both transcendental and empirical schemata in terms of their role in objective knowledge, and knowledge of self.

The first two chapters, then, establish the centrality of imagination and understanding in terms of the correlation of objective, and self-knowledge. By expounding—and, where necessary, revising and extending—Kant, a philosophically viable broad theory of knowledge is established. Its components are decisive also for Kant's aesthetic theory. In Chapter 3, I begin to make the relevant connections by outlining his basic strategy in the third *Critique*, and then offering a detailed analysis of how the relation between imagination and understanding forms the basis of the 'pure aesthetic judgement' (or 'judgement of taste').

This focuses on what I call the *emergent judgement of reflection*. A special emphasis is given to examples which illuminate what the relation between imagination and understanding actually amounts to in the experience of aesthetic forms. More specifically, these examples bring out the significant mediating role of the categories and transcendental schemata in the pure aesthetic judgement.

Chapter 4 considers the privileged epistemological status which Kant assigns to the judgement of taste. The complex arguments with which Kant attempts to establish its 'universal validity' are expounded and criticized in detail, and then presented in a more viable form on the basis of a development of Kant's important insights concerning a horizon of critical comparison.

In Chapter 5, Kant's notion of adherent beauty is analysed. It is argued that in linking beauty and perfection the notion offers both insights concerning the limits of the aesthetic and a basis for understanding perfection as an aesthetic concept with contemporary interest.

Chapter 6 explores Kant's theory of fine art at length. I consider the cognitive structure of the 'aesthetic idea' and, in contrast to most commentators, explore its link to 'originality' and 'exemplariness' in great detail. This means putting an emphasis on the comparative critical and historical horizon in which works of fine art are created and judged. An especially detailed account is offered as to how this might be understood in the specific context of the history of painting. The theory is developed also with a view to negotiating the specific problematics of works of an avant-garde nature.[7]

In Chapter 7, I complete my account of the Kantian aesthetic with a detailed analysis of his theory of the sublime. The chapter follows the general approach first set out in my book *The Kantian Sublime: From Morality to Art*. I discuss the mathematical and dynamical modes of the sublime, and the status of the sublime as an artistic concept. In the course of this, however, I make important and extensive refinements to my original approach. This allows the sublime to be integrated more satisfactorily within the general Kantian aesthetic.

I end the book with a short Finale reiterating the more general significance of the strategy that informs the work as a whole.

Part 1 of Chapter 1 is a much revised version of material from 'Judgment, Self-Consciousness, and Imagination: Kant's Transcendental Deduction and Beyond', in H. Parret (ed.), *Kant's Aesthetic Theory* (Berlin: Gruyter Verlag, 1998), 117–35. Chapter 5 is a revised version of 'The Claims of Perfection: A Revisionary Defence of Kant's Theory of Dependent Beauty', *International Philosophical Quarterly*, 26 (1986), 61–74.

---

[7] It should be emphasized that I concentrate attention on the relation between Kant's aesthetics and the works themselves, rather than addressing the use made of Kantian concepts by Lyotard, Greenberg, and others in their more general discussions of modernity and related topics in the arts. In some respects, these discussions raise the opposite problem to interminablism. They use Kant at a level of generality that loses all real bearings in his actual structures of argument. I have already said as much as I can say on Lyotard's difficulties here in Part 2 of my *Critical Aesthetics and Postmodernism* (Oxford: Clarendon Press, 1993). It should be noted that Lyotard's use of Kant in cultural theory is very different from his more academic study of Kant, *Lessons on the Analytic of the Sublime*, trans. Elizabeth Rottenberg (Stanford, Calif.: Stanford University Press, 1994). This book is as interminablist as anything produced by the Analytic tradition. I will deal with the broader questions raised by Greenberg's use of Kant, and the more sustained and ambitious use of him in Thierry de Duve's *Kant After Duchamp* (Cambridge, Mass. and London: MIT Press, 1996), in a work-in-progress entitled, provisionally, The Phenomenology of Artistic Change.

1

The Transcendental Deduction: Objective Knowledge and the Unity of Self-Consciousness

INTRODUCTION

Kant's aesthetic theory obtains its great strength from two factors. The first is that he provides highly viable characterizations of the logical status of aesthetic and artistic judgements. The second—and it is this factor which gives his theory the *utmost* philosophical depth—is that he is able to link these judgements to the most fundamental aspects of our basic cognitive relationship to the world.

At the heart of this linkage is Kant's recognition that the aesthetic domain enhances the interaction between *understanding* and *imagination*—two logically distinct but phenomenologically inseparable competences. Their reciprocal relation enables objective knowledge of both self and world. The aesthetic is not some, as it were, luxury experience, but one whose grounds engage cognitive competences that are basic to the conditions of knowledge, as such.

Now, whilst Kant's arguments concerning the logical status of aesthetic judgements have been found compelling by many thinkers, his broader linkage to understanding and imagination appear rather more contentious. Indeed, those capacities themselves might be claimed to be little more than an idiosyncratic feature of his mature 'Critical' philosophy, with no validity outwith that context. And it might seem also that this context is *highly* suspect by virtue of a major philosophical problem.

It consists in the fact that Kant holds the understanding and imagination and, indeed, space and time (as forms of intuition) to be *constitutive* of experience. In effect, they *create* the phenomenal world, by giving objective form to a mysterious unknowable realm of 'noumena'.

To say the least, the positing of 'noumena' has been found problematic by the great majority of Kant's interpreters and, even if one were inclined to defend the positing it would raise issues that would require a book-length study in itself, to be dealt with in even the most minimal terms.

However, it is possible to approach Kant in a way which does not necessitate such a problematic engagement. In this respect, one can argue that Kant gets it right in general terms concerning those capacities necessary for *objective knowledge* of the world and the self, but one need not accept the problematic notion that these capacities actually *create* the objectivity of phenomena, as such.

More specifically, this approach holds that *there is a realm of items in space and time that exist independently of their being known, but that if we are to know them the capacities for understanding and imagination, and the unity of self-consciousness described by Kant, are necessary conditions of such knowledge, and are so on very much the lines for which he argues.*

To put this another way, there really are 'things' out there, and the explanation of *what enables us to know them as things connected with one another in unified terms* is of the very profoundest philosophical importance. Kantian *epistemology* can provide the requisite explanation without bringing on board the dubious *ontological* commitment that temporal and spatial forms of things should be regarded as no more than aspects of the human cognitive apparatus.

I shall now offer an initial characterization of the general structure of Kant's philosophical position made with the foregoing qualifications in mind. I will then introduce the complex and special status of the Transcendental Deduction.

At the heart of Kant's 'Critical' philosophy is a distinction between the role of sensibility and the role of the intellect in knowledge. The role of the former is both receptive and mildly active. Through it, particular items ('intuitions') are distinguished, arranged in relation to time, and (if they are 'external') arranged in relation to space also. The function of the intellect (or 'understanding' as Kant more often terms it) is to subsume this manifold of sensible intuitions under concepts, so that it can be recognized *as* a particular item, set of items, event, or sequence of events, or whatever. Sensibility and understanding, in concert, form the *representative power*—the very basis of judgement and knowledge.

The core of the understanding consists of those 'pure concepts' or 'categories' which are fundamental to objective knowledge. Kant holds that there are twelve of them. They are unity, plurality, totality, reality, limitation, negation, substance and accident, cause and effect, reciprocity, existence, possibility, and necessity.[1]

Kant's Transcendental Deduction of the 'categories' is central to his epistemology. To understand the Deduction, it is worth defining first the meaning of its constituent terms. For Kant, 'transcendental' means those factors which are necessarily involved in knowledge of world and self, or in determining the limits of such knowledge The term 'deduction' is used by him on an analogy with its legal sense—as the justification of an entitlement. The task of the Transcendental Deduction (in the very broadest terms) is to show that the categories are fundamental in the sense of being *necessary* conditions of any possible experience.

Kant's proof of this claim is enormously complex and takes two very different forms in the first and second editions of *The Critique of Pure Reason*. Not surprisingly, this complexity is matched by depth of controversy in the interpretation of what his arguments are intended to show, and what they actually achieve.[2]

---

[1] See Kant, *The Critique of Pure Reason*, trans. N. Kemp-Smith (London, Macmillan, 1973), B102–B116, pp. 111–19 for more detailed characterizations of these.

[2] Significant recent readings of the Deduction include Henry Allison, *Kant's Transcendental Idealism: An Interpretation and Defense* (New Haven, Conn. and London: Yale University Press, 2004), chap. 7; Paul Guyer, 'The Transcendental Deduction of the Categories', included as chap. 4 in his important edited collection *The Cambridge Companion to Kant* (Cambridge: Cambridge University Press, 1992). It should be noted that Allison has reservations and Guyer is avowedly sceptical as to Kant's success in the Deduction as such. A complex and in some respects more sympathetic approach can be found in chaps 3–6 of Patricia Kitcher's *Kant's Transcendental Psychology* (New York: Oxford University Press, 1990). Kitcher's account is one which addresses both A and B arguments in great detail, and is particularly attentive to their historical context as well as to the transcendental psychology itself. Eckart Foster's edited collection *Kant's Transcendental Deductions: The Three Critiques and the Opus Postumum* (Stanford, Calif.: Stanford University Press, 1989) addresses the first *Critique* and other works. For present purpose, see esp. the essays by Dieter Henrich and Paul Guyer, and the reply to Guyer by P. F. Strawson. Dieter Henrich's important paper 'The Proof-Structure of Kant's Transcendental Deduction', included in R. C. S. Walker (ed.), *Kant on Pure Reason* (Oxford: Oxford University Press, 1982), 66–81 has had great influence on interpretations of the Deduction. More specifically, his theory that the Transcendental Deduction involves a single proof in two major steps has found wide acceptance. However, even this influential theory must be approached with caution.

He is, I think, right to favour the second edition (or 'B' version) of the Deduction, if only for the fact that its very existence shows that Kant was not completely happy with his first (or 'A') formulation. What is more problematic is Henrich's account of the supposed steps

My approach will hold that the Transcendental Deduction centres on showing that *the objective unification of a sensible manifold achieved through the categories and the objective unity of self-consciousness* (or, as Kant sometimes terms this latter notion, the 'pure' or 'original unity' of 'apperception') are reciprocally dependent. One cannot have the one without the other.

To establish these claims, I shall in Part 1 of this Chapter offer an analysis of Kant's arguments as presented in the revised, 'B' version of the Deduction. I will then, in Part 2 make some critical points and indicate how these might be dealt with—initially by reference to some insights from Gareth Evans. These will enable me to formulate a three-stage reconstruction of Kant's major argument, culminating in

of argument in the Deduction. The first step centres on the fact that (in Henrich's words) 'wherever there is unity, there is a relation which can be thought according to the categories' (Walker, *Kant on Pure Reason*, 70). But Henrich then notes that 'This statement, however, does not yet clarify for us the *range within which* unitary intuitions can be found' (ibid.). For this reason, a second—generalizing—step in the proof is required so as to show that 'every given manifold without exception is subject to the categories' (ibid.). Henrich's interpretation is provocative and searching, and gives emphasis to the fact that Kant explicitly draws two formal conclusions in sections 20 and 26 respectively. However, the pattern of argument between these sections is much more convoluted than allowed for in the 'two-steps' approach. This, in itself, might suggest that the two conclusions just noted are points where Kant, as it were, draws intellectual breath, and are not the substantial points of argumentative gravity which Henrich takes them to be. Indeed, there is a strong case for arguing that Henrich's approach runs aground through *underplaying* a major factor in the Deduction—namely, the significance of 'pure apperception'. My difference with Henrich in this respect has been brought out, indirectly, by Henry Allison in the first edition of *Kant's Transcendental Idealism*. He points to a distinction between the 'objective validity' of the categories and their 'objective reality'. The former pertains to their role as necessary conditions of objective judgement; the latter pertains to the way in which they exist as actual features of our cognitive framework. In my opinion, Henrich, Allison himself (to some degree), and the bulk of commentators in the Anglo-American tradition of analytic philosophy unduly privilege the objective validity of the categories. (This is probably because of a mistrust of 'transcendental psychology' arising from the legacy of Wittgenstein's behaviourist tendencies.) I favour the objective reality dimension rather more, if only because claims to validity can only be *enabled* through the exercise of cognitive structures which are basic to being a finite rational subject. Without such structures, we have ambitious assertions and logical connections, but no grounds for justifying their claims to objective validity. Kant's emphasis on the original unity of apperception and the transcendental imagination is, I would suggest, a tacit acknowledgement that claims to objective validity must be mediated by the objective reality of real cognitive capacities in the subject. This reality is inseparable from the unity of 'pure apperception'. For the distinction between objective validity and objective reality, see Allison, *Kant's Transcendental Idealism*, 133–6.

the experiential necessity of the Kantian categories. Detailed avenues of justification for this final stage will form the substance of Part 3 (again making significant use of ideas from Evans). I will then proceed to a Conclusion which looks ahead to future chapters.

PART 1

Kant begins his argument with the claim that

The manifold of representation can be given in an intuition which is purely sensible, that is, nothing but receptivity: and the form of this intuition can lie a priori in our faculty of representation, without being anything more than the mode in which the subject is affected.[3]

This is, in effect, a re-statement of Kant's major position in the 'Transcendental Aesthetic' of the first *Critique*. All experience is given in time and (in most cases) space. Time and space are 'forms of intuition', that is to say, receptive structures inherent in subjectivity itself. Through them, the human subject is affected by that which is other than himself or herself. The second step in Kant's argument consists in a preliminary outline of the other major structuring capacity to which the manifold of sensible material must be subjected in order to constitute experience. In this respect we are told that

the combination of a manifold in general . . . is an act of spontaneity of the faculty of representation; and since this faculty, to distinguish it from sensibility, must be entitled understanding, all combination—be we conscious of it or not, be it a combination of the manifold of intuition, empirical or non-empirical, or of various concepts—is an act of the understanding.[4]

Kant further declares that

To this act the general title 'synthesis' may be assigned, as indicating that we cannot represent to ourselves anything as combined in the object which we have not ourselves previously combined . . .[5]

The thrust of Kant's initial statements are clear. In order to have experience, we must be able to receive a manifold of sensible intuitions and combine (i.e., 'synthesize') these through the understanding's

---

[3] Kant, *The Critique of Pure Reason*, trans. N. Kemp-Smith (London: Macmillan, 1973), B.130, 151.
[4] Ibid.   [5] Ibid.

spontaneous activity. However, Kant then complicates matters by remarking that 'the concept of combination includes, besides the concept of the manifold and of its synthesis, also the concept of the unity of the manifold'.[6] As I read him, Kant's point here is that in order for the understanding to combine the manifold of sensible intuitions there must exist some further principle of cohesion—the 'unity of the manifold' per se. What makes Kant's position so difficult to interpret is his further remark that

Combination is representation of the synthetic unity of the manifold. The representation of this unity cannot therefore, arise out of the combination. On the contrary it is what by adding itself to the representation of the manifold, first makes possible the concept of the combination.[7]

He goes on to point out, explicitly, that the unity in question here is not that of the categories, because their application already presupposes 'combination'. I would suggest that many of the ambiguities and difficulties of the 'B' Transcendental Deduction stem from this claim. It seems to imply that the synthetic unity of the manifold is a further *logically independent* condition that is required for knowledge of objects, over and above the having of a sensible manifold, and the connective activity of the understanding.

This is not wholly accurate, in that it turns out that whilst this extra ingredient is indeed a condition of the understanding's synthetic activity, it is nevertheless—in an extremely complex way—also a function of it. The elaboration of these two aspects constitute, respectively, the third and fourth stages of Kant's main line of argument. I shall now consider them in turn.

First, the synthetic unity of the manifold as a condition of the understanding's activity. Kant restates this, initially, as 'The Original Synthetic Unity of Apperception'. The following passage gives a useful summary of the relation between this and the understanding:

all unification of representations demands unity of consciousness that alone constitutes the relation of representations to an object, and therefore their objective validity and the fact that they are modes of knowledge; and upon it therefore rests the very possibility of the understanding.[8]

---

[6] Kant, *The Critique of Pure Reason*, trans. N. Kemp-Smith (London: Macmillan, 1973), B 130, 152.   [7] Ibid. B 130–1, 152.
[8] Ibid. B 137, 154.

Here Kant is making the key point that the understanding can only unify a manifold (and thence constitute objective experience) in so far as it is a function of a deeper unity.

The unity in question here is, of course, not the category of unity but rather self-consciousness itself. This mode of consciousness should not be identified with empirical states of self-awareness wherein we are explicitly aware of ourselves as being such and such a person. It is *much* more fundamental; and can be best described as the very *capacity* to ascribe experiences to oneself.

What makes this capacity for self-ascription so decisive is that we have many experiences without being explicitly self-conscious of the fact that we are having them. These moments, however, do not function as gaps or fissures in self-consciousness. For, even if we were not explicitly aware of ourselves in the course of such moments, we could have become so aware. Every normal conscious state of a person admits the possibility of being prefixed with a thought to the effect 'I am thinking/perceiving/imagining this'.

The original unity of apperception, then, is the sheer capacity to ascribe experiences to oneself. Without this capacity, the understanding could not synthesize manifolds. Intuitions can only be collected and combined in a unity; in so far as the agent of combination (i.e., the human subject) itself has unity of consciousness. The capacity for self-ascription of experiences is the basis of this unity. Now the question arises as to how this capacity is itself possible. This brings us to the fourth major stage in Kant's Transcendental Deduction. It centres on the claim that the

act of understanding by which the manifold of given representations (be they intuitions or concepts) is brought under one apperception, is the logical function of judgment . . . All the manifold, therefore, so far as it is given in a single intuition, is determined in respect of one of the logical functions of judgment, and is thereby brought into one consciousness. Now the categories are just these functions of judgment . . .[9]

Kant's point here is that the capacity to ascribe experiences arises fundamentally through the application of the categories. But *why* should this be so? Unfortunately this key question is answered only indirectly by Kant. However, his previous and subsequent observations point in the following direction. The subsumptive and discriminative functions

9 Ibid. B 143, 160.

of judgement per se involve a synthesis of representations according to rules. But, in order for rules to be followed it is presupposed that they be situated in a context which allows operational stability.

This is the function of the categories. They are a framework whose embodiment in particular judgements unifies and stabilizes the manifold in general terms, as well as in terms of the specific representations involved. Whether one is explicitly aware of it or not, a judgement can only be made in so far as it embodies some aspect of this general unity. The categories are basic conditions for knowledge of objects.

Now the key point which must be added to this is that, as pure principles of the understanding, the application of the categories is a 'spontaneous' act of the subject (i.e., produced by he or she rather than derived from some external source). This means that in unifying the manifold through the categories the subject engages in activity which continuously affirms its own identity *as* subject. The self, in other words, becomes aware of its own unity only in so far as it can systematically exercise its capacity to unify the manifold; and this necessarily centres on the use of the categories.

The first four stages of Kant's Transcendental Deduction, then, culminate in the following position. All experience presupposes original synthetic unity of apperception (i.e., the capacity to ascribe experiences to oneself) and this is tied to the understanding's capacity to unify manifolds through the application of the categories.

Now earlier on I noted that many of the Deduction's puzzles stem from Kant's treating the original synthetic unity of apperception as logically independent—that is, a requirement over and above the synthetic activity of the subject. In the most general philosophical terms, it is. For at various points in the Deduction Kant countenances the possibility of an intuitive intelligence: 'An understanding which through its self-consciousness could supply to itself the manifold of intuition—an understanding, that is to say, through whose representation the object of the representation should at the same time exist.'[10] An understanding such as this would not need the capacity to ascribe experiences to itself, since everything it was conscious of would simply be the product of its own cognition. *For a finite subject such as a human being, however, matters are radically different.* Here the business of understanding is not to produce representations but to organize what, through sensibility, is

[10] Kant, *The Critique of Pure Reason*, trans. N. Kemp-Smith (London: Macmillan, 1973), B 138–9, 157.

given to it from an external source. Self-consciousness, in other words, is only possible in so far as the unifying subject, through its activity, distinguishes between that which is its own, and that which is external to it or which exceeds its cognitive purview.

In the context of a finite subject, however, this capacity to ascribe experiences to oneself and the capacity to give objective unity to manifolds are (in ways to be described) *reciprocally dependent* on one another. It is only in a more general philosophical context of intuitive intellects, that they can be regarded as separate.

At this point, then, Kant holds that, in the most general terms, the capacity to ascribe experiences to oneself, and the capacity to unify manifolds through the categories, are, in a finite subject, directly correlated. Put in even more general terms, the unity of the self and the objective world are ontologically reciprocal. One cannot give a full definition of the one without giving a full definition of the other. This is the point of far-reaching philosophical significance which the Deduction is striving to establish.

Interestingly, however, whilst Kant has gone through what I have identified as the four main stages of his arrangement by §21, he does not begin to draw appropriate conclusions of the kind just noted until §§26 and 27. The reason for this is that the trajectory of Kant's arguments is extremely general. He is addressing the objective dimension of the self and the world's structural correlation. In §§24 and 25, he fills in the gaps by a fifth stage of argument which looks much more closely at the subjective aspect of this correlation. Specifically, he is concerned with the question of exactly *how* the application of the categories determines the subject's sensibility.

At first sight, this strategy may seem puzzling. For, given that experience is a function of the understanding's unifying of manifolds presented by sensibility, what more really needs to be added to the account which Kant has already offered?

The answer is *much more*. Kant's organization of the first *Critique* is one which expounds the structure of sensibility and that of the understanding successively. This sometimes gives the impression that the function of these faculties is, ontologically speaking, that of different stages in a process. Of course, they are not. Kant needs, therefore, to explain the real ontological ground of the unity of finite consciousness in more detail, by describing how the application of the categories not only unifies the manifold, but does so by (at the same time) determining the conditions under which the manifold is presented—that is, the subject's own sensibility.

Kant's means of showing this centre on the 'transcendental synthesis of imagination'—or, as he sometimes terms it, the 'figurative synthesis'. By reference to the transcendental role of imagination, Kant is able to distinguish between the logical and ontological status of the categories. At the level of theory, they are simply intellectual or logical enti-ties—essential rules for the unifying of manifolds. However, at the level of practice or concrete cognition, synthesis cannot take place in logical terms alone. It must be mediated by further capacity: that of imagination.

For Kant, imagination is not simply a capacity for reproducing images of items or events on the basis of recollection or association. Rather, it is the very capacity to produce and use imagery itself. Kant describes this generative power as 'the faculty of representing in intuition an object that is *not itself* present'.[11] The reason why Kant regards this as so important is that through mediation by the imagination the understanding's synthetic activity is made 'figurative' or concrete. It is able, as it were, 'to get a hold on' the manifold of intuition by directly determining the subject's sensibility, or, more specifically, his or her 'inner sense' of time.

The links which Kant makes between this figurative synthesis and temporality are, unfortunately, not set out in the requisite detail. I shall, however, now try to develop them more fully. A useful starting-point is Kant's observation that 'Inner sense . . . contains the mere form of intuition, but without combination of the manifold in it, and therefore so far contains no determinate intuition'.[12]

The point here, one presumes, is that a manifold presented in time alone would be a mere heterogeneous flow. There would be no specific sense of moment, or of intelligible succession. To generate such order requires connective activity from the understanding; but, more than this, it requires a capacity to recall what has been and project what might yet come. Without this ability to draw on what is not immediately present, there could be no awareness of the present itself. There could be no *attention*.

Imagination therefore is a precondition of experience. Now, Kant holds that when the categories are applied they do so through the me-diation of imagination. They are able to unify the manifold through, at

---

[11] Kant, *The Critique of Pure Reason*, trans. N. Kemp-Smith (London: Macmillan, 1973), B 151, 165.   [12] Ibid. B 154, 166.

the same time, unifying the conditions under which the subject receives it—i.e., his or her sense of time. Kant's descriptions of this (whilst following the broad trajectory described in the previous paragraph) are, however, somewhat difficult. Consider the following crucial footnote.

Motion . . . considered as the describing of a space, is a pure act of the successive synthesis of the manifold in outer intuition in general by means of the productive imagination . . .[13]

It is clear from the main text that the 'describing of a space' which Kant mentions here can be a perceptual process, and involves the understanding and (therefore) the categories. This suggests that its synthetic activity, the understanding, stimulates and draws on the imagination. It can only carry out its identificatory and discriminatory functions in so far as it generates a temporal framework of ordered succession or continuity. Through this, intuitions are able to endure from moment to moment in an intelligible schema of encounterability and re-encounterability. Imagination, in other words, provides a capacity for attention, recall, and projection—a tracking procedure—whereby the categories can temporally stabilize intuitions and thence enable the identification of patterns of sameness and difference amongst them so as to confer objective unity upon the sensible manifold.

Now, if this was all that Kant was wishing to establish through the transcendental synthesis of imagination, the last substantive arguments of the Transcendental Deduction would, in effect, be a kind of general prologue to the schematism section. (There Kant considers the function of imagination in relation to the application of particular concepts—most notably, of course, the individual categories. I will discuss this in great detail in the next chapter.)

However, the transcendental synthesis of imagination is much more than such a prologue. The reason why is that it is not only central to the general application of the categories, but also to the pure synthetic unity of apperception. The decisive passage is as follows.

I exist as an intelligence which is conscious solely of its powers of combination; but in respect of the manifold which it has come to combine I am subjected to a limiting condition (entitled inner sense), namely that this combination can be made intuitable only according to relations of time, which lie entirely outside the concepts of understanding, strictly regarded. Such an intelligence,

---

[13] Ibid. B 155, 166.

therefore, can know itself only as it appears to itself in respect of an intuition which is not intellectual . . .[14]

Kant's point here is that human subjectivity does not consist purely of understanding. It consists rather of the understanding's combination of a manifold external to the subject, and involves, therefore, both understanding *and* sensible receptivity. Hence, if human self-consciousness is a function of the subject's connective activity, then it must be generated, specifically, by the understanding's action on sensibility's most fundamental mode—inner sense. This, as we have seen, is precisely what is involved when the understanding engages the transcendental synthesis of imagination. Through it, the subject is able to intuit itself *as* subject.

It is important to be clear about the scope of intuition used in this context, in so far as it has both conceptual implications, which Kant does not develop, and ontological implications, which he does. First, the conceptual implications. As I have already argued, the importance for the transcendental synthesis of imagination is that, through it, the understanding is able to stabilize the temporal flow of intuitions in terms of successiveness and continuity. Now, although Kant does not remark upon the fact, similar considerations must apply in relation to the pure synthetic unity of apperception. For we could not ascribe experiences to ourselves if we did not have a clear sense of our relation to present, past, and future.

Again, this is precisely what is achieved through the understanding's determination of inner sense through the transcendental synthesis of imagination. At the heart of the 'I think' in the finite subject is an intuition involving a present attentiveness to an object of thought or perception; and this is only definable in so far as the subject can, through imagination, recall its past and project its possible future perceptual positions in relation to this and other such objects. Imagination, in other words, is the basis of that sense of temporal continuity which makes self-ascription of experiences possible.

In the second version of the Transcendental Deduction, Kant does not develop these conceptual points. Rather, his orientation is much more ontological. Specifically, he emphasizes the causal effect of understanding upon inner sense. Consider the following passage.

Now in order to know ourselves, there is required in addition to the act of thought, which brings the manifold of every possible intuition to the unity

[14] Kant, *The Critique of Pure Reason*, trans. N. Kemp-Smith (London: Macmillan, 1973), B 158–9, 169.

of apperception, a determinate mode of intuition, whereby this manifold is given; it therefore follows that although my existence is not indeed appearance (still less mere illusion), the determination of my existence can take place only in conformity with the form of inner sense, according to the special mode in which the manifold, which I combine, is given in inner intuition.[15]

Kant's point here is that whilst (in terms of his broadest philosophical position) the finite self is not mere appearance, it can only know itself *through* its appearances; or more specifically, by means of the production of appearances through inner sense. The action of the understanding's synthetic activity upon the subject's sense of time is, of course, the foundation of this. As Kant puts it 'we intuit ourselves only as we are inwardly affected by ourselves . . .'[16]

The concept of inward affection is decisive for Kant's notion of the self. It provides a kind of criterion of *belonging*, wherein that which defines discursive subjectivity per se—the understanding—is inseparably bound up with the special condition of finite human subjectivity—i.e., inner sense. One could say that through the 'I think' as such we know *that* we are, and that through the understanding's determination of inner sense this thought is tied to intuitions which convey a full sense of *what* we are.

Kant unfortunately does not say much more about what these intuitions amount to, at this point. This is why (a little earlier) I spelt out the logical implications of his use of the term intuition. These, we will recall, centre on the importance of temporal continuity—the subject's ability to define a present through reference to its own past and possible futures. One presumes, therefore, that to have an intuition of oneself involves continuity in our representations—a continuity which, as we have seen, is a function of the understanding's determination of inner sense through the transcendental synthesis of imagination.

Let me now briefly summarize the stages and substance of Kant's Transcendental Deduction. The first stage is his reiteration of the position established in the Transcendental Aesthetic—namely, that all experience is given in temporal and (usually) spatial terms, and that these forms of sensible receptivity are characteristics of subjectivity—rather than things in themselves.

The second stage consists in the claim, that, in order for experience to be constituted, a further element is required—namely, the connective synthesis performed by the spontaneous activity of the understanding.

---

[15] Ibid. B 157–8, 168–9.   [16] Ibid. B 156, 168.

Kant's third stage of argument is much more complex, for he claims that, in addition to the synthetic activity of the understanding, experience presupposes a further feature. He characterizes this as 'The Original Synthetic Unity of Apperception'—i.e., the capacity to ascribe experiences to oneself.

What makes Kant's exposition especially difficult is that having initially stated this as though such unity of self were a condition of the understanding's activity, it turns out, in the fourth stage of his argument, that this relation is, in fact, one of ontological reciprocity. One can only unify a manifold in so far as one is a unified self, but one can only be unified in so far as through the categories one can engage in spontaneous acts of intellectual unification. The two capacities are correlated. One cannot have knowledge of an objective world without unity of self-consciousness, and one cannot have unity of self-consciousness except through knowledge of an objective world.

The fifth and final stage of Kant's argument involves a phenomenological analysis of what is involved in such exercise. Specifically, he identifies the transcendental synthesis of imagination as a mediating capacity which enables the understanding to determine inner sense. Through imagination, we can recall the past, project the future, and thus define a present object of attention. In this way a framework of linear temporal continuity is generated. Understanding is, thereby, able to unify the manifold, and, in so doing, intuit itself as the ongoing activity of a unified self.

We are thus led to Kant's formal conclusion concerning the Transcendental Deduction: §26 is headed in such a way as to make one accept that a conclusion is about to be given. However, in practice Kant largely reiterates previous arguments and worries, giving some emphasis to the notion of apprehension (which is, in fact, much more adequately described in the first version of the Deduction, as the means whereby the manifold is 'run through, and held together'[17]). It is only in the 'Brief

---

[17] Ibid. A 99, 131. For a succinct review of issues pertaining to Kant's theory of imagination, see J. M. Young, 'Kant's View of Imagination', *Kant-Studien*, 79 (1988), 140–64. A comprehensive and interesting approach can be found in Sarah Gibbon, *Kant's Theory of Imagination: Bridging Gaps in Judgement and Experience* (Oxford: Clarendon Press, 1994). This book explores the role of imagination throughout Kant's Critical corpus. Rudolf A. Makkreel achieves a similar level of comprehensiveness but manages also to negotiate with broader philosophical issues in the outer chapters of his book *Imagination and Interpretation in Kant: The Hermeneutical Import of the Critique of Judgment* (Chicago and London: University of Chicago Press, 1990).

Outline' at the end of §27 that Kant offers his (awkwardly expressed) substantive conclusion. As he puts it

The deduction is the exposition of the pure concepts of the understanding . . . as principles of the possibility of experience—the principles being here taken, as the *determination* of appearances in space and time *in general*, and this determination, in turn, as ultimately following from the *original* synthetic unity of apperception, as the form of the understanding in its relation to space and time . . .[18]

On these terms, therefore, the categories—as pure principles of human understanding—are conditions of any possible experience. This is because their exercise determines appearance objectively in respect of space and time in accordance with the original synthetic unity of apperception. This unity in turn, however, just *is* the understanding in active relation to space and time through (though, to his discredit, Kant does not specifically mention it here) the mediation of imagination.

Putting all this in even more general terms, the upshot of Kant's Deduction is that the experience of an objective world and the unity of subjective experience are ontologically reciprocal. We cannot have the one experience unless we are also able to have the other. Without the exercise of the categories, in other words, there could be no object or subject of experience.

PART 2

I shall now make some critical points. A great weakness in Kant's account is the level of generality at which the Deduction is conducted. As well as opening up all sorts of interpretative ambiguities, it has a very worrying lack of specificity in terms of what roles are played by individual categories in that general correlation of objective and subjective which is at the centre of Kant's arguments. In the 'Metaphysical Deduction' (which comes a little earlier in the *Critique of Pure Reason*) Kant deduces his twelve categories on the basis of an Aristotelian conception of the forms of judgement. Even overlooking the limitations of the Aristotelian conception of judgement *and* its use in this context, many of Kant's

---

[18] Kant, Critique of Pure Reason, B 169, 175.

commentators have also been struck by the artificiality of his exact application of the model.[19]

Given, then, that the Transcendental Deduction offers no further clarification of the individual categories, it seems that we have a theory concerning the logical dependence of object and subject of experience, and some account of the elements involved, but nothing which might give a compelling justification of how these elements function individually, and in concert. Indeed, because of the weakness of the Metaphysical Deduction concern must also arise as to the entitlement of some of the Kantian categories to be assigned a transcendental role at all.

There is a further area of significant difficulty which must be mentioned. It is clear that if the categories are to give objective unity to a sensible manifold, then they must indeed operate within stable temporal conditions. But, why should we accept Kant's insistence that in order to create such stability the categories must also bring about unity of self-consciousness? An 'official' Kantian answer would be that since time is the form of inner-sense in the subject and has no existence 'in itself' then it follows that to unify time just is to unify the subject's consciousness of itself. And, since the means of this unification is imagination, this is, accordingly, a further way in which the categories give unity to subjective consciousness.

This, however, raises the following problem. Even if we overlook the unfortunate lack of detail in Kant's account of the foregoing, it would appear that in order to 'buy into' the central claim of the Deduction, we must also accept the hugely problematic notion of the ideality of time. This might not be an issue for Kant, but if we are searching for a generally viable philosophical outcome to the Deduction, then it is an extreme difficulty.

Given these various problems, we may suspect that Kant's central argument is too restricted to have any broader philosophical worth. This would be a mistake. To see why, consider, in the first instance, the following brilliant passage from Gareth Evans.

---

[19] Allison usefully summarizes central areas of concern in his remarks that 'it fails totally to explain how one could "deduce" the pure concepts of the understanding from the table of logical functions'; and that 'it is difficult to see what sense can be given to Kant's claim to have demonstrated the completeness of the list of categories or to have shown "why just these concepts, and no others have their seat in the pure understanding" ' (Allison, *Kant's Transcendental Idealism*, 124 and 128–9 respectively). Interestingly, in the second edition of *Kant's Transcendental Idealism: An Interpretation and Defense* (n. 4), Allison takes a rather more sympathetic approach, devoting an entire chapter to the Metaphysical Deduction.

The capacity to think of oneself as located in space, and tracing a continuous path through it, is necessarily involved in the capacity to conceive the phenomena one encounters as independent of one's perception of them—to conceive the world as something one 'comes across'. It follows that the capacity for at least some primitive self-ascriptions—self-ascriptions of position, orientation, and change of position and orientation and hence the conception of oneself as one object amongst others, occupying one place amongst others, are interdependent with thought about the objective world itself.[20]

Without referring to Kant, Evans here identifies, in effect, what I have shown to be the basic thrust of argument in the Transcendental Deduction. To understand the world, qua objective, logically presupposes that one has a sense of one's own subjective position and movements as one object in relation to others. Knowledge of an objective world and the unity of self-consciousness, in other words, are reciprocally dependent.

Evans' refreshingly practical emphasis on the subject's positioning and movement allows us to compensate for some of Kant's difficulties. In fact, it allows us to give real substance to the Transcendental Deduction by broadly reconstructing it through three steps of argument.

This is made possible by two enabling points. The first is that (as I have shown elsewhere[21] and as we shall see, in detail, in the next chapter) self-ascriptions of position, etc. *must* involve, at some stage, concept-guided exercises of imagination. Such exercises serve to organize our experience of time, but do not entail that time *itself* must be interpreted as ideal. A key problem is thus eliminated.

The second enabling point is that Evans' way of putting things highlights and fills out a point in Kant's account that is easy to lose track of. This is the fact that the unity of self-consciousness is not just a unity, but is, at least in part, an *objective* one. The 'I think' is a function not just of thought and imagination acting on time per se but coheres as a unity through both the application of the categories and the amenability of phenomena (including the subject's own body) to be understood in orderly and regular terms. In applying the categories, the subject, qua embodied, comprehends itself as a specific finite agent within the objective field of phenomena. On these terms, the subject

[20] Gareth Evans, *The Varieties of Reference* (Oxford: Clarendon Press, 1982), 176. The reference occurs in the context of a discussion of 'Demonstrative Identification' that has only one passing (and unrelated) reference to Kant.

[21] See 'Imagination and Objective Knowledge', chap. 4 of my *Philosophy After Postmodernism: Civilized Values and the Scope of Knowledge* (London: Routledge, 2003).

applies the categories (where appropriate) to itself and in this sense it has objective unity.

With these points in mind, the Deduction can then be made as follows:

(a) knowledge of objects qua objects is only possible through the understanding's structuring of imagination;

(b) this structuring centres on the way in which present attention to an object is informed by the imagination's capacity to project the body's previous relations with this and other objects and states of affairs, and by its anticipations of future or counterfactual possibilities of such relations (this is the objective unity of self-consciousness);

(c) the structuring factor in (a) and (b) is the application of the categories.

Making due allowance for my references to supporting material outside this chapter, points (a) and (b) can be taken as provisionally established. This leaves the task of justifying point (c)—why the structuring activity of the understanding should be identified specifically with Kant's categories.

Some justification can be offered. It will not have the absoluteness or comprehensiveness aspired to by Kant but it will at least make my three-stage reconstruction of his argument broadly viable. It is to this I now turn.

PART 3

What kind of a thing in general is a category? As noted earlier, in strict Kantian terms a category is a concept and, as such, is the kind of thing which is applied in judgement. But, for Kant, the category is, in fact, also a basis of (as it were) *orientation* in judgement—that is to say, it allows judgements to be directed towards definite objects. In his words, it involves 'the *determination* of appearances in space and time in general'.[22]

This implies that whilst we might use categories explicitly as concepts (e.g., when we assert that '*a* is real') their role is much deeper than this, and must, in large part, be *pre-reflective* (though Kant does not, as far as I

²² Kant, *The Critique of Pure Reason*, B 169, 175.

know, put it like this). This means that they can be learned and employed in a basic way without us always being overtly aware of them *as* concepts. And, it is only by virtue of this pre-reflective categorial competence being put in place alongside our learning of empirical concept application that this latter application can be objectively contextualized (a point which I shall return to a little further on).

By exploring this notion of the categories as modes of pre-reflective cognitive orientation, in relation to Evans' emphasis on practical subject-positioning, it is possible to work towards a justification of the claim that it is the categories which must structure the objective unity of the world and self-consciousness.

To show this, I shall first develop Evans' emphasis on the mobility of the embodied subject. This points towards human cognition being understood as a function of sensorimotor capacities co-ordinated as a unified but constantly reconfiguring field. On these terms, the structure of the phenomenal field is correlated with the body's growth and movement, and the acquisition of language.

It is worth emphasizing that, in recent years, significant and sustained empirical evidence has shown that, even in the very earliest stages of infancy, basic cognitive competences are already in place.[23] Shaun Gallagher's important philosophical work has interpreted this (and other evidence) as showing important correlations between these competences and the neonate's having a basic sense of its own body-orientation.[24] However, these cognitive factors are present only in the most very basic terms. Their full correlation requires subsequent experiential development.

In this respect, for example, the child correlates its cognitive capacities by such activities as tracking changes in its perceptual field, and by moving towards stimuli, or by negotiating the way in which they withdrew from reach and/or view.

[23] This is most strongly pronounced in relation to visual cognition. See, for example, the study 'Development of Basic Visual Functions', by J. Atkinson and O. Braddick, in A. N. Slater and G. Bremner (eds), *Infant Development* (Hillsdale, NJ: Erlbaum, 1989), 7–41 and, in the same volume, Slater's 'Visual Perception and Memory in Early Infancy' (pp. 43–71). A more general informative discussion is Daniel L. Stern, *The Interpersonal World of the Infant: A View from Psychoanalysis and Developmental Psychology* (New York: Basic Books, 1985). See esp. chap. 3, pp. 37–68. In what follows, I develop the implications of this material in an existential (loosely Merleau-Pontian) sense. For a link between Kant's transcendental strategies and more 'classical' theories of developmental psychology, see Onora O'Neill, 'Transcendental Synthesis and Developmental Psychology', *Kant-Studien*, 75 (1984), 149–67.

[24] This theme is explored throughout his acclaimed book *How Body Shapes the Mind* (Oxford: Clarendon Press, 2006). See esp. pp. 65–85.

A decisive factor in this process is when the child learns that by changing its own physical position it can gain access to certain stimuli, either by creating them as a result of its actions, or by coming across them. Likewise, it will get a sense of certain stimuli being beyond its control, or dependent on certain sequences of events in order to be encountered. In this way, it will learn what items or states of affairs are stable and independent of the will, which items or states of affairs are not, and the different ways in which these characterizations can be made. The categories emerge, in the course of these practical activities, through the gradual habituation of sensorimotor coordination to the demands made by specific forms of stimuli.

Consider, for example, a simple and repeatable activity such as playing with bricks. The child learns to assemble the *plurality* of parts into the *unity* of a whole structure or edifice, and to disassemble it into its components (i.e., *negate* the achieved whole). As its ability develops, it will form a basic understanding of what is *possible* and what is *not possible* in this activity. It may also learn to face such challenges as using the *total* number of bricks available in the process of construction, or in arranging the elements in such a way that, at some point, it will *cause* the whole edifice to collapse.

Of equal importance in the correlation of subject and objective world is the child's gradual recognition that human beings are significantly different from other material bodies and creatures, and can *reciprocate* its attention and gestures in many different ways.

In all these different cases, repeated interchanges between the child and its environment not only bring about an achieved coordination of the objective and subjective dimensions of experience, but also, by means of this, engage and articulate the child's appetitive being and desires. Through concrete interactions, the child learns the physical and social world, and its own being, in terms of possibilities and impossibilities of realization.

Now the accumulation of these processes involves a gradual learning of the salient characteristics of reality through practical exploration. Such competences are learned through rote and habit as ways of dealing with the world and other people. They embody, I would suggest, many of the Kantian categories in their fundamental pre-reflective form. In negotiating change and habituating oneself to what is enduring and what is subject to the will and what is not, one habituates oneself to the nature of the real, without having explicit 'lessons' about the nature of reality qua reality.

As the examples and points above should have indicated, notions such as substance, cause and effect, existence and non-existence, possibility and impossibility, necessity and contingency, unity, plurality, and totality, and reciprocity are learned not *as* concepts, in the first instance, but as cognitive regularities and expectations arising from repeated practical explorations and interaction with a variety of environments. Indeed, as will be shown in detail in the next chapter, the categories' emergence and application are inseparable from the transcendental schemata of imagination. These schemata enable intuitions to be tracked and anticipated, and provide a pre-reflective *objective orientation*. Through this, basic recognition and then concept formation and application in a fuller sense, get a purchase.

It is, of course, vital to stress that the learning of such competences and the emergence of the categories through them proceed alongside initiation into language. Suppose, for example, that a child learns the word 'dog' and can successfully apply it when an appropriate creature comes in view. In such a case, it is one thing to use a general term and another thing for this to amount to concept-use in a complete sense. For the latter to happen it is surely required that *the general term is understood as applying to appropriate instances in other places and times as well as to those which are given as immediate stimuli*. We need evidence, in other words, that the term has been contextualized in that broader network of factors which determine the *general* character of reality (a point to which I will return in some detail further on).

I would argue that it is the transcendental schemata and categories qua pre-reflective cognitive competences rather than as explicit concepts which initially provide this. They are that layer of learning 'between the lines', as it were, whereby we habituate ourselves to the general character of the real. They are a mode of stabilized orientation which our initiation into language is able both to build upon and to refine.

In terms of the former, for example, in order to follow those rules which are the basis of language acquisition it is presupposed that the child and teacher share some already stabilized communicative terrain—enough, at least, to allow recognition of correct and incorrect ways of rule-following. In terms of refinement, the developed rule-following involved in the acquisition of language allows the categorial competences to be further articulated—to the stage where they themselves can be explicitly formulated and applied *as concepts*.

There is a vital point here which will be returned to in future chapters. The kind of activity wherein the categories gradually emerge as fully achieved competences clearly involves a great deal of trial, error, and experimentation in how the child engages with and comes to comprehend things and events. In fact, the best way of describing this process is as one of *play*.

Play is something that enables the child to try out different avenues of cognitive exploration in a leisurely way. It is something that achieves a deepening cognitive grasp of things and events without this being driven by the pressures of practical goal-orientated activity. And, if play is integrated in processes of learning directed by adults, it does not lose entirely its sense of something that is pleasurable to do apart from any practical ends. *It is something that can be enjoyed for its own sake, and, through this, can be assigned a basic aesthetic character.*

More exact criteria of the aesthetic will be formulated as this book progresses. But, even now, we have enough before us to make an initial connection between the aesthetic qua play and the process whereby the categories are achieved as fundamental cognitive competences. This means that the aesthetic at its most crude and basic level is implicated in the correlated emergence of our objective knowledge of reality, and of the self. Through play we become familiar with objects and events by means of their re-encounterable and/or recurrent aspects, and through the gratification of engaging with or anticipating these aspects we, at the same time, achieve a unified sense of self.

Now it might seem that the processes just described offer, at best, a kind of illuminating ontogenetic descriptive support to Kant's categories in so far as they explain how the categories are acquired as fundamental concepts. However, the description has also further interesting conceptual implications. These serve to justify point (c) in my earlier reconstruction of Kant's argument. For, without the categories as *achieved* competences, there would be no broader context of cognitive generality in which *empirical* concepts could be embedded so as to function objectively. The formation and application of such concepts presuppose that a stable context—*a horizon of mastered 'thingliness', eventfulness, and causality*—is also in place.

To complete the argument, therefore, we must question Kant's categories in more-individual terms. This means asking first whether the list is comprehensive, and second whether each of the categories identified by Kant has the a priori significance which he assigns to it. The criterion for answering both questions centres on whether the horizon of 'thingliness', eventfulness, and causality just described is intelligible without bringing in such an individual category.

A detailed investigation cannot be offered here, but some light can be cast on both questions. In terms of comprehensiveness, there is at least one glaring omission from Kant's categorial table—namely, the 'identity and difference' pairing (which, for him, counts as a 'concept of reflection'). If concept-formation and application of any kind are to take place, it is difficult to see how it could be made sense of in the absence of a capacity to recognize sameness or difference between intuitions. Indeed, one might argue that to recognize *as such* (whether on the basis of categorial or empirical concepts) just *is* to articulate sameness or difference in the sensible manifold. The identity/difference pairing, in other words, is as much involved in giving form to the manifold as are the official categories. It is a major principle of synthesis.

In terms of the a priori credentials of the individual categories, there is at least a case, prima facie, for arguing that unity, plurality, totality, existence and non-existence, possibility and impossibility, substance, and cause and effect, are necessary to the intelligibility of the aforementioned empirical processes. If they cannot be excised from the account without rendering it unintelligible, then their case for transcendental status is indeed justified.

The link between generality and objectivity offers a further avenue of justification of the experiential necessity of Kant's categories. Again, it involves deploying a notion from Gareth Evans. The notion in question is that of a 'Generality Constraint' which determines the 'structuredness' of thought. As Evans puts it, a structured thought of the form a is F should be interpreted as lying at the intersection of two series of thoughts: on the one hand, 'the series of thoughts that a is F, that b is F, that c is F. . . and, on the other hand, the series of thoughts that a is F, that a is H . . .'[25]

It is important to emphasize that the 'series' just mentioned are not phenomenological descriptions of actual thought processes, but rather further implications which are entailed when the thought is formulated in a structured way. A thought has this character when its thinker understands that what is predicated of a subject can also be predicated of other subjects, and that the same subject can be the bearer of many different predicates.

Now, whilst Evans does not raise the point, it would follow that a person whose thought was 'structured' in this sense is one whose use of object and concept terms was informed by a comprehension of

[25] Evans, *The Varieties of Reference*, 104.

their *general ontological and extensional scope* (respectively) and also some key aspects of their interrelation. This is a logical indicator that such comprehension has attained at least the rudiments of objective thought.

There is a correlated insight concerning the self-conscious subject. To put it in Evans' terms, a structured thought of the form 'I am *F*' must lie at the intersection of two series of thoughts to the effect that, on the one hand, 'I am F, and John is F, and Jane is F . . .', and, on the other hand, that 'I am F, I am G, I am H . . . .'[26]

Here, in other words, the subject's *self-understanding* attains a basic objective level of unity when he or she recognizes that other persons can have the same kinds of experiences that they have, and that he or she can be the subject of different kinds of such common experiences. This means, in effect, that the subject becomes conscious of its status as a member of a class of sentient objects who experience the world on broadly similar terms.

On these terms, therefore, the structuredness of thought would be a logical sign of a person having understood the basis of both objective knowledge and the objective unity of self-consciousness. We can then use this as a test of the transcendental status of the individual categories, by inquiring whether or not they are entailed in thought structured by the Generality Constraint. It could be argued, for example, that such understanding directly exemplifies basic categorial competence in a number of areas indicated by Kant (such as unity, plurality, possibility, and substance and accident) and would also involve others (such as cause and effect) as broader contextual factors.

In this section, then, I have completed the three-stage reconstruction of the Transcendental Deduction, by showing how the majority of the categories are implicated in objective knowledge and the objective unity of the self.

CONCLUSION

Now, a summary of the trajectory of this chapter as a whole. I have argued at length that Kant's B version of the Transcendental Deduction attempts to show that our objective knowledge of the world must involve an application of the categories which also brings about the

---

[26] For an example of Evans' own use of the Generality Constraint in relation to self-identification, see ibid. 256.

objective unification of self-consciousness. As joint functions of this application, the objective unity of the phenomenal world and the unity of self-consciousness are necessarily connected to one another. They are implicated in one another's full definition.

Kant's insufficient attentiveness to the categories in their specific characters and interrelations, however, makes this central pattern of argument less than compelling. Despite this, I was able to propose a way in which it might be made more viable by following a clue from Gareth Evans. This consists in the fact that to have knowledge of an objective world that one 'comes across' one must be able to ascribe experiences to oneself concerning one's positions (and changes of position) as one material body amongst others. On the basis of this, I was able to eliminate one of Kant's problems and to give emphasis to the unity of self-consciousness's objective character.

I then set out a three-stage reconstruction of the Transcendental Deduction. This led to a reinterpretation of the categories as pre-reflective cognitive competences. It was argued that they constitute a fundamental orientation towards the world without which empirical concept application is not possible.

A second means of justifying the experiential necessity of the categories was then proposed—again following Evans. This involved identifying his 'Generality Constraint' as a basic logical criterion for objective knowledge of the world and the self, and then suggesting that the majority of Kant's categories are entailed when the Constraint is operative.

Before drawing some broader conclusions, a qualification must be made. My development of Kant's position in this chapter has no aspirations to exhaustiveness. It indicates how at least *some* (perhaps the majority) of his categories might be entitled to the kind of significance which he assigns to them in the Transcendental Deduction. To establish the case in stronger terms would necessitate a much more detailed consideration of the individual categories, discussion of alternative contender-concepts which do not figure in Kant's theory, and a more sustained exposition of the ontogenetic theory of the mobile subject's cognitive development. The link to Evans' Generality Constraint would also need to be filled out in rather more detail (especially in terms of how the individual categories were implicated in it).

This being said, the approach is, I think, one which genuinely follows Kant's major argument and which does show how it might be modified so as to be philosophically viable.

In my reading of the Transcendental Deduction's structure of argument, I have given some emphasis to the subjective dimension, and, in particular, the transcendental synthesis of imagination. Having, therefore, formulated a viable reading of the categories in this chapter, in the next one I will look at Kant's treatment of imagination in the schematism section of *The Critique of Pure Reason* in much more detail. This will show, in particular, how the categories are able to engage with reality.

2

Imagination and the Conditions
of Knowledge

INTRODUCTION

The preceding chapter has shown how, for Kant, the productive imagination plays a central role in our knowledge of the objective world and the unity of the self. This role is not one which has been greatly emphasized by other thinkers, so it is worth considering its structure and scope in rather more depth. The task is all the more vital for the present work in so far as subsequent chapters will show its centrality to Kant's aesthetic theory.

There is a logical starting-point for a detailed investigation—namely, the schematism section of *The Critique of Pure Reason* (which follows on from the Transcendental Deduction). Unfortunately, the schematism is short, notorious for its obscurity, and has not been given much systematic development even by Kant's more sympathetic interpreters.[1]

---

[1] Strawson's influential paper on 'Imagination and Perception' re-established the intellectual respectability of imagination's role in cognition, but did not give centrality to the role of schemata. For an accessible version of the paper, see *Kant on Pure Reason*, ed. Ralph Walker (Oxford: Oxford University Press, 1982), 82–99. A more sympathetic treatment of the schematism itself can be found in chap. 8 of Henry E. Allison, *Kant's Transcendental Idealism: An Interpretation and Defense* (New Haven, Conn. and London: Yale University Press, 2004). Another sustained treatment of the subject is in chap. 2 of Sarah Gibbons, *Kant's Theory of Imagination: Bridging Gaps in Judgement and Experience* (Oxford: Clarendon Press, 1994). Another probing account is Michael Pendlebury's 'Making Sense of Kant's Schematism', *Philosophy and Phenomenological Research*, LV, 4 (1995), 777–97. Pendlebury has also offered a very useful treatment of related issues in a paper on 'The Role of Imagination in Perception', *South African Journal of Philosophy*, 15 (1996), 133–7. My differences with Allison, Gibbons, and Pendlebury centre, primarily, on the fact that they do not adequately address the phenomenology of the schema per se—that is, the relation between the schema's status as a rule and the imaginative product which that rule generates. I have similar problems with Béatrice Longuenesse's otherwise brilliant, sustained analysis of the *logic* of the schematism (and related issues) within the Critical corpus, which is distributed throughout Part 3 of her *Kant and the Capacity to Judge* (Princeton, NJ: Princeton University Press, 1998).

To the casual observer, indeed, it may appear to be little more than a remnant of European idealism's more Romantic aspects.

In contrast, I will argue that the schematism is of decisive importance to the formation of objective knowledge and, more speculatively, to the unity of the self. It has a philosophical significance in excess of its historical context and the confines of Kant exegesis.

To show this involves strategies of great methodological complexity. In order to clarify the surprising scope of the schematism's significance one must combine both analytic and phenomenological approaches.

In Part 1 of this chapter, I briefly consider Kant's rather unsatisfactory introductory treatment of the schematism. Part 2 addresses Kant's more detailed account of transcendental schemata, and offers some important refinements to his position.

I then proceed, in Part 3, to develop Kant's notion of the productive imagination in more detail, making use of a phenomenological outline of the ontogenesis of experience. Through this, it is argued that the transcendental schemata should be interpreted as *retentive and anticipatory procedures* in the productive imagination through which the nascent categories achieve a basic orientation in cognition.

It is argued further that these procedures centre on the productive imagination's capacity to model possibilities of temporally successive appearance. It is only through the realization of this disposition that we can explain how concepts in general are able to apply.

In Part 4, my development of Kant's position focuses on the phenomenology of schematization, and is extended to cover empirical sensible concepts. It is shown how realizations of the relevant imaginative dispositions have an intrinsic general significance which is homogeneous with the generality of sensible concepts. Part 5 extends the importance of schematization to some aspects of the unity of the individual self.

I then proceed to a brief conclusion summarizing the arguments in this chapter, and indicating the general importance of understanding and imagination for this study.

For a survey of the general relation between imagination and knowledge (which picks up themes from the Transcendental Deduction), see chap. 2 of Eva Schaper's *Studies in Kant's Aesthetics* (Edinburgh: Edinburgh University Press, 1979). Schaper does not, however, offer much elucidation of the schematism either here or elsewhere in her book. Jane Kneller's recent study *Kant and the Power of Imagination* (Cambridge: Cambridge University Press, 2007) also has surprisingly little to say about the schematism, preferring instead to view Kant in a broader historical and intellectual context.

PART 1

As we have seen, Kant's arguments in the Transcendental Deduction are complex and require a great deal of work in order to be made viable. I shall focus now on two clear emphases in his arguments. The first is that knowledge of an objective world and a unified self presupposes both pure concepts of understanding (or 'categories' for short) and the second is that the imagination plays a key role in this knowledge.

For Kant, imagination is 'the faculty for representing an object even *without its presence* in intuition'.[2] It has a productive aspect based on the capacity to generate images per se, and a reproductive aspect based on associational connections between images so generated.

The schematism emphasizes the former, and, in particular, its linkage of attention and retention in relation to the sensible manifold (a topic which I will consider in more detail in Part 3).

Kant begins his exposition by claiming that

In all subsumptions of an object under a concept the representation of the former must be *homogeneous* with the latter; i.e., the concept must contain that which is represented in the object that is to be subsumed under it . . . Thus the empirical concept of a *plate* has homogeneity with the pure geometrical concept of a circle, for the roundness that is thought in the former can be intuited in the latter.[3]

He also offers a further example with a few more details filled in, as follows:

The concept of a dog signifies a rule according to which my imagination can specify the shape of a four-footed animal in general, without being restricted to any specific shape that experience offers me, or any possible image that I can exhibit *in concreto*.[4]

Kant also describes the schema as a 'procedure' or 'rule of unity' through which a concept finds sensible application.

But, what distinguishes such a rule from that of the concept on whose behalf it is acting? If we say it is the rule sensibly applied as opposed to abstractly conceived then this tells us nothing, because Kant's whole point is that the schema involves an *additional* factor which enables

---

[2] Kant, *The Critique of Pure Reason*, trans. Paul Guyer and Allen Wood (Cambridge: Cambridge University Press, 1998), A137/B176, 256.   [3] Ibid. A141/B180, 271.
[4] Ibid. A141/B181, 273.

concepts to be applied to phenomena. The concept must 'contain' general characteristics of its object which are 'homogeneous' with the concept.[5]

It is striking that Kant's examples centre on a capacity to represent shapes which are sufficient to characterize *kinds* of spatial object, but not sufficient to present recognizable 'natural' individual instances of those kinds. Indeed,

the schema of sensible concepts (such as figures in space) is a product and as it were, a monogram, of pure apriori imagination, through which and in accordance with which the images themselves first become possible.[6]

It is clear from these first characterizations that, whatever schemata in general might be, the *general* shapes and forms of empirical spatial particulars are involved in them.

However, Kant asserts rather than explains and argues his points. There is one issue in particular which must be clarified before proceeding further. Earlier I noted that the schema must be an 'additional' factor which mediates between concept and phenomenal item. Kant's examples seem to indicate that this is some third term, but if the mediation of such a term is involved this would point towards a fallacy of the 'third man' type where the mediating term would require another mediating term in order for it to apply, and so on, in an infinite regress.

Given this, to be charitable to Kant, the mediating factor should be regarded not as some singular schema but simply the way in which different concepts engage the productive imagination in different ways. For example, to schematize the empirical concept dog we do not need some schematic dog-form as a content of consciousness; rather, the schema consists in the way that the exercise of this particular concept directs the imagination in a different way from what is required by other concepts.

---

[5] Allison, for example, tries to help Kant by distinguishing between 'discursive' and 'perceptual' rules, linking schemata to the latter. On these terms, the schema 'functions to process the sensible data in a determinate way, thereby giving one a sense of what to expect on the basis of certain perceptual "clues". For example, on seeing the front of a house, one naturally expects that it will have sides and a back with appropriate "house-ish" features. Rules of this sort are intimately connected with the perspectival nature of perception and, therefore, with the imagination' (Allison, *Kant's Transcendental Idealism*, 210). Allison is right to link schemata to perspectival factors. However, if the 'sense of what to expect' here is to be more than a mere abstract expectation (i.e., the mere *idea* of a hidden aspect), then it must have some sensible content, that is have an occurrent image character or a dispositional orientation grounded on such occurrent imagery. It is this factor on which the burden of my own analysis falls.   [6] Kant, *Critique of Pure Reason*, B181/A142, 273–4.

On these terms schemata are to be understood as *different operational procedures* determined by the specific demands which particular concepts make upon the productive imagination in order to be formed or applied. They are, in other words, different ways in which concepts engage the productive imagination per se.

This being said, there are still three major questions left unanswered by Kant's introductory characterizations of the schemata. First, in what sense do concepts 'contain' features which characterize their objects; second, in what sense are they 'homogeneous' with such characteristics; and third, *how* do schemata based on these qualities act as 'rules' for concept application?

The bulk of Kant's subsequent exposition addresses the transcendental schemata's role in enabling the categories to be applied. However, it does not answer the aforementioned questions in any direct way. Indeed, he introduces a new factor in so far as the burden of emphasis in the transcendental schemata concerns *temporality*.

In order to work towards answers to the three question, then, we must first consider Kant's treatment of the transcendental schemata in detail—both expounding them, and, where necessary, revising his position.

PART 2

For Kant, the transcendental schemata enable the application of those 'categories' which are the basis of our knowledge of an objective world. The categories consist of unity, plurality, totality, reality, limitation, negation, substance, causality, reciprocity, possibility, actuality, and necessity.

Kant treats the *quantitative* group of categories—unity, plurality, and totality—in terms of a single schema, since they all pertain to 'time-series'. The schema is *number*. It schematizes the relevant categories through 'the successive addition of one (homogeneous) unit to another' and, in this way, exemplifies the fact that 'I generate time itself in the apprehension of the intuition'.[7]

The qualitative group of categories—reality, limitation, and negation—is again dealt with in terms of a single schema which pertains to the 'content of time'. It consists of degrees of reality as expressed through *variations in the magnitude of sensation*. In Kant's words,

the schema of reality, as the quantity of something in so far as it fills time, is just this continuous and uniform generation of that quantity in time, as one descends in time from the sensation which has a certain degree to its disappearance or gradually ascends from negation to its magnitude.[8]

Kant's remaining categories are given individual as well as group characterizations. They can be summarized as follows.

The relational categories comprise substance, causality, and reciprocity, and concern the 'order of time' in the connection of perceptions. Substance's schema is that of *the permanent which endures through temporal change*. As Kant puts it, 'in it alone can the succession and simultaneity of appearances be determined in regard to time'.[9] Causality is schematized through 'the succession of the manifold in so far as it is subject to a rule'.[10] Reciprocity is schematized as the simultaneous rule-governed interactions of a substance's accidents with the accidents of other substances.

Finally, the group of modal categories. This consists of possibility, actuality, and necessity. They describe the 'sum total of time'. The schema of possibility involves 'the agreement of the synthesis of various representations with the conditions of time in general'.[11]

On these terms, for example, a thing cannot possess opposite properties at the same moment in time; it could only have these at successive stages of its existence. Possibility is schematized, therefore, in terms of *the consistency between the specific properties of a thing and its occupying a specific location in time*.

The schema of actuality is more straightforward. It consists of 'existence at a determinate time'.[12] Necessity's schema is also relatively clear in nominal terms. It involves the 'existence of an object at all times'.[13]

I shall now analyse Kant's treatment of the schemata in more detail. Consider first the time-series categories—unity, plurality, and totality. Kant's assertion that 'number' is their common schema is curious and not at all compelling. The named schemata characterize different ways in which the *relation* of parts in a whole might be understood. Numbers, in contrast, mark out quantitative scope of an

[8] Kant, *Critique of Pure Reason*, B182/A143, 275.   [9] Ibid. B183/A144, 275.
[10] Ibid.   [11] Ibid.   [12] Ibid. B184/A145, 275.   [13] Ibid.

accumulation of units. Whilst this scope might be considered in relation to a whole, it is not a necessary factor per se, in so far as one can often—indeed, mainly—characterize things as unities, pluralities, or totalities, without our attention to their parts having to involve any element of enumeration. It is also strange that Kant takes only one schema to be involved in the time-series categories.

His position here might be developed as follows.

If something occupies space and time then, qua spatio-temporal, it is composed of a continuum of parts. If one wishes accordingly to comprehend the character of a specific spatio-temporal unity, plurality, or totality as given in perception, it follows that one must, *in principle*, be able to apprehend the continuity of its parts *as* a continuum, if called upon. This requires at least some procedure of *successive* apprehension.

In the case of a spatial item or state of affairs, this apprehension is relatively open. The continuity of parts in a spatial item or state of affairs can be scanned successively in any direction. In the case of an event, in contrast, the sequence of its 'parts' qua temporal must follow an exact order of succession. Its phenomenal continuity is strictly linear.

Now, it is clear that we cannot perform such successive apprehensions of phenomenal continuity for every object of perception: our cognitive capacities would be overwhelmed. However, we at least know that the item's phenomenal continuity can be tracked through successive apprehension, as required. Having such a procedure at our disposal is a condition of our being able to negotiate sensible items and states of affairs, qua sensible.

I would suggest then, that unity, plurality, and totality can be schematized in terms of a single procedure, but that it concerns the successive apprehension of continuity of parts, rather than number.

Let us turn now to the cases of reality, limitation, and negation. Kant's treatment of these time-content categories is especially weak. The concepts of 'reality' and 'negation' are fundamental to the possibility of experience (in ways which will become clearer as I proceed) but the categorical status of 'limitation' is much harder to justify, and, for present purposes, can be set aside.

It should also be noted that Kant's treatment of a group of categories in terms of a single schema is, again, not compelling. Neither is his characterization of this schema in terms of quantitative variation of the magnitude of sensation, specifically. Further factors are involved. I will now try to develop Kant's approach to take account of them.

Rather than treating reality and negation as two separate concepts, it is more useful, phenomenologically speaking, to treat them as paired—since each is involved in the full definition of the other, and the transitions between the two are of the utmost importance in our understanding of phenomenal change. Kant is right to identify the transitional factor here with variation of magnitude, but it has three quite distinctive aspects, each of which can be regarded as a schema in its own right. I shall now consider these.

The first is variation of *physical* magnitude. Anything which occupies time is capable of being physically diminished in quantity until there is nothing left of it. We move from a given reality to its negation.

However, there is also a qualitative version of this. It arises when some item is added to or subtracted from, in such a way as gradually to change it into some other kind of thing (e.g., when a liquid is 'watered down' to such a degree that it becomes no more than water).

A second schema involves variation of *perceptual* magnitude. It has a spatial and a temporal aspect. Broadly speaking, the closer things come towards us in the spatial field, the bigger they will appear to be, and, correspondingly, the more they move away from us, the more their magnitude will appear to diminish, accordingly.

Likewise with time. The nearer an event is to us in time (either past or future), the more influence it will tend to exert on what we do in the present. And, reciprocally, the further away in time it moves, the less it will tend to exert such influence.

The third schema is the closest to Kant's own characterization. It involves variation of the magnitude of sensation. Over and above the perceptual criteria just outlined it is clear that how things impact on our senses—our feeling of them—can have greater or lesser degrees of intensity according to the nature of the impact and the constitution and sensitivity of our sensory receptors.

The schemata which Kant characterizes individually, are rather more straightforward. That of substance—the permanent which endures through temporal change—pertains to invariance of form throughout the different appearances which an item takes. This invariance centres on features which characterize the phenomenal structure of that specific kind of item. (The re-identifiability of an item as an individual also involves features which are distinctive to it qua individual, but these empirical properties are not relevant to transcendental schematization.)

The schema of causality centres on temporal transformations amongst items and states of affairs. Changes of this kind happen in a rule-governed way which through the productive imagination's power of attention and recall can be tracked and negotiated before being explicitly recognized through concepts.

In the case of reciprocity, imaginative attention and recall (with the emphasis on the former) are directed not so much towards the temporal *trail* of events and the anticipation of outcomes but rather towards a sense of how things which are physically proximal can mutually modify one another—in causal terms or through simply limiting each other's space of action.

Finally, the modal schemata. These are orientated towards temporal coherence in the perceptual field. If something is possible, it must have attributes which are consistent with how a thing of that kind is located in time.

A living being, for example, cannot come into existence at its death, and then move through time towards its birth. Likewise, a pebble cannot be physically transformed into particles and then, a moment later, be reconstituted as a pebble without any intervening process of physical action upon it. The possibility of things is dependent on their properties being acquired consistently with the passage of time.

The schema of actuality is simpler than this. For, if something exists, it must occupy some portion of space at some time or other. (A world of sounds cannot be used as a counter-example here, since sound is intelligible only in terms of the perturbation of space-occupying phenomena.)

Necessity's schematization is a little more complex. It is difficult to make sense of Kant's notion of necessity as 'the existence of an object at all times'. However, such necessity *can* be comprehended in terms of factors which constrain the existence of all spatio-temporal items and states of affairs, qua spatio-temporal. For example, no material body can occupy the exact same spatial coordinates as another at the same time. No material body can move from one part of space to another without continuous traversal of the intervening regions.

Having expounded and developed Kant's account of the transcendental schemata, I shall now consider the productive imagination in more detail, with a view to presenting his general theory in a viable form. This will involve a phenomenology of the ontogenesis of experience which brings into play a key factor which Kant neglects—namely, *anticipation*.

Through this approach, the transcendental schemata will be characterized more exactly as *retentive and anticipatory procedures* whose power derives specifically from imagination.

PART 3

As we have seen, for Kant, the imagination is a capacity for representing things which are not themselves given in immediate perception. This capacity is of the most vital importance. For, whilst the imagination is dependent on what is given in time and space, in Kant's terms, time and space *themselves* are intimately connected with the workings of the productive imagination. Indeed, as we have seen, he even implies that imagination is somehow involved in the actual *production* of space and time.

The point of philosophical substance here does not require that we go as far as Kant on this last point. There is a more economical alternative which holds that imagination is simply a necessary condition for *knowledge* of spatio-temporal phenomena. This is because the embodied subject exists in space, and perceives things in space, through *movement* (be this from one position in space to another, or a simple process of eye-movement in scanning an object).

By definition, movement of any sort entails temporal succession. To experience such succession in a coherent order requires that our sense of what is immediately present must be informed by a sense of what has gone before. We must be able to *retain* some of the previous relevant perceptions. *Attention entails retention.*

However, there is another factor not emphasized by Kant, but which must also be brought in—namely, *anticipation*. To see why this is so, I shall first undertake an outline phenomenology of the ontogenesis of experience.

All animals can deal with their environments in the sense of being able to negotiate specific kinds of stimuli, in specific ways, for specific ends. Such behaviour is not based on developed conceptual abilities and rational planning (which are enabled through mastery of language) but neither is it mere instinct in the way that less-developed life-forms (such as insects) negotiate their environments.

One might say that even though animals do not possess objective knowledge they do have, nevertheless, *objective orientation*. They can negotiate their environments in a way that is informed by some sense of what the world's objective physical features allow or disallow vis-à-vis the creature's own capacities.

Human beings, of course, have objective knowledge of their world. However, knowledge and rational planning do not simply happen in an instant. They have to be learned. And, if the linguistic abilities on which such knowledge is founded are to develop, it is presupposed that some stable proto-cognitive factors enabling such development are already in place. There must be some form of *objective orientation*.

In the previous chapter, I linked this to the categories in their *nascent* pre-reflective form. The categories are rules for recognizing objective structure in sensible manifolds. But, *if such rules are to get a purchase on phenomena, they must, at the same time, involve ways of negotiating the manifold in terms of coherent patterns of temporal succession.* This is the function of the transcendental schemata.

Such procedures do not exist independently of the categories. One presumes, rather, that the urge to cognitive unity embodied in the different categories is what orientates us towards specific patterns of temporal succession which have to be dealt with if the nascent categories are to develop and issue in full objective knowledge. The transcendental schemata, in other words, are specific ways in which the categories determine productive imagination.

Again, a wealth of striking relevant empirical evidence has been summarized by Gallagher. He notes that neonates have

sensitivity to motion parallax—when the infant moves its head, nearer parts of a three-dimensional object seem to move more than further parts. [Indeed,] Neonates are capable of discriminating between different geometrical shapes, such as triangles, squares, and circles . . . Their vision is also characterized by shape constancy, that is, across changes in orientation or slant neonates are capable of recognizing the real shape of an object . . . Neonate vision also shows feature constancy, that is, the ability to recognize invariant features of an object across certain varying features, such as moving versus stable objects.[14]

The recognitions of different patterns of invariancy, variancy, and unity across time suggest that the basis of categorial discriminations and correlated transcendental schemata as perceptual tracking procedures are in play—however crudely—more or less from birth. The neonate is, as it were, prewired to negotiate experience's character as both temporal and centred on phenomena which are spatial, or inseparably related

---

[14] Shaun Gallagher, *How the Body Shapes the Mind* (Oxford: Clarendon Press, 2006), 164–5.

to space-occupying bodies (as in the case of subjective states, such as thought or feeling).

Now, whilst, for Kant, space and time play a receptive role in our cognitive framework, they are not wholly passive. Their properties determine how the items which are presented in them will appear. Of course, all perceptual items and states of affairs are different at the individual level, but there are basic features vis-à-vis space occupancy and its temporal conditions which determine the structure of their appearance in general terms.

In relation to the ontogenesis of experience, the mastery of these structuring features involves learning operative skills in relation to perceived items and states of affairs. These build on the innate propensities summarized by Gallagher, and involve a capacity to retain some sense of the previous appearances of the item which is currently being attended to.

However, the role of temporality in the gradual achievement of objective knowledge is surely as much, if not more, *future orientated*. How we negotiate the manifold is informed by *anticipations of* how, under different conditions of temporal succession (determined by the perceiver's orientation and movement, or the movement of objects), certain aspects of appearance will develop in such and such a way but not others, or will issue in such and such outcomes but—again—not others.

Through attention informed by retention, and anticipation, the child learns to negotiate the 'thingliness' and eventfulness of the world in a basic way even though it has not yet learned to understand these in terms of explicit categories and empirical concepts.

Basic sensori-motor negotiations of this kind centre on such things as constancy and invariance of spatial form and size (and, thence, identity) in things across variations of light conditions, and across different distances. We must comprehend the regularity of events and become aware of the capacity of some things and events to act upon us, and we upon them. We must form a sense of which things can be dealt with as discrete unities, and which things are easier to negotiate as aspects of some greater whole.

The basic levels of *recognition* involved here are the nascent categories. But, in order that conditions for such basic idioms of recognition are in place, we also need to *track* the relevant salient patterns of temporal succession in the sensible manifold.

As we have seen, Kant's transcendental schemata centre on the successive perception of extent or duration, substantiality, causal regularity, variations of magnitude, and patterns of temporal consistency amongst phenomena. These are precisely the temporal 'tracking' procedures—involving retention and anticipation—which the achievement of objective orientation requires.

They have their origins in perceptual habits acquired through the gradual coordination of the body's mental and sensori-motor powers in a unified field. For example, through repeated handling of such things as toys, and interactions with other people, the child becomes able to anticipate what their hidden perceptual aspects might be like, and finds ways to disclose them or have them disclose themselves, if not immediately accessible.

Likewise, it can retain a sense of its own past, and anticipate its possible future movements on the basis of these interactions. It learns an operational schema of possibilities in terms of how specific things, and their contexts of occurrence and location, have and might be expected to appear—but without yet identifying these *as* appearances of individual things or particular contexts of occurrence.

If this approach is correct, then we might characterize the transcendental schemata more specifically, as *pre-reflective procedures which involve a sense of how phenomena have appeared, and anticipate how they might come to appear under specific conditions of temporal succession.*

The nascent categories provide the recognitional dimension of objective orientation, whilst the transcendental schemata are the temporal tracking procedures—specific demands exerted on the productive imagination—which enable such recognition. Without these procedures we could not achieve objective knowledge because we would have no perceptual sense of there being any objects to know.

On these terms, then, the fact that a child has learned the 'thingly' character of things, and the eventful character of events, in these operational terms means that its ability to form *explicit* category and empirical *concepts* is in place. The acquisition of explicit concepts through language both feeds into and extends this basic objective orientation.

Now it might be admitted that retentive and anticipatory procedures of the kinds described are, indeed, necessary for the formation of objective knowledge. But it might also be argued that this position does not, *of itself*, justify Kant's connection of these with imagination specifically. Might they not, for example, be explained sufficiently as a function of attention informed by memory traces alone? Why should imagination be invoked at all?

An answer has already been given. In humans, objective orientation develops into concept acquisition. Since concepts, by definition, must apply to individuals in places and times beyond the limits of the present perceptual field, this means that, in order to form and apply them, human anticipatory procedures must be informed by a broader representational power—one which enables the projection of situations beyond the contents of the present perceptual field. Memory traces are simply not enough here.

And neither can the requisite trans-ostensive power be explained in terms of concepts of a more rudimentary *ur*-kind. At some point, an extra-conceptual factor will have to be invoked so as to explain the trans-ostensive leap which enables concept formation. If this were not the case, we would be caught in a vicious regress of concepts required to ground conceptuality and concepts to ground the concepts which ground conceptuality, ad infinitum.[15]

There is, as far as I can see, only one way to avoid such regress. It is to link human anticipatory procedures to imagination's capacity to produce quasi-sensory images. There is no other candidate for this role available.

Given some object, one can recall its previous states, and anticipate that it has hidden aspects or possible relations which will become perceptually available in correlation with the percipient's or object's changes of position. One does this in the fullest sense through the occurrent projection *in imagination* of their possible regularities, persistencies, and variations of appearance.

However, two important qualifications should be made to this. First, such imaginative activity does not *reproduce* the hidden or successive aspects or past appearances of its intended object in exact detail. It is literally a quasi-sensory *schematization* of possibilities of appearance. It is, in important respects, *selective*.

If, in contrast, the relation between imagination and its objects were one of exact correspondence, then images would obtrude upon the immediately given in a way that would collapse the distinction between actual and possible immediate perception, and thus render our perception of reality incoherent.

Second, as the subject becomes habituated to objective past or future vectors of phenomenal change, his or her perceptual negotiations

---

[15] For a lucid summary of the problem here, see Gibbons, *Kant's Theory of Imagination*, 8.

of them rarely require the occurrent exercise of imagination. Such occurrent employment settles—through sustained perceptual familiarity with the relevant dimensions of appearance—into a *disposition*. This means that it is not made occurrent in every cognitive act, but can be so realized as perceptual circumstances demand.

I am arguing, then, that in order to avoid infinite regress in the explanation of concept formation's trans-ostensive aspect, we must suppose the mediation of imagination as a disposition to represent that which is not given in perception. This disposition (directed towards specific aspects of past or possible future appearances) is the basis of the transcendental schemata.

We now have a general answer to the first of the key questions noted in Part 1. It is that of the sense in which schemata are 'contained' within concepts. In the case of transcendental schemata, we see that they are not 'contained' in the sense of being occurrent in every concept-application. Rather, they are dispositions which allow the tracking of specific general vectors of temporal succession in phenomena, thus rendering the unity of the manifold amenable to recognition. The very fact that they project phenomenal characteristics beyond the immediately given perceptual field means that it is through schemata that we become actively aware of the world's rich and enduring *phenomenal* structures and processes. They orientate us towards that *fabric of appearance* which (as we shall see in more detail in the next chapter) is the focus of the pure aesthetic judgement.

Further analysis of schemata-as-dispositions can also answer the other two outstanding questions from Part 1. These concern the sense in which schemata are 'homogeneous' with sensible concepts and the sense in which they provide 'rules' for such concepts.

To formulate these answers, however, we must offer a more detailed phenomenology of imagination's occurrent character in the schematization of concepts. This will also allow the approach to be extended to the schemata of empirical sensible concepts.

PART 4

To have a sensible concept in the fullest sense entails comprehension of its *extensional scope*—that is, the fact that it can be applied not only to directly perceived items, but also to different individuals which share the same properties, and which are distributed across, and perceivable by, different observers, at different times and places.

Objective orientation achieved through the nascent pre-reflective categories and their transcendental determinations of imagination already goes some way towards explaining how extensional scope can be understood as a basis for explicit individual concepts.

For if, say, a child learns the 'thingliness' and eventfulness of phenomena by habitual procedures, it is reasonable to suppose that, as a factor in such activity, it will, at the same time, learn some individual characteristics of specific kinds of things and events, and, in this way, be prepared for their explicit, conceptually mediated recognition.

These can involve instances of the categories, or of empirical sensible concepts. In either case, we are dealing with schematization that is more specifically focused than in the transcendental schemata's pre-reflective orientational role.

For example, when a ball is encountered, the child anticipates, on the basis of habitualized experience, that it will easily move if pushed, and will rebound from things if pushed hard enough.

But, in such experiences the child does not yet distinguish between individual balls and 'ballhood' per se. There is a general factor of a specific kind embodied in the individual encounters, but this has not yet been made the basis of an explicit concept.

The potential of such a *tacit generality* to be raised to *explicit* concept status is augmented by another aspect of the transcendental schemata. Earlier it was argued that without such procedures there would be no way of explaining how the trans-ostensive dimension of concepts could emerge. Such a dimension is basic to the comprehension of any concept's extensional scope.

Now, as retentive and anticipatory procedures, the transcendental schemata are simply habitual ways of dealing with structural features of things and events. However, the imaginative dispositions in question must, qua dispositional, be capable of sometimes being realized occurrently. The phenomenology of this is extremely instructive.

For example, suppose that, given a partial perspective on a building, one imagines what its hidden aspects and interior might be like. And, suppose also that one has never seen this actual building before. Under such circumstances, one's imaginings of the aspects and interior are consistent with the given stimuli, but whether or not they accurately represent the hidden aspects is another matter entirely.

However, the decisive point is the mere fact of some *general phenomenal consistency* in such imaging. They are schematic procedures which are consistent with enough phenomenal features to define the kind of thing in question. This is *all* that is required in order to negotiate the 'thingliness' of the thing in basic terms.

Indeed, in its productive form, imagination just *is* a quasi-sensory capacity for the modelling of possible appearances of specific kinds of sensible item. It need not be constrained by exact correspondence with existing sensible items, and, indeed, cannot be—given the schematic and stylized character of images per se (a topic I will return to in more detail a little further on).

Through this imaginative modelling, our sense of the phenomenal world's perceptual continuity within and beyond the immediate field will never have gaps. Given some portion of reality, we can imagine how it might be configured in areas to which we do not have immediate perceptual access.

Indeed, as long as an image sequence constitutes a logical schematic continuation of the given and presents how it *might* appear or might have appeared, then, in a key sense it does not matter if our subsequent explorations or recollections show the imagery to be not entirely accurate. In such cases, even though our modelling may be factually mistaken, it is at least coherent in having articulated a *possibility* of appearance.

This primacy of *general consistency* over exact correspondence in the exercise of the transcendental schemata opens up a broader possibility. For, whilst such modelling of appearances is learned initially in an ostensive context, its general character means that it can gradually be used *autonomously*—that is, as a basis for modelling kinds of phenomenal item or event other than those given in the immediate perceptual field.

For the child, encounters with perceived items may lead to daydreams or fantasies involving the imaginative fabrication of things or situations other than those which are present to perception. Through this, the child models possibilities of appearance which are not derived from direct empirical experience but which, nevertheless, share some general phenomenal traits with it.

Even if its imaginings are of specific individuals, these contain general characteristics of shape, size, and detail which can also be developed easily into the imagining of other individuals of the same kind—even though these 'general' individuals are not clearly separated from the one originally represented.

Interestingly, there is a bias towards generality even in the case of specific imagined individuals. Suppose, for example, that a child imagines its mother. One presumes that if the child's linguistic capacities are developed the image will be able to satisfy specific descriptions—e.g., 'mother when she meets meet me from school'.

But, if the image is just of mother per se (and especially if the child's linguistic capacities are not developed) it will involve some of her identifying general phenomenal characteristics, but not as given under some exact time and place of perceptual encounter.

Indeed, even in the case where the child can imagine 'Mother when she meets me from school', various kinds of core phenomenal content will be consistent with the image's realization. If the image is not a sustained sequence of imagery, then it must have appropriate synoptic/schematic features. Its selectivity will demand an element of generality.

One does not mechanically reproduce past appearances, one *generates* them as consistently as possible with the specific description of them. If the description entails more than one event, then the generalizing factor will be all the more pronounced. But, even in recollections of a single event, interpretation rather than exact mechanical reproduction is involved. (I will return to this point in more detail in Part 5.)

In this way, then, possibilities of appearance come to be modelled with *a significant degree of autonomy from the actual*. Such autonomy means that the child's cognitive power is now extended radically, and that its introductions to language are informed by a decisive trans-ostensive representational factor.

Reciprocally, the acquisition of language allows key recognitional distinctions to be made at the level of imagination and perception. Specifically, the child is able, gradually, to distinguish between imaginative fantasies per se and imagined real possibilities and between kinds of thing, their individual instances, and the relation between these elements.

Imagination's capacity for modelling appearance in general is, then, complementary to explicit concept formation. This encompasses not only the general sense of 'thingliness' and eventfulness that is directly involved in category formation, but extends also to our acquisition of empirical sensible concepts.

A further key aspect of productive imagination is also relevant to both these dimensions of conceptualization. For the extensional scope inherent to the notion of a concept means not only that a set of phenomenal properties can be instantiated by many individuals in different places and times, it means also that these are, in principle, accessible to different observers, *under different perceptual conditions*. If a concept is to be comprehended qua concept, these possibilities of different observational conditions must inform its articulation.

Now, in schematizing the previous or hidden aspects of a given object, there is, of necessity, qua schematic character, an element of *selective* interpretation, and this is true even if the object's hidden aspects are ones which have actually been experienced previously.

The element of schematic selectivity is, of course, even more pronounced in those cases of imagining items or states of affairs which are not immediately given, or of which we have not had direct previous experience.

This leads to the decisive point. The very fact that phenomenal items and states of affairs are schematized through selective interpretation has great significance vis-à-vis objective cognition. It means that the schema characterizes its object from the imaginer's point of view. There is a core of objective properties which determines what is selected, but *how* these properties are characterized is down to the individual imaginer's subjective perspective upon them.

Given, therefore, that in imagination, conceptual content cannot be separated from subjective orientation, the image has the potential for exemplifying the general fact that such a content is encounterable under different perceptual conditions.

This point should now be linked to the other key intrinsic features of the productive imagination's occurrent imagery—namely, its tacit concrete universality, its orientation towards general phenomenal consistency rather than exact correspondence with the object, and its potential to be used independently of that which is given in immediate perception.

If we connect all these points, it is clear that the occurrent exercise of imagination, *as such*, has an inherent dimension of generality. This answers the second question left unanswered in Part 1. *Sensible concepts are 'homogenous' with general features of their objects because they are enabled through the mediation of imagination—a cognitive capacity whose occurrent exercise, itself, tends (through its schematic character) towards some generalization of the intended object's phenomenal features.*

It is surely this homogeneity which provides a basis for learning of general linguistic rules and which, reciprocally, the acquisition of language refines (thus enabling the full formation and application of concepts based on a sense of their extensional scope). Imagination provides the mediating trans-ostensive dimension which allows concepts to be articulated.

This relates directly to the third question left unanswered from Part 1—namely, the sense in which schemata are 'rules' for applying concepts. If my arguments are correct, it is clear that schemata are necessary to the *formation* of concepts. However, it is less clear as to how they might be regarded as rules for the *application* of concepts, in the mature language-user.

It comes down to this. Could we recognize, say, a saucer or a dog as an instance of the relevant concept, in the absence of a disposition to schematize it in terms of sensible core properties which define the concept in question?

The answer is 'no'. For whilst schemata need not always be involved occurrently in the conceptualizing of sensible items, every such concept must be, nevertheless, in principle *schematizable*—that is, it is entailed that if one has a concept of a sensible item one must be able also to imagine what an instance of that concept might be like in general terms.

This is true even of concepts which one has never actually seen an instance of, or of fictional entities. One may know the notion of a 'hippogryph' only as a mythological term per se. But if—through description—we know what kind of thing such an entity is, then it becomes possible to schematize how it *might* appear even though we have never seen such a creature in actuality.

The point is, then, that for a language user to comprehend a sensible concept *as such*, the concept must be schematizable—the user must, through imagination, be able to model how an instance of it might appear in general sensible terms (irrespective of whether or not such an instance is present in the immediate perceptual field).

If, in contrast, a subject could only negotiate the basis of such a concept's appearance through recognition of immediately given instances of it *in concreto*, then that subject would, surely, not yet have mastered the relevant concept in its full extensional scope. Its recognitional capacities would be more animal than human.

To understand a *sensible* concept, in other words, cannot be separated from the capacity to schematize an instance of what it might be like qua sensory—however bare such a schematization might be. One must know it as a possible appearance—that is, in terms of the sensible conditions under which it occupies space and time.

To reiterate, then, the application of concepts to sensible manifolds does not, of itself, necessitate the occurrent mediation of schemata, but since schematization is so intimately bound up with the trans-ostensive basis of concept acquisition and application, one cannot separate the having of a sensible concept from the dispositional capacity to schematize it in imagination (if cognitive circumstances demand).

Schematizability rather than schemata, as such, provide a rule—or, better, a *criterion*—for comprehending the general sensible scope of a concept's application. Even though the criterion here is psychological, it could be also be expressed in public terms if the subject were able to follow commands of the form 'draw a picture of an x—not a particular x, just an x'. Through being able to do this, the subject would provide publically accessible evidence of knowing 'what it is like' for the term to apply in general sensible terms.

It should be emphasized that as well as serving as a logical criterion of the subject's comprehension of a concept's sensible scope, the schemata also has a much more mundane, but phenomenologically vital role.

Our everyday cognitive life is replete with recognitional acts involving concepts. And, whilst perceptual contexts rarely *demand* that the correlated dispositions to schematize are exercised occurrently, they often are—purely by chance or association. We may, for example, be thinking of some kind of thing and find that an image exemplifying some characteristic appearances of things of that kind happens to come to mind.

Happenstances of this kind are quite common and important. For, through them, something which is a necessary formal condition of cognition comes also to enrich the general phenomenal texture of subjective experience. The significance of schematization vis-à-vis self-knowledge can, indeed, be taken much further. It is to this possibility that I now turn.

PART 5

As we have seen, to schematize is to be selective, but with a subjective emphasis. Even in their exemplification of general features schemata are manifestly *stylized*—i.e., have a particular character.

This has some remarkable implications for *self-knowledge*. Kant does not consider these, but they are generally consistent with his approach.

They converge on what follows from the intrinsic connection between stylization, imagery, and memory.

It is all too easy to think of memories as faded copies of 'original' experiences—i.e., as their decayed indexical residue. However, this is a woefully incorrect model. To see why, we must first note a distinction between 'fact memory' and 'corporeal memory'. The former is a recall based exclusively on description whilst the latter involves memories with some sensible—that is to say, imaginative—content.

As our experience increases, a specific factual description may be rendered less amenable to present recollection, but success in recollecting it does not require that we sort through our past experiences until it is found. What happens, rather, is that what is accessible to memory can be *schematized* in a way which is consistent with what that memory describes in factual terms. Such corporeal memory is projected on the basis of our present interests. Its style is indelibly shaped by these.

It is this very factor which is central to personal identity. Memory is at its most real for us when it is projected as image rather than conceived as fact alone. However, because of the gap between the image and its referent, this means that the present context of projection must interpret the memory from its own point of view. How the past appears is thereby inseparable from the present.

And, of course, there are many areas of our past of which we may have some factual knowledge without being able to recall in sensible terms what the experiences in question were like. However, in such cases, we can project imagery which is consistent with what we know, and in this way even unknown aspects of the past are filled in through the fact of their being schematized in relation to present knowledge.

This might serve as the basis of a more general theory of personal identity. Indeed, some unexpected further elements can also be filled in by reference to the objective dimension of experience.

As an entrée to this, however, we must draw another inference from the nature of the image per se, which Kant does not. It concerns an implicit reference to the personal identity of anyone who schematizes.

If, as we have seen, any image is stylized, then it exemplifies (to some degree) a personal perspective on things. In the previous few arguments, I have emphasized this perspective as being interpretative and present-orientated. But, there is another implicit aspect which centres on *perceptual possibility*.

To schematize is to exemplify conditions which are consistent with a concept's sensible application. If this is so, then, reference to a possible observer is entailed in so far as sensibilia are, by definition, in principle accessible to perception.

It is important to stress the 'possible' aspect here. For the schema-product does not have to exemplify actual concept instances which we have actually experienced. The general observer implied in schematization, is, rather, one which, by definition, *notionally* includes the one who performs it. Even though he or she does not intend such specific reference in order for the schematization to occur, it is nevertheless phenomenologically entailed.

There is, therefore, an inescapable 'possible for me' clause built into schematization. It is not just that it is this particular 'I' who projects the schema, but also that *what* is so projected is one aspect of a world of possible concept occurrence and application which must include myself qua concept-user.[16] Indeed, the stylized character of the schema will tend to underwrite the implicit subjective reference factor here.

This intimacy of subject and concept achieved through schemata has a further decisive significance.

Earlier, I emphasized the necessary cognitive role of the transcendental schemata—as an enabling factor in the formation of objective knowledge. Given, therefore, the foregoing account of the nature of imagery, this means that in so far as objective knowledge necessarily involves schemata, our conception of the object is inseparable from the having of *possible* personal perspectives upon it, even though it does not explicitly draw upon our actual experiences of it. A disposition to model the scope of concepts will, when made occurrent, issue in exemplars not only of the concept in question but of a personal way of modelling it.

Now, for Kant, the kind of connective 'synthetic' activity bound up with concepts of self and world per se has a basically formal significance. It involves a unified self as a necessary condition of objective knowledge through its involvement in the application of the categories (the doctrine of 'pure apperception', as Kant calls it).

However, the foregoing analysis has opened out an entirely new prospect. For it is clear that the imagination's schematizing activity *exemplifies the spontaneity of the self* qua *individual cognitive agent*. By understanding transcendental and empirical knowledge of objects *and*

---

[16] This point is also recognized (but without being significantly developed) by Wilfrid Sellars in his 'The Role of Imagination in Kant's Theory of Experience', in Henry W. Johnstone (ed.), *Categories: A Colloquium* (University Park, Pa.: Pennsylvania State University Press, 1978). See esp. pp. 236–7.

states of self-knowledge as necessarily linked to this activity, we link them to the exemplification of the individual self as well as to subjectivity in formal terms.

The ramifications of this are of great interest, both within Kant's philosophy and in broader terms. In relation to the former, the schematism may now offer the basis for a rethinking of Kant's notoriously opaque conception of personal identity.

At the very least, it certainly extends and consolidates his basic strategy in the transcendental deduction—i.e., showing that subject and object of experience are reciprocally dependent through their involvement in the application of the categories. His emphasis on schemata fills in key details, and my development of it gives further credibility to its overall claims.

In more general terms, there is something about the role of schemata which links the past, present, future, and counterfactual states of a subject. Schematizing is done in the present and, whatever its content, exemplifies something of the personal perspective of the cognitive agent.

Kant notes that it is not the business of imagination to furnish intuitions but to organize the manifold of sensible perceptions.[17] But, in the schemata we have a factor necessary for the objective organization of experience which acts upon time *through*, in part, the subject's unique perspective upon it. The exemplification of this might not amount to a perception of the self in Kant's or any other terms, but it may be about as close as we can get. There is perhaps room for an exemplificational theory of personal identity to be constructed around it.

I shall not pursue this possibility here. The key point is that if this analysis is correct then imagination is not only a necessary condition for knowledge of an objective world but, through its role in this, is also implicated in the unity of the self.

CONCLUSION

In this chapter, then, I have explored the role of the schematism in that reciprocity of objective and self-knowledge which is achieved through the categories. In particular, we have seen how the transcendental schemata consist of tracking procedures based on dispositions to imagine temporal

---

[17] See Kant, *The Critique of Pure Reason*, B179/A140.

successions of appearance. They are procedures arising from demands made by specific concepts on the productive imagination.

Through such demands, the unity of the manifold becomes accessible to recognition. Without these dispositions and their occurrent realization as quasi-sensory images, there would be no viable explanation of how concepts acquire their trans-ostensive scope.

In the course of discussing the schemata of empirical concepts, I showed further that schematization through quasi-sensory imagery has a number of intrinsically general characteristics. In concert, these are highly complementary to concept formation. It is, indeed, this intrinsic generality which gives the schema's occurrent realizations some homogeneity with that of sensible concepts.

Finally, I argued that schematizing activity might also be taken to encompass key aspects of memory, and to exemplify the activity of the self at the level of individual cognitive being as well as in terms of its formal unity.

There is a supremely important conclusion which must be reiterated for the purposes of subsequent chapters. It is that *understanding and imagination (and the relations between them) are central to objective knowledge and its correlation with both the unity of the self and the character of individual subjectivity.*

It should also be recognized that the relation of understanding and imagination means that cognition is not simply a process of classification through judgement. In order for any empirical judgements to take place, we need the categories and those perceptual tracking procedures which are provided by the schemata. As we have seen, schematization is a selective and stylized process. Its projection of content in accordance with a concept is an inherently *creative* one. Overt acts of recognition involve a correlation of phenomenal unity and diversity, achieved through understanding and imagination.

Given this, it is hardly surprising that the cornerstone of Kant's aesthetic theory turns out to be the heightened and creative interaction of understanding and imagination. His aesthetics reaches deep into the factors which enable knowledge of self and world. In particular, the role of the categories and transcendental schemata is of decisive significance in mediating the aesthetic judgement, as will be shown in many examples in the following chapter. It is to this rich cognitivist aesthetics I now turn.

3

Pure Aesthetic Judgement: A Harmony of Imagination and Understanding

INTRODUCTION

Kant's aesthetics are set out in their most comprehensive form in Book I of the third *Critique*. As well as characteristic difficulties connected with his jargon and complex conceptual architectonics, there is also a problem of significant repetition and use of synonyms. In terms of the latter, for example, the 'pure aesthetic judgement'[1] is also known as the 'judgement of taste'.

These specific usages encompass reference to both the features of phenomena which occasion aesthetic responses and to the feelings which are involved in this. On other occasions, Kant refers to the former through the synonyms 'subjective finality', 'purposiveness without purpose', the 'form of finality', and 'formal finality'.

In this chapter, I shall, in Part 1, freely outline Kant's basic strategy concerning the aesthetic, as set out in the Preface and Introduction to the third *Critique*. His general approach to judgement will be revised

---

[1] An incisive, in-depth critical survey of the first-wave of important literature on this topic can be found in Hannah Ginsborg, *The Role of Taste in Kant's Theory of Cognition* (Cambridge, Mass. and London: Harvard University Press, 1990), 45–101. A useful review encompassing more-recent material is Paul Guyer's chapter 'The Harmony of the Faculties Revisited', in Rebecca Kukla (ed.), *Aesthetics and Cognition in Kant's Critical Philosophy* (Cambridge: Cambridge University Press, 2006), 162–93. Guyer identifies, initially, two broad approaches to the problem. The 'precognitive strategy' seeks to ground the harmony of the faculties on those factors which precede and thence enable normal processes of conceptualization. Guyer suggests that Henrich, Crawford, Ginsborg, and Makkreel favour this approach albeit with significantly different perspectives upon it. The other major approach to the harmony of the faculties is from a 'multicognitive' viewpoint. This centres on the idea that beautiful manifolds allow of different ways of being conceptualized such that our judgement does not involve a definite concept per se. This view is linked by Guyer to Fred Rush and, in a slightly more qualified way, to Allison. In *Kant and the Claims of Taste* (Cambridge, Mass. and London: Harvard University Press, 1979), Guyer himself favoured the precognitive interpretation but

in important ways.² Part 2 will begin addressing the substance of his theory by considering the *disinterested* character of the pure aesthetic judgement.

Part 3 will focus on the harmony of imagination and understanding which is intrinsic to Kant's all-important notion of *subjective finality*. It will be argued that Kant's exposition is unnecessarily restrictive. To render his approach more viable, I will then, in Part 4 offer a phenomenology of beautiful forms which render the temporal dimension of

---

has now revised his position. Specifically he holds that whilst aspects of both major approaches are consistent with Kant's texts, a number of problems accrue to both. Chief among these is the point that 'the very idea of a state of our cognitive powers that does not involve any determinate concepts is dubious' (Kukla, *Aesthetics and Cognition*, 178). This necessitates, accordingly, a third 'metacognitive' approach. It holds, specifically, that 'in the experience of beauty in an object, we recognize that the ordinary conditions for cognition of such an object are satisfied but also feel that our experience of the manifold presented by the object satisfies our demand for unity in a way that goes beyond whatever is necessary for the satisfaction of those ordinary conditions' (Kukla, *Aesthetics and Cognition*, 187) The problem with this, however, is that it makes the pure aesthetic judgement dependent on the mediation of the concept of an object, even though the factors which make the object beautiful are not sufficiently described by that concept. It is telling in this respect, that Guyer's main examples here are derived from art, and I think that what he is doing is, in effect, looking at the harmony of the faculties on the basis of fine art, rather than on the basis of that which Kant himself emphasizes emphatically—namely, the beautiful forms of nature. This emphasis by no means rules out a link between the harmony of the faculties and fine art, but, as we shall see in Chap. 6, it requires a very different interpretation than is involved in the case of beauty. Kant is right to privilege the pure aesthetic judgement's relation to beauty, because its disinterested character means that it is a pleasure in how things *appear*, and constitutes, indeed, the logically most basic form of pure aesthetic judgement. To follow Guyer's strategy would distort this, through introducing the constraints of a definite concept. My own approach to the harmony of the faculties is emphatically 'multicognitive'. It holds that whilst the pure aesthetic judgement does not involve any definite concept as an outcome, definite concepts involving the categories and transcendental schemata are involved in it in a ceaseless play of interactions. The only commentator who allows a significant role for the categories is Rudolf A. Makkreel in his *Imagination and Interpretation in Kant: The Hermeneutical Import of the Critique of Judgment* (Chicago and London: University of Chicago Press, 1990); see esp. pp. 26–58. On p. 56, he links the categories to aesthetic judgement but does not follow this up with any sustained account of their phenomenological function in this context. This is also true of Malcolm Budd, who affirms the significance of the categories for aesthetic judgement, but only in passing. See p. 6 of his 'Delight in the Natural World: Kant on the Aesthetic Appreciation of Nature', *British Journal of Aesthetics*, 38 (1998), 1–18.

² There is a short and a longer version of the Introduction to the third *Critique*. These are both presented in Immanuel Kant, *Critique of the Power of Judgment*, trans. Paul Guyer and Eric Matthews (Cambridge: Cambridge University Press, 2000). I will use this translation, with parallel references to the *Critique of Judgment*, trans. Werner Pluhar (New York: Hacket and Co., 1987) and *Critique of the Power of Judgment*, trans. James Creed Meredith (New York: Oxford University Press, 1978). For an especially thorough analysis of the meaning and structure of Kant's general framework of ideas in these Introductions, see Henry Allison, *Kant's Theory of Taste* (Cambridge: Cambridge University Press, 2001), 13–64.

the pure aesthetic judgement in a more consistent way than Kant himself does. Particular emphasis will be given to the role of the categories and transcendental schemata.

In Conclusion, I will develop his position in relation to the ontogenesis of cognition (based on the approach taken in Chapters 1 and 2).

PART 1

Kant's introductory position centres on the point that human being (by virtue of its free and rational capacities) is the 'final end' of nature. This is because, without the existence of the free rational being, nature would be devoid of any worth.

Now, if freedom is the basis of nature's worth, a difficulty arises. A free being's sensible (and thence natural) aspects present great obstacles to the exercise of freedom in its highest form—namely, morality. Natural drives make us tend towards selfish motives, and even if they involve other-regarding feeling, these cannot provide authentic moral motivation because feelings of this kind are (according to Kant) based, ultimately, on mechanistic processes bound up with our animal nature rather than our free rational being.

Kant deals with this difficulty in an extremely complex way. To make sense of it, we must consider the notion of an 'end' (with its synonyms 'purpose' and 'finality'). The notion is derived from human rational activity and artifice. In general terms, an end is an intended outcome, brought about through adopting the appropriate means. Given this outcome, one might regard the achieved end as, in effect, the causal ground of the means and materials which are involved in its realization.

For reasons which will become clear, Kant also uses 'end' *analogically* in relation to the forms of organic nature and the system of nature in general. In this context, we might note, initially, that an end consists of general, *kind-defining* features which we assume—on the analogy with human artifice—to be a causal ground, of which the individual objects whose kinds are defined by these features, are, in effect, the outcomes.

In Kant's terms, they are 'final in relation' to the 'end' defined by such general features. (The individual rose, for example, is final in relation to the end constituted by 'rosehood' per se.)

For Kant, when thinking of nature as a system, we take this approach to a higher level. Nature is regarded as a *teleological* hierarchy of individuals, species, and genera, each level of which is 'final in relation to' factors in the levels above. It is as if natural forms had been designed to serve the purposes defined by the concept which they instantiate, and that these, in turn, are final in relation to more general concepts of natural phenomena.

The question arises, then, as to *why* we should consider nature on this analogical basis.[3] Kant's answer is complex, and centres in the first instance on the notion of judgement.[4]

In general terms, judgement involves the identification of something as having such and such a character or being in such and such a relation.[5] For Kant, there are two basic directions to such classification. We may simply recognize the something as an instance of such and such a concept. When recognition is grounded in this way, on a concept that we already have, Kant calls it a 'determinative judgement'.

The second direction of conceptualization arises when we negotiate something whose appropriate classification is not immediately apparent. Here we have to search out a concept which fits our interest in the particular. Kant calls this the 'judgement of reflection'.

Unfortunately, Kant does not probe judgement any further in psychological terms. But, there are a number of important qualifications which need to be made if the *real* nature of judgement is to be clarified. For example, when we search out a concept for a particular, it is not that we lack *any* concept of it. We must know that there is 'something' for which more precise classification is needed, and this initial, *orienting* determinative judgement concerning the 'something' acts as a springboard for its more exact classification.

[3] For a succinct discussion of some of the difficulties raised by Kant's analogy between artifice and nature, see Guyer, *Kant and the Claims of Taste*, 54–67.

[4] The most thorough study of Kant's notion of judgement over the whole range of the Critical philosophy is Béatrice Longuenesse's *Kant and the Capacity to Judge* (Princeton, NJ: Princeton University Press, 1998). This account, as Longuenesse puts it, is 'mainly devoted to elucidating Kant's intentions and results' (p. 14). My great problem with her and most other contemporary Kant interpreters is that through emphasizing judgement as a logical procedure (based on the use of predicates) the psychological dimension is rather neglected. To be fair to Longuenesse, the logical function is, indeed, what judgement in its normal sense is about. But, in the Kantian aesthetic context, it behooves us to be much more attentive to psychological issues—especially when these offer possible clues to the elusive cognitive character of aesthetic judgement.

[5] See Kant, *Critique of the Power of Judgment*, 66–7 (Pluhar, 18–19; Meredith, 18–19). In Longuenesse, *Kant and the Capacity to Judge*, we find an emphasis on Kant's notion of the 'merely' reflective judgement (discussed at pp.163–6). In this, she touches on issues relevant to the key notion of the *emergent judgement of reflection* (which I am about to introduce). However, her discussion is constrained by the points that I described in n. 4.

However, it is important to make a distinction, also, between dispositional and occurrent judgement. For example, orienting determinative judgements of the kind just described are not made in an explicit way in the normal course of things. Rather they are grounded in a network of cognitive dispositions which give a general unity to our experience of the world. (This network, of course, constellates around the categories.). It is only when circumstances demand, that such judgements are explicitly occasioned in the form, say, of the overt recognition that 'here is something whose more precise character needs to be determined'.

However, what neither Kant nor his interpreters consider are those further situations when the immediate 'something' is particularly elusive in terms of finding a more-exact concept for it. In these circumstances, the orienting determinative judgement can lead to *cognitive deliberation*—in the form of subjecting the particular to close scrutiny or perceptual exploration, or both—in order for its more precise phenomenal character to be determined, and thence brought under an appropriate, more precise concept.

It is vitally important to identify the factors involved in this deliberation. They centre on how the particular in question presents its structural features. And this means both the particular range of structural features which are specific to it and also the particular way in which these features are instantiated.

For example, any phenomenal manifold will be unified in some respect. The character of this unity will be determined by such things as specific combinations of shape, volume, and mass; and by the relation between these features and the distribution of parts in the manifold. Do they, for example, cohere as a loose plurality, or as a unified totality, or simply as a whole where the relation of parts is not so well defined? In what sense do these parts define the character of the whole? Are they the attributes of a thing; are they merely a plural assemblage? What is the character and order of their spatial distribution? Do they, for example, form a hierarchy; do they balance one another, or do some seem to limit or even negate the perceptual role of others in how the manifold presents to the senses? Are the features of the manifold which we perceive its invariant and substantial aspects, or are some of them just effects determined by the particular conditions under which the manifold is perceived? Are any of these features such that we could remove or change them without changing the character of the whole—that is, are some absolutely necessary to its identity in a way that others are not?

If we are seeking to conceptualize a state of affairs involving more than one thing, then matters get more complex. We have to negotiate, also, the character of the causal or other kind of relation between these elements within the broader perceptual manifold. Does this state of affairs have a distinctive group identity or is it a mere plurality? Does it make sense to say that its total nature is presented immediately, or is the relation between the parts or elements in the state of affairs one which suggests extension beyond the immediately perceptible? Are there variations of magnitude in how the elements in the state of affairs relate to one another, and, if so, what sort of magnitude is involved? Is it based on the real character of the elements or is it one which is determined by the position which the perceiving subject takes upon the manifold?

I am arguing, then, that when we seek to conceptualize some item whose identity is challenging, we interrogate its particular character in relation to structural factors on the lines just described. This gives us a more complete sense of what this particularity involves, so that we have information that assists in the conceptualization of the manifold in more exact or appropriate terms.

Such interrogation is not intelligible except through the occurrent involvement of relevant categories and transcendental schemata. To determine a particular's character qua particular is to follow the distinctive ways in which its empirical properties exemplify phenomenal structure. And this amounts to sustained attention based on a back-and-forth movement between the categories and the individual properties of the manifold. Only through this cognitive elucidation of the particular's phenomenal character will we find a more appropriate concept or concepts for its description. All in all, the categories and transcendental schemata play a vital *mediating* role in the accomplishing of more deliberative instances of empirical judgement.

This leads to a remarkable conclusion. When judgements of reflection occasion sustained cognitive deliberation of this kind, there is not one judgement involved but, rather, *many individual ones.* Sustained perceptual scrutiny necessitates many small acts of recognition and appraisal in relation to the manifold, and it is as the outcome of these multiple acts that the more appropriate concept *emerges.* This multiplicity is, however, not experienced *as* a multiplicity. The whole series is based on the intention to find a more appropriate concept, and it is *the psychological continuity from intention to recognitional outcome,* here, that gives the multiplicity its psychologically unified character as a single judgement.

I shall call these cognitively complex structures '*emergent judgements of reflection*'. Sometimes they will occur quite consciously, in that we are aware that there is a cognitive problem which is troubling us. For the most part, however, we will enact them without being aware explicitly that we are so doing—and the more so in those cases where the particular's form is so *engrossing* as to absorb our attention entirely. (As we shall see in due course, this character is of decisive significance in explaining beauty.[6])

With this revision of Kant's notion of judgement in mind, we can now return to his own main avenue of approach to the reflective variety. It centres on the contingency and complexity of natural forms. For the reflective judgement, organic nature presents a great challenge, in so far as it is a teeming mass of hugely complex individuals and processes whose *systematic understanding* requires sustained judgements of the utmost intricacy. This is why Kant holds that we *must* think of nature on the model of human artifice, or, more specifically, *as if* it had been designed so as to facilitate cognition of it.

A teleological presupposition of this kind is a necessary, and thence an a priori, principle of reflective judgement. It is necessary because without it (one presumes) our cognitive capacities would be overwhelmed by the overwhelming complexity of the specific idioms of organic life, and the processes which link and sustain them. Putting this in terms of my earlier revision of Kant's approach to judgement, one might say that the *emergent judgement of reflection* is guided by the concept of an end as its appropriate outcome. The teleological principle is a guiding a priori principle of cognitive economy in our conceptualization of natural forms.

---

[6] In her important book *Kant on Beauty and Biology* (Cambridge: Cambridge University Press, 2007), Rachel Zuckert argues that in so far as the categories are 'necessary universal concepts' 'they do not provide us with any means of recognizing among sensible properties in their contingent, particular, heterogeneous character' (p. 294). But, to discriminate perceptually between any elements in a manifold—to explore it—*just is* to see how its fabric of particularity is structured. The particularity of a configuration only reveals its particularity when one investigates the individual way in which it manifests those structural features which give form to the manifold—such as having just these invariant features, or just this configuration of parts, etc. Zuckert seems to interpret contingent and individual properties as if recognized *in vacuo*. But, qua phenomenal, they instantiate also more-general features bound up with the objective structure of the manifold. We can doubtless recognize such properties in terms of logical recognition without explicitly invoking the categories and transcendental schemata, but if this recognition requires perceptual deliberation in order to be achieved, then even contingent features have to be characterized in terms of how they exemplify more-general features. The recognition and explanation of difference presuppose some context of sameness in relation to which the differences can be made specific.

It is this principle which allows the first bridge between freedom and nature to be made. For Kant, our capacity for theoretical knowledge is driven by an 'interest of reason' which strives to understand its object in the most total and comprehensive terms. Hence when—in reflective judgement—we follow teleological connections in the understanding of nature, we will be led, eventually, to the most complete or 'final end'. This is the feature which forms the purpose of nature as a whole system. And the feature in question is humankind in its definitive character as free rational being. In Kant's words:

> only in the human being, although in him only as a subject of morality, is unconditional legislation with regard to ends to be found, which therefore makes him alone capable of being a final end, to which the whole of nature is teleologically subordinated.[7]

On these terms, to think of nature teleologically leads us to think of the supreme end which is the ground of all the rest. For Kant, only humans are qualified for this role, in so far as they follow moral precepts determined by their own autonomous rational being. The a priori principle of reflective judgement, in other words, leads us to understand that whatever obstacles nature presents to moral life freedom (and, thence, our moral being) is the final end of nature.

A detailed exposition of this theoretical understanding forms the substance of Part II of the third *Critique*—namely, the 'Critique of Teleological Judgment'. However, to understand its relevance for aesthetic judgement, we must address the second bridge which Kant makes between freedom and nature.

Again, it is extremely complex, and involves features of Kant's architectonic thinking which I will not go into. Matters can, however, be summarized in terms of the following substantive points.

Kant holds that individual reflective judgements of nature are directed towards *objective finality* (e.g., when we judge, say, that 'this is a flower' or that such and such a set of life forms serve such and such a purpose in relation to the existence of other life forms). Because such judgements involve 'ends'—following the analogy with artifice—Kant assumes that successful realizations of such judgements (as is the case with successfully realized artifice) will involve a sense of pleasure in the outcome.

In the case of most examples of such judgement, the pleasure aspect will be so small, or something which we are so habituated to, as to pass

---

[7] Kant, *Critique of the Power of Judgment*, §84, 302–3 (Pluhar, 323; Meredith, 100).

unnoticed. However, in those judgements which involve what Kant calls *subjective finality*, the pleasure factor is massively to the fore.

The grounds of such judgement centre on the relation between understanding and imagination. In previous chapters, we have seen how this relation is the basis of all objective knowledge, and the unity of self-consciousness. In the third *Critique*, Kant now suggests that judgements which enhance the cooperation of these two capacities can be regarded as final in relation to, or as serving the purpose of, cognition in general.

We reach the decisive point. Kant claims that

If pleasure is connected with the mere apprehension (*apprehensio*) of the form of an object of intuition, then the representation is thereby related not to the object, but solely to the subject, and the pleasure can express nothing but its suitability to the cognitive faculties that are in the play in the reflective power of judgement, in so far as they are in play, and thus merely a subjective formal purposiveness of the object.[8]

The point is that sometimes we take pleasure in the mere intuition of a perceived item (i.e., in the way it appears to perception). This is the judgement of subjective finality. Its pleasurable character is grounded not on the object being judged as an instance of some definite objectively final concept, but, rather, in the way that perception of its form enhances the interaction of imagination and understanding—an interaction which is recognized only through a feeling of pleasure.

And, since this interaction is the general basis of reflective judgement per se (and, indeed, of all cognition), then we can regard forms which facilitate such interaction as *subjectively* final or purposive in relation to the a priori principle of reflective judgement itself. They serve the 'purpose' of cognition in general by stimulating the interaction of those two capacities which are basic to it.

Forms which bring about this pleasure are called *beautiful*. It is *as if* they had been designed with the purpose of facilitating cognition in general. And the 'pure' aesthetic pleasure arising from judgements of beauty has a highly distinctive status. For in so far as it is pleasure, it is bound up with our sensible animal nature, but in so far as it is grounded in a harmony of subjective cognitive capacities, it has some connection with conditions involved in the exercise of freedom.

As we shall see in the next chapter, the connection goes deeper still. The pleasure arising from the enhanced interaction of imagination

---

[8] Kant, *Critique of the Power of Judgment*, VII. 75–6 (Pluhar, 29–30 ; Meredith, 30).

and understanding has claim to universal validity. It is a higher pleasure—that is, more than mere animal gratification. By means of it, an aspect of our sensible nature finds some harmony with our existence as free rational beings. This forms the second bridge between nature and freedom.

My exposition of Kant's introductory approach to the aesthetic in the third *Critique* is now complete. It is now time to look in much greater detail at the substance of his theory.

PART 2

Part I of the third *Critique* is the 'Critique of Aesthetic Judgment'. I shall devote attention to Book I—'The Analytic of the Beautiful'.

Kant approaches aesthetic judgement on the assumption that it has four aspects or 'Moments', each corresponding to those which traditionally define the forms of judgement per se. These are the qualitative, the quantitative, the relational, and the modal.

He deals with these in turn. However, his approach does not involve any clearly developing structure of argument. To grasp the essentials, it is better, rather, to assemble ideas and connections which, to some degree, cut across Kant's order of presentation.

As we have seen, the aesthetic involves a feeling of pleasure. For Kant, there are two forms of judgement based on this—the 'material' (also called the 'empirical' or 'impure') and the 'judgement of taste' or 'pure aesthetic judgement'.

Material aesthetic judgements arise from the 'agreeable'—that is, that which is found pleasant in sensation. For Kant, this also encompasses the 'charming' and the 'emotional'.[9]

---

[9] An extensive and instructive discussion of these notions in terms of the internal structure of Kant's philosophy can be found in Allison, *Kant's Theory of Taste*, 131–8. In terms of more-general philosophical worth, however, it is surely the case that Kant's theories of the charming and of the emotional are terribly dated, and should be discarded. He regards, for example, the pleasure in colour as an instance of the charming, and thence one whose origins are causal rather than cognitive. Now, whilst our preference for one particular colour over another may rest on purely personal preference, to take a pleasure in the perceptual relations between colours can go beyond this—in so far as the more such relations are involved in the pleasure the more it is grounded on the harmony of imagination and understanding. Kant's theory of the emotions is equally off the mark. It is now acknowledged universally, in philosophical circles and beyond, that whilst the emotions may involve disruptive outbursts, their major function is to facilitate the cognitive unity of experience. Indeed, Antony Damasio

The key criterion of such material aesthetic judgements is that they are, in effect, reports concerning the causal impact of stimuli which are found pleasurable or otherwise. Their significance in these respects is determined only by the personal preferences of the one who experiences them.

Now, if something is found agreeable, Kant holds that we have an 'interest' in it. This means that the 'real existence' of the object which gives rise to the interest is a matter of concern.

Suppose, for example, that we are hungry and see a tasty looking pie in a shop window. If it turned out that the pie was merely an advertising prop made out of plastic, our anticipation of agreeable gustatory sensations would be thwarted. Agreeable sensations only arise from real causal impacts on the relevant senses. We have, accordingly, an interest that the objects which promise to deliver them are likewise real. Mere appearances will not do.

Kant also raises another issue which relates to feeling and interest whilst not being a material aesthetic judgement. It is our liking for the 'good', in the sense of things which are useful, or that which is intrinsically good, and desired for its own sake (e.g., morality). In respect of these senses, Kant observes that 'Both always involve the concept of an end, hence the relation of reason to (at least possible) willing, and consequently a satisfaction in the existence of an object or of an action, i.e., some sort of interest'.[10]

On these terms, then, our pleasure in the good entails that we know it in relation to an item or action of an end-orientated kind, and that we desire that this end should be realizable in actual, concrete terms. In either case here, our liking is dependent on beliefs concerning real existence—that is, that these sorts of items or actions will lead to the right sorts of material outcome.

Kant's thinking in this area, then, can be summarized in a general point. Much of our pleasure in things is determined by the appropriate causal impacts on our senses or by their use-value or significance for practical and/or theoretical reason. It is pleasure grounded on the real existence of its object.

---

argues that they have a further positive significance for our rational being in so far as they provide 'somatic markers' that enable reason to function much more effectively in immediate practical contexts. For more on this, see A. R. Damasio, *Descartes' Error: Emotion, Reason, and the Human Brain* (New York: Penguin Putnam, 1994).

[10] Kant, *Critique of Judgment*, §4, p. 93 (Pluhar, 49; Meredith, 46).

Our pleasure in the beautiful is very different. Such 'pure aesthetic judgements' are 'contemplative'.[11] Indeed, 'Taste is the faculty for judging an object or a kind of representation through a satisfaction or dissatisfaction without any interest. The object of such satisfaction is called beautiful'.[12]

A great deal of mischief has been caused by Kant's characterization of the pure aesthetic judgement in terms of its 'contemplative' and 'disinterested' character. The problem is not that these terms are mistaken. It is rather that, considered on their own, they tend to suggest that the aesthetic judgement is based on the taking up of some kind of detached psychological attitude.[13] This view is vulnerable to the sceptical view that there is, in fact, no such attitude,[14] and that reports based on mere introspective affirmation by proponents of the attitude, are wholly inadequate to establishing the case for it.

I will return to the problem of disinterestedness and the contemplative at a number of points as my study develops. However, even now, the illusion of the aesthetic 'attitude' can be dispelled. For, whilst Kant may raise difficulties through his characterization of disinterestedness, there is a simple formulation of it—entirely consistent with the major thrust of his arguments—which bypasses the sceptical problems.[15]

It consists of an emphasis on *disinterestedness as a logical rather than psychological criterion of the aesthetic*. This holds, simply, that in order to take pleasure in the way a form appears to the senses per se *it is not logically presupposed that we believe the object to have any broader practical significance or value for us*. In fact, in the strictest terms, mere illusion or

---

[11] Ibid. §5, p. 95 (Pluhar, 50; Meredith, 48).

[12] Ibid. §5, p. 96 (Pluhar, 53; Meredith, 50).

[13] A technical discussion of disinterestedness illuminated with ideas from Kant's moral theory can be found at Guyer, *Kant and the Claims of Taste*, 167–206. The account is spoiled slightly by Guyer's linkages of art to disinterestedness on those occasions when we are indifferent to the work's status as a unique thing. Indeed, he makes the interesting point that if we like reproductions and are not bothered about the fact that they are only reproductions then this is a sign of our disinterestedness (pp. 201–2). In fact, he argues that the equal pleasure derived from a reproduction 'may be a salutary criterion when concern with such matters as the novelty, rarity, or value of works of art all too often overshadows genuinely aesthetic appreciation of objects' (p. 202). However, as we shall see later on, questions of novelty impinge on *all* modes of aesthetic appreciation in a positive way and especially so in terms of the 'originality' of fine art.

[14] An extremely influential version of this view has been proposed in a number of works by George Dickie. See, for example, the chapters in the second part of his *Art and the Aesthetic* (Ithaca, NY and London: Cornell University Press, 1974).

[15] If I understand him correctly, Guyer's account of disinterestedness tends in a similar broad direction.

appearance will do just as well—if our pure aesthetic judgement really is based exclusively on how a form presents to the senses.

Put like this, there is no need to appeal to psychological attitudes. 'Disinterestedness' picks out the logical grounds of the pure aesthetic judgement. The term 'contemplative' simply emphasizes the fact that such judgements are directed to how phenomenal configurations appear rather than their location in a broader nexus of practical and theoretical interests.

This qualification of Kant's position is actually very complementary to a broader aspect of his theory. For, it is quite clear that the pleasure we take in the beautiful is involuntary—that is, not something which we can choose to have or not have, at whim. True, one can put oneself in a position where beautiful forms can be encountered, and in some cases we can look for such form in phenomenal configurations which are significant also in other respects (a factor which will be explored at length in Chapter 5's discussion of 'adherent' beauty). However, whether a form is judged to be beautiful or otherwise is determined by an enhanced interaction of imagination and understanding, and this, of course, depends on the character of the configuration itself, rather than what we choose to find there. The beauty of a configuration is independent of the will.[16]

I am arguing, then, that if it makes sense to posit a pleasure based just on the form of appearance, then its disinterested and contemplative character is logically entailed. The Kantian aesthetic's real philosophical substance has to be sought in the *way* beautiful forms engage perception. Everything else follows from this.

The basic factors involved have already been indicated in my outline of Kant's introduction to the third *Critique*. These centre on the notion of *subjective finality* and its synonyms. I shall now address these in much greater detail.

PART 3

As we saw in Part 1, the logical ground of pure aesthetic pleasure—and thence the object of the pure aesthetic judgement, is a set of complex

---

[16] There is, of course, a strong voluntary factor in terms of which aspects and relations we choose to attend to in our perception of beautiful forms, but what we find there is constrained by what the manifold allows. Beauty enables our perceptual choices rather than being enabled by them.

cognitive relations based on the appearance of the sensible manifold. This involves 'subjective finality' or 'purposiveness without purpose'. Kant declares that 'Beauty is the form of the purposiveness of an object, in so far as it is perceived in it without representation of an end'.[17] In a note to this remark, he observes further that 'A flower . . . e.g., a tulip, is held to be beautiful because a certain purposiveness is encountered in our perception of it which, as we judge it, is not related to any end at all'.[18] As an instance of a natural kind, we might simply judge *that* the flower is a tulip. This would be a judgement of objective finality. The great majority of judgements of natural phenomena have this character. They are, one might say, *discursively rigid* in so far as they involve classifying a particular sensible manifold and linking to other such manifolds within the broad interests of our everyday knowledge of the world.

However, in our pure aesthetic judgement of the flower, attention is focused exclusively on how it coheres as a phenomenal *particular*. We are preoccupied by the form of its *individual* appearance, rather than this form's identifying significance vis-à-vis class or kind membership.

In his discussion of what this involves Kant gives great emphasis to the role of feeling as a recognitional factor. As he puts it,

an objective relation can only be thought, but in so far as it is subjective as far as its conditions are concerned it can still be sensed in its effect on the mind; and further, in the case of a relation that is not grounded in any concept . . . no other consciousness of it is possible except through sensations of the effect that consists in the facilitated play of both powers of the mind . . . [19]

This presents a severe interpretational problem. In Kant's narrow terms, cognition involves the application of definite concepts. Hence, if it is recognized only by the feeling of pleasure or displeasure it gives rise to, then, strictly speaking, the pure aesthetic judgement is not cognitive.

But, this is unnecessarily restrictive. Even though a definite concept is not involved, the pure aesthetic judgement is grounded in cognitive activity of a complex sort. As we shall see in Part 4, this gives some entitlement to the view that it is recognized, primarily, by the pleasure it gives rise to. However, in order to emphasize its distinctness from the causally based material aesthetic judgement, Kant must allow that it is a cognitive judgement of a special kind.[20]

[17] Kant, *Critique of Judgment*, §17 n. 120 (Pluhar, 84; Meredith, 80).   [18] Ibid.
[19] Ibid. §9, p. 104 (Pluhar, 63; Meredith, 60).
[20] Kant does concede this in §57, I think. See ibid. 215 (Pluhar 211; Meredith, 206).

It is imperative, therefore, to clarify, carefully, what it is about the beautiful form's appearance which facilitates the play of imagination and understanding, and to explain in more detail the nature of the cognitive activity which this play involves. Only on this basis will it be possible to understand, eventually, why the pure aesthetic judgement is recognized primarily through feeling.

Kant himself, unfortunately, offers little direct help with these tasks. However, he does provide some important clues which can be followed up. For example, towards the beginning of the 'Critique of Teleological Judgment' he mentions in passing that

One has good reason to assume . . . the possibility of the connection of the particular experiences in one system of nature; where among its many products those can also be expected to be possible which, just as if they had actually been designed for our power of judgment, contain a form so specifically suited for it that by means of their variety and unity they serve as it were to strengthen and entertain the mental powers (which are in play in the use of these faculties), and to which one has therefore ascribed the name of *beautiful* forms.[21]

Kant tells us no more about 'variety and unity' in this context. But, the 'variety' factor, at least, consists surely of the heterogeneity of the manifold in terms of individual parts, texture, and details of appearance—that is, such things as colour, or ways of reflecting light.

The unity factor is rather more complex. If it is not that of definite reflective or determinative concepts considered individually or in concert, then it must centre on *alternative but complementary possibilities of unifying the manifold*. The importance of this is shown by Kant's occasional remarks concerning how imagination and understanding are engaged by beauty. He suggests, for example, that imagination's role is

productive and self-active (as the authoress of voluntary forms of possible intuitions); and although in the apprehension of a given object of the senses it is of course bound to determinate form of this object and to this extent has no free play (as in invention), nevertheless it is still quite conceivable that the object can provide a form that contains precisely such composition of the manifold as the imagination would design in harmony

---

[21] Ibid. §61, 233 (Pluhar, 235; Meredith, 3: Part II). The question of variety and unity understood in terms of its broad cognitive significance is actually the central thematic of Zuckert, *Kant on Beauty and Biology*.

with the lawfulness of the understanding in general if it were left free by itself.[22]

These remarks are vital, but extremely opaque. To make sense of them demands, in the first instance, consideration of the understanding's ordering of the sensible manifold.

Whatever else it might involve, the 'lawfulness of the understanding in general' must mean its capacity to conceptualize. This involves an orientation towards the manifold's basic phenomenal structure achieved through the mediation of relevant categories (and transcendental schemata) and classification in terms of its more specific empirical character.

Now, unfortunately, Kant does not himself explore what this lawfulness must involve in the specific case of the pure aesthetic judgement. And, his commentators have, I think, not been at all willing to see where the argument leads in terms of what this *really* involves in phenomenological terms. The focus of attention must be the formal properties of phenomenal appearance. These consist of such features as part, whole, line, shape, mass, volume, density, size, position, and temporal variations in terms of which of these aspects are attended to, and in what combination. More specifically, this means *attentiveness to the manifold's objective structural features* (as described through the categories).[23]

---

[22] Kant, *Critique of Judgment*, General Remark, 124–5 (Pluhar, 91; Meredith, 85–6). In Malcolm Budd's important papers 'Delight in the Natural World: Kant on the Aesthetic Appreciation of Nature', *British Journal of Aesthetics*, 38 (1998), 1–18 and 'The Pure Judgment of Taste as a Reflective Judgment', ibid. 41 (2001), 247–60 an interpretation is proposed much of which is viable. However, the passage from Kant just cited brings out my major disagreement with Budd. He does not, I think, give due attention to what the role of imagination amounts to in concrete terms. In the first paper, for example, he notes that 'the imagination is not free to manufacture whatever form it pleases but is tied to the production of a determinate form' (p. 7). He goes on to argue that this form is what the imagination produces when guided by the faculty of understanding's 'monitoring function' (ibid.). These points, unfortunately, misrepresent both imagination and understanding. In the passage under consideration, Kant talks of 'voluntary forms of possible intuitions'. This means that the role of imagination is to provide alternative orientations *through time* in how we attend to the beautiful configuration, and, in this, is directed by the understanding's open, explorative cognitive *activity* rather than some passive 'monitoring function'. In my notion of the emergent judgement of reflection, I try to do justice to this active dimension.

[23] Béatrice Longuenesse notes, confidently, that 'Kant is adamant that judgments of taste are not cognitive judgments, and that as aesthetic judgments, they do not rest on categories' (Kukla, *Aesthetics and Cognition*, 195). But it might be insisted with equal confidence that Kant is rather less clear on these issues than Longuenesse suggests. Indeed, given that Kant relates

This may involve no more than simple recognition in terms of specific categorial concepts. But, if the aspects are embodied in a *distinctive individual phenomenal configuration* then there may be something about the character of this configuration which allows us to explore such structural features in more sustained and complex perceptual terms. We are concerned with *the way* in which its formal aspects

the pure aesthetic judgement to the 'lawfulness of understanding in general' quite explicitly, then it would be bordering on the incredible if this were not to be understood as involving the categories and transcendental schemata in some mediating role or other. My account of the emergent judgement of reflection (in its open-ended mode) shows exactly what this involves, in a way that is consistent with both Kant's position and the more general viability of his theory. The account can be used, also, to develop further the critical points made against Rachel Zuckert in n.6. It is important to do this, since she has offered a profoundly searching account of the phenomenology of aesthetic judgement which finds no use for the categories or transcendental schemata. True, she acknowledges that aesthetic judgement 'may well have to occur within the broader context of objective experience governed by categorial rules' (Zuckert, *Kant on Beauty and Biology*, 297) However, she discounts any more-active involvement in the pure aesthetic judgement. This approach is characteristic of most other commentators also, but Zuckert has a distinctive perspective on it. She argues that 'our representation of an object as beautiful concerns its contingent, empirical, and diverse properties. Thus, those properties that may ground their conformity to the categories are not, as such, relevant to aesthetic judging, nor can categorial judgment ground a representation of beauty, viz., of a unity amongst an object's contingent, diverse, empirical properties as such' (p. 199). In these remarks, unfortunately, Zuckert does not consider the distinction drawn earlier between the dispositional and occurrent function of the categories. The former is the enduring cognitive horizon within which all our judgements are enacted, but in the emergent judgement of reflection they are engaged occurrently—precisely because in order to make sense of the particularity of a manifold we must explore those general features which it is particular in relation to. Difference does not exist *in itself*. We need to know what sort of shape, what intensity of texture, what reciprocity of parts in relation to a whole give this configuration its distinctiveness. In the case of beautiful forms, this exploration, however, does not issue in some culminating definite concept. The configuration enables a sustained exploration of alternative ways in which structural features might be taken to cohere at the level of appearance. Categories and transcendental schemata, in other words, play a *mediating* role. It is interesting that when Zuckert herself characterizes the phenomenology of the pure aesthetic judgement it is in the following terms—'In order to represent an object as beautiful, we must . . . represent heterogeneous sensible properties as internally related to one another, as reciprocally unified, as always already part of a whole, as always already means towards that end (or as reciprocally ends and means).[Indeed, we do so] imaginatively, without conceptual guidance—by representing these properties as at once presented at different moments, *and* as part of an anticipated future whole; in aesthetic experiencing we must imaginatively anticipate the future as an end, engage in projective imaginative activity, structured by the form of purposiveness as a form of time relation' (p. 302). But, it is difficult to see what might be made of all this activity without involving the emergent judgement of reflection. To discriminate the different aspects of a manifold just *is* to negotiate it in relation to how it mediates and is mediated by categorial features, attended to through time, on the basis of the transcendental schemata. All the cognitive factors which Zuckert describes in relation to aesthetic judgement are examples of the emergent judgement of reflection in its conceptually open-ended, intrinsically pleasurable, mode.

are aligned, and the different ways in which this alignment might be perceived.

To focus on this is to address actual and *apparent* possibilities for unifying the manifold. It is to treat the formal aspects as *vectors of perceptual exploration* both individually and in combination. Even in objects with determinate forms, their appearance can be unified in different ways, on the basis of which, and how, formal aspects are made available for perceptual attention and exploration by the individual configuration.

What we are dealing with here is a distinctive variety of that *emergent judgement of reflection* whose character I described, at length, earlier. In most employments, these judgements involve perceptual deliberation that has a definite concept as both its outcome and as the intended meaning which gives continuity to the many discriminations that lead up to this outcome. However, in an emergent judgement of reflection of a purely aesthetic kind, the process of perception is *open ended*. It involves an interplay between categorial concepts and alternative possibilities of schematization opened up by the individual empirical character of the sensible manifold.

Beautiful forms, in other words, engage the structural and particular factors which are involved in the achievement of objective knowledge, but they do not compel convergence on any definite concept as a cognitive outcome of deliberation. It is in this sense that the pure aesthetic judgement involves the 'lawfulness of understanding in general' rather than the employment of its constituent factors in a rigidly discursive correlation.

As we have seen earlier, the categories and transcendental schemata mainly function as a dispositional network of cognitive orientations. They are engaged explicitly only when circumstances demand. Their occurrent employment is the exception rather than the rule. In the pure aesthetic judgement, this is reversed. For here, the object's individual configuration is mediated actively by its relation to the structural richness of the phenomenal manifold. But for the requisite perceptual exploration to happen we *must* be able to track the form's temporally successive appearances, in terms of the formal aspects/perceptual vectors described.

Now, there are many occasions when we judge something to be beautiful 'at a glance'. But, even if we happen not to attend to it in detail on *this* occasion, our fleeting acknowledgement of it *as* beautiful entails that it is something worth attending to perceptually at some time or other. Beauty, in other words, is inseparably linked to the need for sustained 'apprehension' and perceptual exploration.[24]

It is this which makes the categories and transcendental schemata so important. The perception of relations between the formal aspects described earlier and the texture of the manifold requires those mediating strategies of structural cognitive discrimination enabled by the categories, in tandem with the complex tracking procedures which the schemata provide.

These centre on such features, we will recall, as the scanning of a phenomenal item's continuity of parts, its invariant structure maintained through successive appearances, variations of magnitude (physical, perceptual, and sensational), its causal interactions, the active coexistence of elements in a manifold, and its temporal consistency in terms of space occupancy. In normal emergent reflective judgement this exploration culminates in relating the particular to some definite concept. The pure aesthetic judgement, in contrast, is open-ended in this respect. Its form is such that, the more we attend to it, and discriminate the manifold, the more apparent vectors of unity in its appearance are revealed. Its character as an aesthetic unity remains open, through each perceptual encounter with it.

That the aesthetic significance of the categories and transcendental schemata is not emphasized by Kant himself, nor by much of the interpretative literature, is down, in part, to rather static conceptions of the scope of beautiful form.

Kant's own examples include flowers, shells, ornamental designs, and intertwining foliage. His exclusions from the beautiful are sometimes extremely surprising. We are told, for example, that

beautiful objects are to be distinguished from beautiful views of objects (which on account of the distance can often no longer be distinctly cognized). In the latter, taste seems to fasten not so much on what the imagination apprehends in this field as on what gives it to invent—that is, on what are strictly speaking the fantasies with which the mind entertains itself while it is being continuously

---

[24] This answers Guyer's claim that not all beauty need involve a play of imagination and understanding. The point is that, even if such a play does not happen occurrently in relation to a given form, it would be a contradiction in terms to describe that form as beautiful but not worth looking at in a sustained, explorative way at some time or other. It must have the *capacity* to engage us in such terms, and, thence, occasion the play of imagination and understanding. See Guyer's 'The Harmony of the Faculties Revisited', in Rebecca Kukla (ed.), *Aesthetics and Cognition in Kant's Critical Philosophy* (Cambridge: Cambridge University Press, 2006) 188–9.

aroused by the manifold which strikes the eye, as for instance in looking at the changing shapes of a fire in a hearth of a rippling brook, neither of which are beauties, but both of which carry with them a charm for the imagination, because they sustain its free play.[25]

These remarks are as bizarre as they are mistaken, in so far as they restrict, stipulatively, the scope of the beautiful to immediately proximal spatial objects and, by implication, spatial objects in the form of static items seen from one viewpoint.

This is not only counter-intuitive in the grossest terms, it is completely at odds with the dominant thrust of Kant's own account of beauty. For, if something brings about the free play of imagination and understanding then it is subjectively final in relation to cognition and must be beautiful—notwithstanding abrupt technical stipulations to the contrary. Objective finality may accrue to items individually considered or to relations between classes of them but, even on Kant's own terms (let alone more generally), subjective finality cannot be restricted in these terms.

What makes Kant's position even more wretched is that even his own static spatial examples require active temporal mediation if imagination's freedom in 'composing' the manifold is to emerge.

When we enjoy a beautiful flower, it is not a single perceptual viewpoint which is involved, but an active one which explores the flower's manifold under different aspects. Its unity and distribution of parts encompass three-dimensions; hence it *must* be attentionally explored through time in order for the relation between alternative apparent possibilities of unity in the manifold to be apprehended in terms adequate to the pure aesthetic judgement.

Some of Kant's own examples introduce temporality in a further sense, in so far as intertwining foliage, decorative ornamentation, and the like make considerable use of visual rhythms and repeated forms whose progression and/or phenomenal configuration not only have to be successively scanned even within a single viewpoint but often suggest visual continuation beyond the immediately given.

Even something as static as a shell exemplifies this. Its whorls and trace-iridescence, for example, are not simply there. The whorls may appear to be coiled and thence suggest the possibility of an uncoiling which gives the shell's 'invariant' form the suggestion of virtual animation

---

[25] Kant, *Critique of Judgment*, General Remark, 126–7 (Pluhar, 94–5; Meredith, 89).

beyond its given aspects. Again, the iridescence appears to act as a veil over the physical surface of the shell, with the suggestion of a real *and* an emerging 'phantom' surface simultaneously.

The role of temporal factors becomes more emphatic still, if we do full justice to Kant's notion of a 'beautiful view' of objects. This should be taken to encompass not only our shifting perceptual perspectives on beautiful forms but those situations where the objects in question are complex, and/or are enhanced through being enjoyed as individual elements in a more-extended configuration, or in an arrangement of individually beautiful forms.

In many cases of this kind a manifest temporal factor is an aspect of the formal configuration itself. In this respect, for example, consider such phenomena as the wind animating foliage and leaves, or waterfalls, or clouds in the sky.

The example of cloud formations is especially instructive. In strictly empirical terms we know such formations to be accumulations of water vapour suspended above the earth and dispersed in correlation with broader climatic changes. In teleological terms, they are not defined by the concept of an end in relation to individual cloud forms but they can be judged teleologically in so far as we take their relation to sunlight and the effects of their precipitation to be final in relation to organic growth and survival processes.

However, let us suppose that a gloriously tempestuous sunset presents a sustained spectacle of visual beauty vis-à-vis shifting cloud formation. What exactly is going on here, phenomenologically speaking?

It may be that clouds seem to take on definite shapes which last for a while, only gradually to change into different forms or, indeed, formlessness. At one moment they are tightly packed masses but then come to vary in the density of their appearances.

The light playing through the clouds grows and diminishes in its intensity of brightness and creates extremely complex gestalt effects. First, perhaps, a set of light billows defined against a dark ground is seen but a few minutes later the form has reconfigured to suggest an entirely different figure of dark billows set against a light ground.

At certain points, the clouds in the distance touch the upper regions of the hills, appearing to merge with them and then detach, unsettling our sense of which visual impression is real and substantial and which is just cloud appearance, and perhaps leading us to care neither one way nor the other—given the beauty of the spectacle per se.

It may be as well that we are also engrossed by the extraordinary play of contrasting colours and the striking way in which a rainbow appears both to join and to divide elements in the shifting manifold of colours, shapes, and masses.

If it should be asked why we perceive the clouds in the terms described, it is because they show us different possibilities for unifying complex structures of appearance. We find different ways—in terms of line, shape, mass, density, etc.—for the manifold to be regarded in perceptual terms.

Now, it is vital to emphasize that the complex beautiful phenomenon just described is not exceptional. We have all experienced such cloud formations. And what I have been describing on a large scale in relation to them also holds true, in more focused ways, for small-scale static beautiful objects.

As we saw earlier, context is important in that spatial items have to be seen from different angles, and their phenomenal continuity has to be scanned if they are to be the subjects of a pure aesthetic judgement. There are also complex suggestions of visual rhythmic continuities which—even within a single viewpoint—are suggestive of visual continuation into possible contexts beyond the immediately given.

I have argued, then, that Kant's own sense of the scope of the beautiful requires significant expansion. In particular, it must embrace temporal factors (bound up with the transcendental schemata and the categories) much more consistently and affirmatively.

One important task remains. We have seen that for Kant the pure aesthetic judgement is experienced not as a definite act of cognition but rather through the pleasure or displeasure which it occasions. The phenomenology of beauty which I have just described offers a basis for explaining why the aesthetic judgement has this 'felt' character. I shall now fill in the details.

PART 4

The examples which I have discussed cast interesting light on the notion of 'subjective finality'. It is clear, for example, that the formal richness of beauty (even within the bounds of a single object or state of affairs) offers *multiple ways for unity to be perceived* at the level of appearance. Through this, the *general* unifying function of the understanding is powerfully exemplified.

It should be emphasized that the unities involved here are mainly apparent: they exist at the level of appearance as disclosed from different perceptual viewpoints. They are organic wholes in terms of how the manifold's formal and textural aspects *cohere* at the strictly *perceptual* level.

Unity, here, is dependent on the exact relation between the dominant aspect or aspects, and the others, in respect of the manifold's heterogeneous elements, and how these are apprehended in perception.

Now, it might be asked why we are even entitled to talk of 'coherence' and 'organic wholes' in relation to 'apparent' structures?

An answer is forthcoming on the basis of the percipient subject's sense of its own body and the importance of other creatures and vegetal life in its interactions with the world. These mean that its general objective orientation is especially attentive to organic forms and processes. Cognition is at home with both teleological structure *and the mere appearance of it*.

This latter point may seem surprising, but it is true in so far as the appearance of teleological structure allows the discriminatory powers of understanding, and the tracking powers of imagination, to be exercised *autonomously*—that is, in a context based on a high level of perceptual input, but which is not constrained by the pressure of solving immediate practical life-problems using determinate teleological concepts.

Freed from such pressure, the mere appearances of different vectors of apparent organic unity in a manifold, emerging from different perceptual orientations towards it, offers an exceptional and concentrated stimulus to our cognitive capacities.

The manifold offers, as it were, rich possibilities of different 'trial runs', thus opening out multiple possibilities of interaction between imagination and understanding, instead of the discursive rigidity of ordinary cognition. In this sense, the emergent judgement of reflection in its aesthetic form is, indeed, 'final' in relation to the end of cognition, generally.

It is important to reiterate, here, the decisive role of the transcendental schemata and categories. In the shifting cloud formations, for example, just about all these schemata and the categories are brought forth in a relaxed explorative rather than a rigidly discursive way.

In the case of the shell, we must scan its continuity of spatial parts, and the invariant shape which informs its different appearances. The coiled energy of its whorls suggests an unfolding beyond the given, and its trace-iridescence may appear to be distributed with different intensities of visual magnitude as we apprehend different regions of its surface. Even in this simple spatial example, the transcendental schemata enable different emphases of unity in terms of how the shell appears to perception.

Once we acknowledge the inescapable *temporal* dimension in imagination's 'composing' of the manifold it becomes clear the tracking procedures involved in transcendental schemata and the relevant directing categories are engaged in complex ways by even the simplest beautiful forms. They open up different possibilities for unifying the manifold's appearance.

We can now clarify why it is mainly through a feeling of pleasure that this cognitive activity is recognized. If the pure aesthetic judgement culminated only in the application of a definite concept or concepts it would be characterizable in *just* those terms—as an act of recognition. But, as we have seen, there is, literally, so much going on in pure aesthetic judgements, cognitively speaking, that we simply cannot keep up (in introspective terms) with the details of this activity. All we experience *in conscious terms* is the feeling of pleasure.

To do justice to the cognitive dimension here, we should regard its role as *intuitive*. Sometimes 'intuitive' is used to mean unanalysable or even ineffable insight. But, not all intuition is ineffable. Indeed, there is a much more commonplace variety which might be called '*explicable intuition*'.

Examples of this include such things as the knowledge that no material body can occupy two different sets of spatial coordinates at the same time and that to move from one point in space to another necessarily involves the continuous traversal of spaces in between.

Sometimes facts such as these have been learned explicitly, but often they will have been learned more indirectly, and will link up with many other facts concerning the conditions of space-occupancy, to *influence our everyday behaviour without us being consciously aware of them as a body of knowledge, or that they are presently influencing us.* They inform our orientation without having to be present to mind explicitly.

Similar considerations hold in those cases where we respond to the implications of something, even though the entire chain of inferences on which the response is based has not been followed in explicitly conscious terms.

The great bulk of our cognitive activity operates in these intuitive terms. However, what separates this intuition from the ineffable variety is that the ineffable has a component which cannot, *of its nature*, be put into words sufficiently. The intuitions involved in most cognitive activity, in contrast, can be analysed and explained in sufficient descriptive terms—*if the right circumstances and analytic frameworks present themselves*. They have the character of *explicable intuition*.

The pure aesthetic judgement has *both* these intuitive aspects. Qua singular, the aesthetic whole which it apprehends is ineffable in that the character of its unity can only be comprehended fully through direct perceptual acquaintance. (One criterion of this is that aesthetic meaning qua aesthetic cannot be paraphrased in linguistic terms.)

Now, what enables the pleasure which we take in this particular is that set of rich cognitive relations which has been described at length. The uniqueness of the configuration is ineffable, and these cognitive relations are so complex, as to be known only intuitively. On these terms, therefore, at *a direct conscious level*, the feeling of pleasure is all we have.

However, the aforementioned cognitive relations are not, logically speaking, a closed book in *general* terms. Given the theoretical context provided by Kant (and my phenomenological development of his position), they are *explicable intuitions* even if we have no immediate and explicit understanding of their workings. They centre on the enhanced interaction of imagination and understanding. Such a general characterization of them is not, of course, sufficient to explain their individual aesthetic appeal, but it at least allows us to explain the *grounds* on which they are found appealing.

I have argued, then, that Kant's approach to the pure aesthetic judgement is, in substantial terms, a viable one. All that is required is the freeing of his points from some of their rigidity of technical exposition, and, in particular, finding a proper role for the categories and transcendental schemata.

As a Conclusion, I will develop, briefly, some of the ramifications of this approach in a way which is consistent with Kant's account, albeit on lines which he himself may not have been willing to countenance. This will involve relating his theory to the general ontogenetic approach taken in previous chapters.

CONCLUSION

In Kantian terms, the aesthetic unity of a manifold is determined by the interplay between its form and the different possibilities of cognitive exploration which this interplay creates. The implication here is that a dimension of *freedom* in judgement is—in contrast with judgements of objective unity—at least partially *constitutive* of aesthetic unity. In Kant's phrase, they involve 'voluntary forms of possible intuitions'. In such judgements, imagination's tracking and projective activity is not as a mere facilitator of recognition but as an equal player. It is stimulated to follow its own basic nature as a productive cognitive capacity.

Such aesthetic unity is free—but it is not chaotic. There must be some element of stabilization in the manifold which enables perceptual exploration to take place. As we have seen, the perceptual exploration involved in aesthetic judgement requires attention of the most active sort. This means that the schemata's tracking potentials are invoked—but in terms of multiple, shifting schemata rather than the specific one or two which might be demanded by a definite objective concept. The categories and their schemata are engaged in flexible and experimental ways.

In a sense, the beautiful configuration is cognitively unstable, but this does not amount to a loss of intelligibility in perception. Rather, it involves a felt sense of *cognition in the making*—of the birth and convergence of the possibility of perceptual sense in the manifold. The pure aesthetic judgement is a kind of felt image of the ontogenesis of sensible experience itself.

Of course, this goes far beyond Kant's own position in the third *Critique*. However, its development has rich theoretical consequences. These emerge if we link the foregoing account to the ontogenetic approach taken in my first two chapters.

Infants interact with their environments on the basis of curiosity—actively searching out and exploring different patterns of relation and order. These explorations are guided by the propensity to mimic and the effects of guidance from more senior agents. However, encouragement from adults is not a sufficient explanation of why such behaviour is *so* pervasive and persistent in infants.

Mimicry, for example, may be an innate propensity, but the complex uses to which it is put bespeak a deeper motive—namely, the exploration of possibilities of order for their own sake. The propensities involved here are even present in neonates. In summarizing some of their cognitive capacities, Gallagher notes, for example, the following features

Preference for some objects over others (e.g., moving objects rather than stationary objects; three-dimensional rather than two-dimensional objects; high-contrast rather than low-contrast stimuli; patterns with curved rather

than straight lines) . . . Active searching for visual stimulation . . . Ability to
habituate to one stimulus and show preference for novel stimuli.[26]

These propensities are developed much further through the infant's
playful negotiations of its environment, and interactions with other
persons. Indeed, as it acquires language, and is socialized, the dimension
of playful physical negotiation of things becomes a vehicle for play in
the sense of creating 'make-believe' situations.

I am arguing, then, that infant behaviour involves much more than
the satisfaction of physiological needs and pleasing adults. It needs a
world of perceptual and imaginative play. Some philosophers (such as
Schiller) have linked play to the aesthetic, but the infant level which
I have described is of special importance in this respect. The motive
for such behaviour is aesthetic in the purest sense of all. All that the
infant has is a network of phenomenal configurations whose character
it explores playfully. By way of such exploration it exercises those cognitive competences—understanding and imagination—through which
it will eventually organize the emergent manifold into a world. Its
explorations are *disinterested* in the sense that it makes no distinction
between play and the real. The latter is, as yet, only nascent in the
former.

The sense of a specifically objective world arises as the infant coordinates its sensori-motor activities in a unified field. This unity is a
function of innate capacities, natural growth, aesthetic exploration, and
the initiation into language and socialization. Through this it achieves
that 'objective orientation' which I described in Chapter 2 and, eventually, a full sense of itself as both material body and person in a world of
other material bodies and persons.

At this point, an objection must be considered. I am arguing that
aesthetic responses are basic to the development of that objective
orientation which is a function of the categories and transcendental
schemata. But, since I have argued also that the aesthetic requires
such orientation in order to be cognitively stabilized, is this not blatantly circular? The answer is 'no'. For here we are dealing with a
reciprocal relationship. Objective orientation and aesthetic exploration
come into existence *together* as innate propensities, mutually modify-
ing one another in a very gradual process of development, mediated
by the growing child's achieved coordination of its sensori-motor
capacities.

---

[26] Shaun Gallagher, *How the Body Shapes the Mind* (Oxford: Clarendon Press, 2006), 164.

Here we are talking about aesthetic exploration and activity of a very basic kind, rather than pure aesthetic judgement. In such basic activity, the learning of phenomenal structure and the pleasure of doing this for its own sake are inseparable. As the child becomes more mature, such learning becomes more of a routine, and the intrinsic pleasure arises only in relation to more attractive/interesting kinds of phenomenal configuration. Experience gradually divides into the everyday world of recognized objects and events (and those practical abilities which are required to deal with them) and those more privileged moments when some aspect of phenomena is found perceptually interesting in its own right. At this stage, pure aesthetic judgement arises—as a more *selective response* to the phenomenal structures made accessible through objective orientation.

This being said, it might be objected further that claims of the foregoing kind are surely dependent on concrete evidence derived from empirical studies of child development. However, the approach which I have taken is consistent with the wealth of material summarized by Gallagher. More importantly, it finds *conceptual* justification through a process of elimination. This is because, given a pleasure in cognitive exploration as such, aesthetic factors are the *only* ones which can explain its grounds.

For example, the pleasure involved in such cognitive exploration is not just an *instinctual* gratification. Such gratifications have as their grounds the satisfaction of specific bodily needs, but a pleasure in cognitive exploration for its own sake has grounds which are much more open. It might be argued that such pleasure is tied to the instinct for survival and security. However, whilst this psychological drive may become quasi-instinctive once an infant has learned to discriminate threatening stimuli, it is difficult to make sense of such a notion at the neonate stage. Indeed, if there were such an instinct, one would have thought that the soliciting of new stimuli, or a preference for complex ones, is actually somewhat at odds with a need for security and survival.

The other main avenue of potential explanation of the grounds of infant pleasure in cognitive exploration would be that of fulfilling a practical goal. Now, there is no doubt that factors of this kind do influence infant and child behaviour—especially when informed by language and the wish to please grown-ups. In adult life, the pleasure of goal-realization is locked into a nexus of means/ends strategies which gravitate, ultimately, around what is demanded by the needs of security and survival in the broadest sense.

With infants and children, the opposite is the case. In early infancy, such a nexus does not exist at all; we have only pleasure in cognitive exploration for its own sake. And, when the child does receive initiation into strategies relevant to survival, its *play* activities, nevertheless, do not converge on the *actual* realization of these relevant strategies. Rather, such realizations are enacted and enjoyed *as play*, and without reference to what they would actually involve if realized in 'real life'.

On these terms, then, the only viable contender in conceptual terms for explaining the infant's pleasure in cognitive exploration and its more developed play activities, is that of the aesthetic. With this in mind, I turn now to my earlier point concerning the pure aesthetic judgement as a tacit replay of the origins of sensible *experience*. The points just made suggest that the aesthetic is a major factor in the calibration of categories and schemata in the ontogenesis of cognition. They emerge together in a basic playful cooperation—bound up with *ur*-aesthetic exploration—and develop into gradually more specialized employments.

If this view is correct, it must surely have some bearing on the character of aesthetic experience in adults. As well as the intrinsic pleasure of the enhanced interaction of cognitive capacities, this interaction exemplifies also the origins of cognition and the birth of self-consciousness. It might be asked what sense of exemplification is involved here. I would argue that it is *intuitive*, in the sense described earlier (namely, that of complexity which is felt without being recognized), but—and this is the decisive point—it can be explained if the right circumstances are available.

In many respects, it is much better that these origins are not revealed in so far as their tacit presence gives the best aesthetic experiences an enigmatic character. However, in an academic study of the present kind, such revelation is of importance. For it underlines the central theme of the present work—namely, that the Kantian aesthetic is not simply a pleasure in how things appear to the senses but one which arises from the most fundamental features of our cognitive engagement with the world—whilst being always more than *just* cognition.

4

The Universality and Justification of Taste[1]

INTRODUCTION

For Kant, the pure aesthetic judgement is unique amongst idioms of pleasure in that it can claim validity beyond mere personal preference. However, since it is not grounded in 'definite' concepts, the validity in question cannot be given a strictly objective justification.

The basis of such validity is to be sought, rather, in the pure aesthetic judgement's embodiment of those universal subjective conditions which enable knowledge formation. Kant's proofs of this are amongst the most complex arguments in the third *Critique*. They converge on the relation between imagination and understanding, and their links to morality. In his discussion, Kant tends to adopt the usage 'judgement of taste' rather than the synonym 'pure aesthetic judgement'. I will follow this usage.

[1] In her book *The Role of Taste in Kant's Theory of Cognition* (New York and London: Garland Publishing, 1990), Hannah Ginsborg approaches this topic via the harmony of the faculties. However, my approach differs radically from her own by virtue of the fact that she reads the universal communicability of the pure aesthetic judgement as synonymous with its claim to universal validity—a position which she has reaffirmed on a different basis in the course of a more-recent essay on 'Thinking the Particular as Contained under the Universal' included in Rebecca Kukla (ed.), *Aesthetics and Cognition in Kant's Critical Philosophy* (Cambridge: Cambridge University Press, 2006), 35–60. In contrast to her, I emphasize that universal communicability is a factor which centres, in the first instance, on the transcendental status of that general harmony of cognitive capacities discussed in the previous chapter. This harmony embodies the universal cognitive conditions which *enable* aesthetic pleasure. The claim to universal validity, in contrast, pertains more to the epistemological status of the actual pleasure which is occasioned by this harmony. By collapsing this distinction, Ginsborg tends to confuse both. It should be emphasized that it is not only this which sets my approach apart from Ginsborg. For, I assign decisive importance to a factor which she scarcely considers—namely, that any claim to universal validity involves an *evaluative*—and thence, comparative—dimension. (This emphasis separates my approach, also, from that of other commentators, such as Schaper, Crawford, Guyer, and Allison.) I will develop my arguments concerning this topic, at length, in Part 5 of this chapter.

Part 1 addresses Kant's preliminary steps towards an epistemological justification or 'deduction' of the judgement of taste's claim to universal validity. In Part 2, his most focused attempt at this is expounded, reviewed, and argued to be unsuccessful.

Attention is then paid, in Part 3, to Kant's alternative morality orientated version of the deduction—a strategy which is continued in Part 4, with specific reference to his culminating arguments concerning beauty as a symbol of morality. Significant weaknesses in Kant's position are highlighted.

In Part 5, I revise Kant's epistemological strategy, supplementing it with an important but understated factor from the moral version. This involves comparative factors, whereby judgement is improved through relevant forms of experience and practice. On the basis of these, the deduction can be put in a viable form. Part 6 explores this further.

By way of a Conclusion, I return briefly to the general connection between taste and morality.

PART 1

Kant holds that judgements concerning agreeable sensations (such as the taste of food or the charm of favourite colours) are based solely on personal preference. It makes no sense to demand universal assent for them, or to ask for justification. Such judgements merely report involuntary responses to causal impacts on the senses.

Of course, against Kant, one might point out that there are *connoisseurs* of food and wine and the like, and that such persons can make fine discriminations regarding quality and the skills and subtleties in terms of which comestibles have been prepared. But, in the final analysis, what counts is whether one likes the food or not, and that is a private matter.

In the case of feeling occasioned by the good, its validity or inappropriateness is determined by definite concepts bound up with questions of 'real existence' (in the sense outlined in the previous chapter).

The pleasure we take in beauty is different from both the agreeable and the good. Kant summarizes its status, tersely, as follows

That is beautiful which pleases universally without a concept.[2]

---

[2] Kant, *Critique of Judgment*, §9, p. 104 (Pluhar, 64; Meredith, 60).

This is not a statement of empirical fact but rather one of epistemological status. The pure aesthetic judgement has *a claim to universal validity* despite not involving a definite concept. Further on, Kant observes that

The judgment of others, when it is unfavourable to our own, can of course rightly give us reservations about our own, but can never convince us of its incorrectness.[3]

Insisting on our own judgement in such matters is warranted prima facie, in so far as judgements of taste are singular, and cannot be 'proven' by the application of objective concepts. However, for the claim to universal validity to be justified, a stronger explanation is required. For Kant, this means specifically, a *transcendental deduction*—that is, an argument or arguments which justify their object by linking it to the a priori conditions of experience.

In §38 of the third *Critique*, Kant offers such a 'Deduction of Judgments of Taste'. However, this section turns out to be of little help, since it is no more than a general summary of arguments offered in more detail earlier on.[4]

These arguments occur mainly in the Second and Fourth Moments of the 'Analytic of the Beautiful'. In the Second Moment, for example, Kant makes an important initial move as follows

For one cannot judge that about which he is aware that the satisfaction in it is without any interest in his own case in any way except that it must contain a ground of satisfaction for everyone. For since it is not grounded in any inclination of the subject (nor in any other underlying interest), but rather to the satisfaction that he devotes to the object, he cannot discover as grounds of the satisfaction any private conditions, pertaining to his subject alone, and must therefore regard it as grounded in those that he can also presuppose in everyone else; Consequently he must believe himself to have grounds for expecting a similar pleasure for everyone.[5]

---

[3] Ibid. §33, p. 165 (Pluhar, 147–8; Meredith, 139–40).

[4] It goes without saying, of course, that many commentators would disagree with this claim. For a discussion of the positioning and structure of the Deduction, see Guyer, *Kant and the Claims of Taste* (Cambridge Mass. and London: Harvard University Press, 1979), 256–78. In chaps 7 and 8 of *Kant's Theory of Taste* Allison offers an especially detailed analysis of arguments broached by Kant in relation to the 'necessity' of taste, and in the official deduction (see pp. 144–59 and 160–92 respectively). This material contains very cogent critique of alternative approaches (such as Guyer's and Savile's), but does not succeed in negotiating the problem of the claim to universal validity except within the strict boundaries of Kant's philosophical architectonics.

[5] Kant, *Critique of Judgment*, §6, pp. 96–7 (Pluhar, 54; Meredith, 50–1).

Here, Kant thinks through the logical consequences of disinterestedness. If one finds something beautiful, and if the grounds of the judgement are genuinely disinterested, then one is entitled to the universal assent of others to this verdict.

It must be reiterated that this is not an empirical expectation, but is rather, in effect, the belief that others *ought* to agree with one's estimate of the form as beautiful. If they do not, then (as Kant makes clear at various points in the 'Analytic of the Beautiful'[6]) this may be due to their judgements having been 'tainted' by factors bound up with the agreeable and the good.

At this point, the claim to universal validity is, in effect, a claim mainly about the logical structure of the judgement of taste. And, in this, Kant is supported by ordinary usage to the degree that it is rather more common to say 'this is beautiful' per se than it is to prefix the phrase with 'it seems to me that' or 'I think that', or some other qualifying idiom.

One might, of course, insist that 'what I call beautiful is intended *only* as a report of personal preference' or that 'yes, it's a beautiful form, and I'd expect some other people to like it, but this doesn't amount to a demand that all people should like it'.

But, Kant's whole point is that if something is judged as beautiful on *disinterested* grounds then this means that in its basic form the judgement suspends any *personal* reference. It aspires to universal validity, as it were, by default.

However, this is only a beginning. If the claim is to extend beyond the mere logical form of the judgement of taste, Kant must show next that there are cognitive factors common to all humans, which are a basis for justifying what the judgement claims. He takes us in this direction, as follows,

The subjective universal communicability of the kind of representation in a judgement of taste, since it is supposed to occur without presupposing a determinate concept, can be nothing other than the state of mind in the free play of the imagination and the understanding (so far as they agree with each other as is requisite for a cognition in general): for we are conscious that this subjective relation suited to cognition in general must be valid for everyone and consequently universally communicable, just as any determinate condition is, which still always rests on that relation as its subjective condition.[7]

---

6 See, for example, ibid. §38, p. 170 (Pluhar, 155; Meredith, 146–7).
7 Ibid. §9, p. 103 (Pluhar 62; Meredith, 58).

An objective concept is 'universally communicable' in that there are shared public rules for its correct and incorrect applications. However, in the foregoing remarks Kant is pointing out that the interaction of imagination and understanding has a *subjective* universal communicability, in so far as it is the basic condition for cognition of any sort. Human beings agree on concept application because they share common cognitive capacities qua rational subjects. The key step in a deduction, accordingly, will be one which can ground the judgement of taste on 'universal communicability'.

This is found in most detail in the Fourth Moment. I shall now consider Kant's relevant arguments there.

PART 2

Kant declares that 'That is beautiful which is cognized without a concept as the object of a necessary satisfaction'.[8] In §21, we find the sustained basis for his deduction of this claim. Kant's reasoning is, however, extremely complicated, and I will analyse it initially in terms of a set of summary points. They are as follows.

(i) Cognitions, judgements, and attendant beliefs concerning their veracity must be universally communicable otherwise true judgements—in the sense of a correspondence between cognition and its objects—would not be possible.

(ii) The universally communicable dimension of cognition includes the subject's 'mental state'. This involves two things: (a) the general accord of the cognitive capacities; (b) these capacities being combined in a 'proportion' relative to the nature of the object cognized. (One assumes that by this Kant means that objects are such that their presentation in cognition will demand different kinds of alignment between imagination and understanding. Small spatial items, for example, will be recognizable at a glance, whereas larger ones or ones of unusual appearance will require more-sustained apprehension from the imagination and more explorative unifying activity from the understanding.)

(iii) There must be one universally communicable proportion which is best fitted to stimulating the general interaction of the cognitive

---

[8] Ibid. §22, p. 124 (Pluhar, 90; Meredith, 85).

capacities, and which is recognizable only through the feeling of pleasure which it occasions.

(iv) Kant's conclusion. In so far as this pleasure arises from a 'common sense'—i.e., a mental state which is universally communicable—then it too must be universally communicable. Hence, the demand that others ought to assent to a judgement of taste based on this is justified.

I shall now review these points.

(i) is viable in general terms in that it would be difficult to see how true judgements would be possible if we were unable to apply concepts and to agree on whether this application had been successful or not. A similar verdict can be made on point (ii). Sub-points (a) and (b) are basically logical refinements of (i) in so far as any cognition involves the general accord of the faculties and (if *particular* true judgements are to be possible) their configuration in some proportion relative to the objects involved. However, point (iii) is where the strategy breaks down. In Kant's own words,

> there must be one [proportion of combination between imagination and understanding] in which this inner relationship is optimal for the animation of both powers of the mind (the one through the other) with respect to cognition (of given objects) in general; and this disposition cannot be determined except through . . . feeling.[9]

What makes this problematic is that whilst points (i) and (ii) are genuine transcendental points about the logical presuppositions of knowledge, point (iii) centres on an assumption which *exceeds* what is established by (i) and (ii). The assumption is that only *one* proportion in the general accord of the cognitive capacities is best suited to stimulating the feeling of their harmonious interaction.

In relation to this, we should recall that, for Kant, the proportion of the cognitive capacities is relative to the objects that are given. If (as suggested earlier) this means that the proportion of the faculties varies according to the contrasting kinds of phenomenal configuration involved, then, if only one such proportion is conducive to their stimulated interaction, it would follow that only one kind of phenomenal configuration can be beautiful.

The question is: what kind? Kant does not provide any examples or arguments to justify the claim. Given this, it would be entirely reasonable

---

[9] Kant, *Critique of Judgment*, §21, p. 123 (Pluhar, 88; Meredith 83).

to say that the proportion which works for one subject might not work for another. What works in stimulating the accord of imagination and understanding may be based, in principle, entirely on the individual's personal cognitive history.

On these terms, even if a judgement of taste is directed exclusively towards purposiveness without purpose, and even if it is genuinely disinterested, one cannot demand that others ought to assent to it. The proportion of imagination and understanding involved may be stimulating for us, but routine, and even *restricting*, for others.

There is an apparent way out for Kant here, if one does some work on his behalf. In this respect, even if—unlike Kant—a person held that beauty is exclusively in the eye of the beholder, this surely could not be so in *absolute* terms. It would be counter-intuitive for there not to be *some* criteria determining the logical scope of beauty as a concept.

Indeed, whilst beauty is focused on the individual perceptual encounter it is learnt in a social context and this entails initiation into correct and incorrect ways of applying the term. This again reinforces the sense that there must be some boundaries to what can be counted as beautiful, and that if an individual departs from this, he or she is using the notion of beauty in a misleading way.

Given these points, Kant's basic insight about a privileged proportion now appears better founded, even though he himself offers no justification for it and does not explain its exact character. But, we can take matters at least a little further in this respect. To do so, we must recall a passing comment (discussed in the previous chapter) which Kant makes at the start of 'Critique of Teleological Judgment'. It holds that beautiful forms involve a combination of 'diversity and unity'.[10]

This is about as good a contender as one might get for the elusive proportion. It has the merit, at least, of identifying that aspect of the phenomenal manifold which gives rise to beauty. Unfortunately, it is still rather too broad, in that any such manifold involves some combination of diversity and unity in its structure simply by virtue of being recognized as a manifold.

The problem already noted, therefore, is repeated here. For, if a person has cultivated their capacities for cognitive discrimination, it makes perfect sense to suppose that he or she may be more sensitive and discerning vis-à-vis the appreciation of diversity and unity

---

[10] Ibid. §61, p. 233 (Pluhar, 235; Meredith, 3: Part II).

in the manifold than a person whose capacities have not been so developed.

Given this, the objections raised earlier still apply. The diversity and unity which engage one person may be too simple and straightforward to stimulate the accord of imagination and understanding in others. We know where to look for beauty in the manifold, but whether it is found there or not is left open to individual taste. There are no grounds to warrant our judgement's claim to universal validity.

Kant's deduction, therefore, still fails. A likeness of the faculties can be transcendentally justified, in principle, and one's particular judgement of taste might be disinterested and based exclusively on formal qualities of diversity and unity, but this still leaves considerable scope for divergences of response according to different levels of cultivation amongst those who judge aesthetically.

Now, whilst Kant's *epistemological* strategy, based on 'universally communicable' mental states, is not successful, I shall show later on that it can be adapted in a viable direction. Before that, however, it is necessary to consider another strategy which Kant adopts, based on moral considerations.

PART 3

Kant's moral strategy is more complicated than the epistemological one just described. In the most general terms, it holds that the judgement of taste's claim to universal validity is justified by virtue of its relation to morality.

However, the more exact understanding of what this amounts to, and its strategic position in terms of Book I of the third *Critique*, is extremely controversial. Some scholars interpret it as a continuation of the deduction, or as an alternative approach, which Kant uses to compensate for the limited scope of his previous arguments.[11]

My own opinion is determined by a key structural fact. After §38, Kant begins to develop the moral implications of the judgement of taste

---

[11] A notable statement of the view that moral factors complete the deduction is R. K. Elliott, 'The Unity of Kant's *Critique of Judgment*', in Elliot's collection of essays *Aesthetics, Imagination, and the Unity of Consciousness*, ed. Paul Crowther (Aldershot: Ashgate, 2006), 3–20. Guyer is the most effective critic of this position—holding the moral dimension to be only a supplement to Kant's epistemological arguments. See his *Kant and the Claims of Taste*, 351–7.

as his overriding thematic. As we will recall from the previous chapter, bridging the gap between freedom and nature is one of the major goals of the third *Critique*. Beauty is connected to our existence as sensible beings, but the free play of the cognitive capacities which grounds pure aesthetic pleasure means that it is connected also with our existence as free, rational, moral beings.

According to Kant, the cultivation of taste enhances our susceptibility to moral awareness (a topic to which I will return). Given this, it is hardly surprising that the possibility of links between moral significance and taste is never far from Kant's central exposition, and that it occurs as an important thematic in its own right in the later sections of the 'Critique of Aesthetic Judgment'.

It is in this context that we should locate Kant's further thoughts about the universal validity of taste. It is not that he attempts to 'complete' the deduction by linking beauty and morality. Rather, he makes that linkage *itself* a central theme in the later stages of the 'Critique of Aesthetic Judgment' for strategic purposes.

The moral version of the deduction is formulated as, in effect, a support-factor in this strategy rather than as an attempt to complete an earlier unfinished argument. More specifically, it offers a more comprehensive *metaphysical* setting for the epistemological grounds of the claim to universal validity.

Kant's moral version of the deduction is extremely scattered. But it has, perhaps, two major aspects—an accumulation of points showing that morality and taste are mutually beneficial to one another and have a shared metaphysical ground, and a more focused argument concerning 'Beauty as a Symbol of Morality' (in §59) which links these points together.

The first indicator of the moral approach is found as early as §22, where Kant considers a connection between the necessity of the judgement of taste and the presupposition of a 'common sense'. The common sense here consists of the claim to universal validity understood in terms of an '*exemplary*' or 'ideal standard'.

What Kant is getting at through this is that the epistemological structure of the judgement of taste is not exhaustive of its a priori significance. In this respect he remarks as follows.

This indeterminate norm of a common sense is really presupposed by us: our presumption in making judgements of taste proves that. Whether there is in fact such a common sense, as a constitutive principle of the possibility of experience, or whether a yet higher principle of reason only makes it into a regulative principle for us to produce a common sense in ourselves for higher ends . . . this we would not and cannot yet investigate here; for now we have only to resolve the faculty of taste into its elements and to unite them ultimately in the idea of a common sense.[12]

Here Kant is positing two (apparently) different grounds for the judgement of taste's transcendental justification. On the one hand, we can show that the common sense is constitutive of the possibility of experience itself, or, on the other hand, we can show that it is a 'regulative principle'—in so far as the assumption of universal validity for judgements of taste is, in fact, *final* in relation to the a priori higher ends of reason (bound up with morality and the final end of nature itself).

These points require two technical comments. First, the common sense can only be construed as a constitutive principle in so far as this encompasses both the claim to universal validity *and* its sustaining cognitive grounds in the universal communicability of the harmony of the faculties and their specific proportions.

The other point is that whilst Kant presents the two possibilities as an either/or they are in fact not mutually exclusive. The common sense can be both constitutive (in the inclusive terms just described) and also regulative in so far as the claim to universal validity serves additional higher purposes in the broader, *moral*, scheme of things.

And, in fact, Kant does not explore these *as* alternatives. Rather, in the outer sections of the 'Critique of Aesthetic Judgment' his account switches emphasis from the 'constitutive' epistemological approach to the morality-orientated 'regulative' one. I shall now consider this latter emphasis.

It centres on the fact that whether or not any judgements of taste actually achieve universal validity is not the key issue. What is important, rather, is that taste can, in principle, be developed—with the attainment of universal validity as an ideal goal or 'regulative principle'. The reason we know that taste has this character is because of its complicated links with morality as the 'final end' of existence.

Of special importance is §40, which is actually entitled 'On Taste as a Kind of *Sensus Communis*'. Here we are told that '*sensus communis*' is the subjective sense possessed by each of us that makes communication possible. It is

a faculty for judging that in its reflection takes account (*a priori*) of everyone else's way of representing in thought, in order *as it were* to hold its judgement

¹² Kant, *Critique of Judgment*, §22, p. 124 (Pluhar, 89–90; Meredith, 85).

up to human reason as a whole and thereby avoid the illusion which, from subjective private conditions that could easily be held to be objective, would have a detrimental influence on the judgment.[13]

On these terms, in such judgement we abstract from our own limits and sensations by 'attending solely to the formal peculiarities of his representation or his representational state'.[14]

In §34, Kant notes that critical activity is relevant to the correction and broadening of judgements of taste. This, as we shall see in Part 5, is of decisive importance. That Kant does not develop it means that the notion of *sensus communis* in §40 remains somewhat abstract, with too much emphasis on the subject's viewpoint.

It also means that Kant loses an opportunity for linking the *sensus communis* to some important subsequent points in which he describes our capacity to develop an *interest* in beauty. Judgements of taste, of course, are disinterested vis-à-vis their logical grounds, but this does not conflict with the fact that, in terms of broader life choices, we may develop a settled propensity for their active solicitation.

This interest has both empirical and a priori ramifications. In §41, for example, it is shown to be of empirical import in facilitating sociability, in so far as the judgement of taste's claim to universal validity involves communicating our feelings to others.

More importantly, it is characterized as an 'Intellectual Interest in the Beautiful' (to which Kant devotes §42). We are told, for example, that

to take an *immediate interest* in the beauty of *nature* (not merely to have taste in order to judge it) is always a mark of a good soul, and that if this interest is habitual, it at least indicates a disposition of the mind that is favourable to the moral feeling, if it is gladly combined with the viewing of nature.[15]

Kant claims, then, that a habitual interest in beauty can be taken as indicative of a susceptibility to moral feeling. He is insistent that only natural beauty has this significance. An inclination towards the beauties of art or other artefacts will be dependent, primarily, on factors connected to human goals rather than aesthetic form for its own sake (a position which is extremely problematic as we shall see in the following chapters).

13 Ibid. §40, p. 173 (Pluhar, 160; Meredith, 151).
14 Ibid. §40, p. 174 (Pluhar, 160; Meredith, 151).
15 Ibid. §42, p. 178 (Pluhar, 165–6; Meredith, 157).

Now, whilst, according to Kant, this morally significant interest in natural beauty is a rare thing, it constellates around an obvious analogy. In Kant's terms,

> [the] immediate interest in the beautiful in nature is not common, but belongs only to those whose thinking is either already trained to the good or especially receptive to such training; and then even without clear, subtle, and deliberate reflection, the analogy between the pure judgement of taste, which, without depending on any sort of interest, allows a pleasure to be felt and at the same time to be represented a priori as proper for mankind in general, and the moral judgement, which does the same thing on the basis of concepts, leads to an equally immediate interest in the object of the former as in that of the latter—only the former is a free instrument, the latter is grounded on objective laws.[16]

The point is that if one has a developed commitment to morality or if one is susceptible to such a development, then the structural analogy between taste and moral judgement will enhance our capacity to cultivate our 'interest' in the former.

At this stage, then, we have five important, if rather scattered, points:

(a) *'sensus communis'*, in the sense of the judgement of taste's aspiration to universal validity;
(b) an interest in the beautiful;
(c) this interest as an indicator of susceptibility to moral feeling;
(d) the analogy between morality and taste;
(e) the analogy as a basis for morality to stimulate an interest in beauty.

Now, points (a) and (b) are consistent in terms of Kant's general approach. However, there are many obscurities involved in (c), (d), and (e) and even more so in respect of how all five points relate to one another.

For example, Kant sometimes appears to imply that it is the *sensus communis* which leads us to think of the analogical connection between taste and morality, but at other times (such as in §59), he gives the impression that it is recognition of the analogy which leads us to posit the claim to universal validity in the first place.

---

[16] Ibid. §42, p. 180 (Pluhar, 168; Meredith, 160). Malcolm Budd clarifies many of the issues involved here in his 'Delight in the Natural World: Kant on the Aesthetic Appreciation of Nature, Part II: Natural Beauty and Morality', *British Journal of Aesthetics*, 38 (1998), 117–26. Unfortunately, his account lacks comprehensiveness as it gives no consideration to the arguments concerning Beauty as a Symbol of Morality, from §59.

The idea of the link between beauty and a susceptibility to moral feeling is especially weak. For, whilst there may be some very general points of analogy between them (a possibility to which I will return), it cannot be inferred from this, a priori, that an interest in beauty is indicative of a developed moral propensity. Neither can it be inferred that the analogy between morality and beauty will allow the former to stimulate interest in the latter. The two *are* different—they involve, in Kantian terms, a priori 'causality', but of *different kinds*. Such connections cannot be inferred at the empirical level either—except on the basis of accumulated evidence (which, of course, Kant does not provide).

The points which I have discussed are key factors in the build-up to §59, where Kant offers what is, in effect, the most focused statement of the moral version of the deduction. However, there is one other major concept involved. It allows Kant to unify the foregoing material in interesting ways, and, in some respects, is the focal point of the final sections of the 'Critique of Aesthetic Judgment'. I shall now consider this concept and the use which Kant makes of it in §59.

PART 4

In the arguments just addressed, Kant emphasizes the transition from morality to beauty. However, in §42, he also acknowledges a reciprocal dynamic from beauty to morality. It is based on our admiration for natural beauty in terms of the apprehension of purposiveness without purpose. Hence, 'since we never encounter it [i.e., purposiveness without purpose] externally, we naturally seek within ourselves, and indeed in that which constitutes the ultimate end of our existence, namely the moral vocation'.[17]

On these terms, whilst our experience of 'subjective finality' is one of purpose, it is not, of course, objective teleology. It may be that the 'as if designed' character of objective finality becomes taken for granted, that we overlook its a priori origins, but in the pleasure of beauty this dimension becomes more accessible. We sense the moral vocation which is the final end even of nature's existence.

In the culminating sections of the 'Critique of Aesthetic Judgment', Kant refines this insight in a quite specific way. It is, for example,

---

[17] Kant, *Critique of Judgment*, §42, p. 181 (Pluhar, 168; Meredith, 160-1).

of decisive significance for the resolution of the so-called 'antinomy of taste'.

This antinomy is a rather artificial import derived from Kant's sense of the architectonics of his Critical philosophy as a whole rather than any direct requirement of argument for his aesthetics. Indeed, his formulation of the antinomy is somewhat obscure.[18]

One real point of substance, however, is Kant's claim that, whilst the judgement of taste is apart from any concept in terms of its logical grounds, its *metaphysical basis* (though it should be emphasized that Kant himself does not use that phrase) is founded on a *rational concept*.

In this respect, we will recall Kant's earlier point that the apprehension of purposiveness without purpose in nature makes us attentive to its ultimate ground in our moral vocation. This vocation—and the cognitive capacities which are necessary for its engagement with sensibility—are aligned by our free and rational being.

Now, in the Antinomy, Kant says that the judgement of taste must involve some concept or other, 'For if one did not assume such a point of view, then the claim of the judgement of taste to universal validity could not be saved.'[19] But the concept in question here is a '*rational*' one, and is not involved in the *logical* ground of the judgement of taste,

yet at the same time by means of this very concept it [i.e., the judgement of taste] acquires validity for everyone (in each case, to be sure, as a singular judgement immediately accompanying the intuition), because its determining ground may lie in the concept of that which can be regarded as the supersensible substratum of humanity.[20]

This 'supersensible substratum', then, is Kant's last key concept. It involves our free rational being *and* its capacity to align our cognitive capacities so as to realize our ultimate vocation in a natural and physical arena. Instead of emphasizing morality in isolation, the supersensible allows theoretical capacities to be included as factors operative within our moral vocation. It is an inclusive rational concept which integrates the cognitive and moral aspects of our existence as free rational beings.

We can now clarify the relation between the supersensible substratum and Kant's epistemological deduction. The claim to universal validity

<hr/>

[18] Guyer is also unimpressed by Kant's raising of the antinomy, and offers an effective discussion of it at *Kant and the Claims of Taste*, 331–50. The only drawback is that he treats the substrate almost exclusively as a theoretical concept, whereas my sense is that it is the principle of unity wherein our existence as creatures of theoretical *and* practical reason is integrated.   [19] Kant, *Critique of Judgment*, §57, p. 216 (Pluhar, 212; Meredith, 207).   [20] Ibid. (Pluhar, 213; Meredith, 208).

is, for Kant, justified by the accord of our cognitive capacities and a privileged proportion which is conducive to their interaction. However, this accord does not just happen. The reason why there is such a thing as cognition *at all* is because of our moral vocation—which is the *raison d'être* of existence per se.

It follows, therefore, that the accord of the faculties, which is the logical ground of taste's claim to universal validity, *itself* presupposes something more ultimate—namely, the supersensible. This involves our free rational being's capacity to align epistemological and moral factors, and is thence the ultimate *metaphysical ground* of taste's claim to universal validity. The assumption of this notion on a priori grounds enables the most *complete* philosophical justification of that claim.

In §59, Kant links the supersensible substrate to points which repeat, or are similar to, those which I outlined in Part 3. This enables him to offer an argument concerning 'Beauty as a Symbol of Morality' which is the most complete formulation of the deduction in its moral version.

Kant introduces his ideas with a few important definitions. He observes, for example, that 'Symbolic exhibition uses an analogy' 'the first to do this demonstratively, the second by means of analogy'.[21] This can involve the use of intuitions, but, with 'symbolic hypotyposes', this is not the case. Rather, these involve

expressions for concepts not by means of a direct intuition, but only in accordance with an analogy with it—that is, the transportation of the reflection on one object of intuition to another, quite different, concept, to which perhaps no intuition can ever directly correspond.[22]

Now, in the case of beauty's symbolic relation to morality, we are dealing with a case of this sort. As Kant puts it,

the beautiful is the symbol of the morally good, and also that only in this respect (that of a relation that is natural to everyone, and that is also expected of everyone else as a duty) does it please with a claim to the assent of everyone else.[23]

This claim occurs as the start of a more intricate chain of reasoning. Again, I will summarize the salient points—in the order that Kant presents them.

(i) Beauty is a symbol of the morally good, and only because we think of it in this light (an analogy which is 'natural' for us,

---

[21] Ibid. §59, p. 226 (Pluhar, 227; Meredith, 222).
[22] Ibid. §59, p. 227 (Pluhar, 228; Meredith, 223).   [23] Ibid.

and which we expect others to make also, as a 'duty') can our pleasure in beauty claim universal validity.

(ii) This claim makes us aware of the superiority of our rational side over our merely sensuous being, and we assess the worth of other people too in terms of how their judgements aspire to this exemplary status.

(iii) The morally good is an 'intelligible' supersensible substrate which grounds the very alignment of our cognitive powers.

(iv) Without this 'intelligible' ground, 'contradictions would emerge between their nature and the claims that taste makes'.[24]

(v) Pure aesthetic judgements are analogous with moral judgements in respect of their characteristics of immediacy, disinterestedness, and universality.

(vi) Indeed, 'Taste as it were makes possible the transition from sensible charm to the habitual moral interest without too violent a leap by representing the imagination even in its freedom as purposively determinable for the understanding and teaching us to find a free satisfaction in the objects of the senses even without any sensible charm'.[25]

The general thrust of Kant's points here are in directions already encountered. However, it is possible to create a more focused structure of argument by considering the points in an order different from that of Kant's presentation.

In foundational terms, the key point is the significance of the *supersensible substratum*. This integrates our moral being and the alignment of cognitive capacities in a way which provides ultimate justification of the judgement of taste's claim to universal validity. It is a 'definite' concept, but one which is rational and metaphysical rather than sensible, thus allowing the cognitive dimension of the claims of taste to be made specific without contradiction.

It is here that beauty's symbolic relation to morality is decisive. The analogy between judgements of morality and taste is a familiar one which we would expect any rational agent to recognize. And it is by reference to this symbolic kinship that we recognize taste's claim to universal validity.

In turn, the fact that an idiom of feeling can have this rational dimension shows that even at the level of sensibility humans have a vocation that leads beyond *mere* causally based pleasures of the senses.

[24] Kant, *Critique of Judgment*, (Pluhar, 229; Meredith, 224).
[25] Ibid. §59, p. 228, (Pluhar, 230; Meredith, 225).

Presented in this order, and clarified a little, Kant at least has a logical structure of argument. Indeed, it allows us to understand his concluding remarks (in the very last paragraph of the 'Critique of Aesthetic Judgment'):

taste is at the bottom a faculty for the judging of the sensible rendering of moral ideas (by means of a certain analogy of the reflection on both), from which, as well as from the greater receptivity for the feeling resulting from the latter (which is called the moral feeling) that is to be grounded upon it, is derived that pleasure which taste declares to be valid for mankind in general, not merely for the private feeling of each, it is evident that the true propaedeutic for the grounding of taste is the development of moral ideas and the cultivation of the moral feeling; for only when sensibility is brought into accord with this can genuine taste assume a determinate, unalterable form.[26]

On these terms Kant has shown that taste's universal validity is conversant with morality, in both symbolic terms, and that of its metaphysical grounding. By virtue of this conversance, one who enjoys beauty is disposed towards morality as well. In accordance with the primary intention of the third *Critique* as a whole, nature and freedom are bridged.

Now, whilst Kant's strategy is clear, his argument concerning beauty's symbolic relation to morality is not compelling. The points concerning the supersensible substrate as a metaphysical basis for the universal validity of taste are at least intelligible (though in need of considerable further discussion and critical modification). However, there are pressing difficulties with the other points, both individually and in concert.

First, we have already seen the problems of assuming that propensities for morality or taste will be beneficial for one another through their effect upon feeling. A worry also arises in that, whilst the points of likeness in beauty's symbolic relation to morality are plausible, the question of whether or not the recognition of it is 'natural', let alone something which we might expect from others as a 'duty', is contentious to say the least.

An even bigger problem arises from the specific use to which Kant puts the analogy. He suggests that it is only in so far as we 'refer' the beautiful to the morally good that our liking for the former can include the claim to universal validity. But, what does the term 'refer' mean in this context?

---

[26] Ibid. §60, p. 230, (Pluhar, 232; Meredith, 227).

One possibility is that unless we *recognize* the symbolic relation to morality we will be unable to comprehend taste's universal validity. But, unfortunately, Kant does nothing to show why such recognition is necessary. If anything, it seems counter-intuitive.

And, if the recognition is insisted upon, then a vicious circularity arises. For Kant includes the universality of the judgement of taste as one of the factors on which beauty's symbolizing of morality is based. On these terms, in other words, the universal validity whose recognition Kant is trying to explain is assumed as an element in its own explanation.

Given the considerations broached in each Part of this chapter, then, it is clear that Kant's epistemological version of the Deduction, and his subsequent moral version, do not succeed. However, whilst this negative verdict holds for the letter of Kant's arguments, their content and spirit allow for possibilities of revision which go a long way towards meeting his goals. It is to these possibilities that I now turn.

PART 5

I will start with an analysis of what I take to be the root cause of Kant's problems. The judgement of taste has two ontologically inseparable but different aspects, which Kant conflates. On the one hand, there is taste's universality, and on the other hand, there is its claim to universal validity. I will deal with these in turn.

In Kantian terms, universality is based on that privileged proportion between imagination and understanding, wherein their interaction is optimally stimulated. Earlier, I proposed that the only viable candidate for this proportion is diversity and unity in the phenomenal manifold.

In one sense, this structure is *so* basic that it characterizes all perceptual manifolds to some degree. However, in those cases which are found beautiful, it engages cognitive capacities that are intrinsic to knowledge of self and world per se. In the convergence of these two factors, taste finds genuine universality in terms of its *scope of application*. The ramifications of this are brought out effectively by Guyer, as follows.

Although the theory of the harmony of the faculties may not be enough to fully justify the claim to universal validity . . . this theory does explain how we may take a pleasure which is truly independent of individual interests and concerns, and which is rooted in an objective—that of the unification of manifolds in general—which must surely be attributed to everyone.[27]

This universality is of heightened contemporary importance. In recent times, the aesthetic has tended to be treated in some quarters as a culturally specific western preference, or as something which amounts to no more than a signifier with social kudos for those who supposedly have 'taste'. It has been regarded as inseparable from the 'elitism' of the white, male middle-class, and its societal hegemony.[28]

However, Kant's approach shows otherwise. The formal configurations which he emphasizes are not those of high art but, rather, natural forms and basic decorative patterns. These are the focus of beauty. The grounds of the pleasure taken in them is not bound up with a specific set of cultural preferences but is something available to all humans qua human through its grounding in the interaction of basic phenomena structure and cognitive capacities.

It may be that a person's material circumstances are such as to restrict the development of taste in any sustained way, but this is the fault of the circumstances rather than of taste itself. The cultivation of taste offers intrinsic gratifications which can enrich an individual's mode of inhering in the world.

Now, Kant's great error is that he identifies the criteria of universality which I have just described with the judgement of taste's claim to universal validity per se. However, universal *validity* involves *an extra factor* which Kant does no direct justice to.

This consists of an at least tacit estimate of the *quality or value* of a specific relational form. In judging something to be beautiful we are not simply describing diversity and unity, we are judging that a particular way of presenting this relation has a distinctiveness which cannot be appreciated simply by describing the *kind* of diversity and unity in question.

Its specific character engages our cognitive capacities in an enhanced way that most instances of the relation do not. Beauty is an evaluative rather than a descriptive term. The judgement of taste, accordingly, is selective, and involves, of necessity, a comparative aspect.[29]

---

[27] Guyer, *Kant and the Claims of Taste*, 328.

[28] Pierre Bourdieu, for example, takes this approach in many of his most influential works. See esp. *Distinction: A Social Critique of Taste*, trans. Richard Nice (London: Routledge, 1979).

[29] In relation to this, Guyer makes the following interesting point. 'Too much familiarity with a given manifold, or kind of manifold, may make its unification entirely as expected as

Kant himself does not negotiate this evaluative character in appropriately direct terms. Rather, he holds that because the judgement of taste is based on purely cognitive and disinterested grounds (i.e., with no interference from extra-aesthetic factors) then this is sufficient for characterizing it as something which others ought to assent to as well.

However, as we have seen, this is not at all sufficient. The particular nature of diversity and unity in the manifold still allows for great variation in terms of how individuals respond to it. *If a Kantian aesthetic is to be viable, therefore, a second major structural step is required. We must link it to procedures that might justify the claim to universal validity, by testing it at a public level. This involves a comparative critical horizon which the judgement of taste must engage with, of necessity, in so far as it claims universal validity.*

The horizon might be explained as follows. If someone challenges our judgement, it is up to them to provide formal evidence to show why our favoured form is supposedly deficient vis-à-vis beauty. Equally, in response, we might offer some formal evidence of our own to defend the claim.

If the evidence against a claim is not found convincing, then we can maintain our position and offer further evidence, or else ask for opinions from other informed parties.

In fact, the only way in which a challenged claim to universal validity can be resolved significantly is through sustained critical *rejection* by a

---

would its subsumption under a concept. But if the nature of the aesthetic response requires uniqueness, what is needed is uniqueness of representations relative to the subject, and not uniqueness of the objects of taste themselves. Truly aesthetic appreciation of an object concerns the character of its representation rather than the uniqueness of its existence. For this reason, considering whether one could obtain the same pleasure from a perfect representation of an object as from the object itself might indeed be a useful criterion for the judgment of taste' (Guyer, *Kant and the Claims of Taste*, 202). In the first part of this passage, Guyer is, in effect, making a point about the empirical significance of a comparative context. If a beautiful form is to stand out as beautiful, it must be unique in the sense of not simply exemplifying a formal structure to which we have become habituated in terms of our personal experience. My point, however, is that uniqueness in a comparative sense can also act in more universal evaluative terms in so far as it is possible for taste to become more educated and developed. Guyer implies that if the role played by the comparative context is based on anything more than personal experience then it must involve strictly objective criteria. In the subsequent pages, I will show that this is not the case. (It should be noted further that the notion of uniqueness that Guyer uses in the second part of the passage is not the comparative experiential one described in the first part. The second sense of uniqueness is an ontological one, based on the distinction between an original form and a reproduction of it. Hence, it rather distracts from his point of substance concerning the potential of experientially based, comparative uniqueness.)

body of informed opinion. An accumulation of formal evidence and widespread approbation will never conclusively validate a claim, but if a significant weight of evidence mounts against it, then (in spite of what Kant himself says) we would have reasonable grounds for revising our judgement.

The question arises as to the nature of the 'formal evidence' involved here. And the answer is that it is a function of the comparative dimension.

That Kant himself does not clarify comparative criteria, at any length, is easy to understand in one respect. It may seem too close to a 'standard of taste' based on judging something to be beautiful through its conformity to established norms or rules. This, of course, would be inconsistent with the judgement of taste's apartness from 'definite' concepts, and its correlated cognitively 'free' aspects.

However, it is possible to make sense of the comparative dimension in a way that does not impinge on the primacy of the particular. This involves placing an emphasis on taste being something which can be *cultivated* in a public context.

In this respect, for example, if a person's experience of some relevant formal relation is developed, embodiments of it which may have previously seemed, say, 'fussy' or 'confused' may now be found stimulating.

Concerning such development, Kant himself actually points us in the right direction. In this respect, for example, I noted in Part 3 that he raises a point which should have been made a great deal more of. It occurs in the area of the 'Critique of Aesthetic Judgment' where he begins assembling his moral version of the deduction. The point concerns how critics can 'correct and broaden' the judgement of taste. This demands that they 'could and should reason about . . . the investigation of the faculties of cognition and their functions in these judgements and laying out in examples the reciprocal subjective purposiveness'.[30]

The possibility of such critical mediation is vital in a way that Kant does not bring out. To say a formal configuration is elegant and exhilarating is not just a report of how one feels. If called upon, I should be able to point out some of the formal features which led me to this judgement and—more importantly—compare it with less felicitous configurations in order to justify my appraisal.

Given this, it is quite possible that someone else who did not find the form beautiful hitherto now comes to see the point by means of my

---

[30] Kant, *Critique of Judgment*, §34, p. 166 (Pluhar, 149–50; Meredith, 141).

'argument', and changes his or her own verdict accordingly. They *learn to feel* the form in a new way.[31] Whilst taste focuses on the subject's own perceptual horizons, the context of public expression is a key factor. Those beautiful forms which we place in our habitat or grow in the garden, or which are found in places which we choose to visit, all express our taste at a public level. And, in the course of everyday interactions with others and visitations of their spaces, an informal exchange of judgements of taste becomes a key factor in the growth of culture.

However, it is vital to emphasize that the public dimension does not entail that we are dealing with 'proofs' and deciding issues of taste through conformity with general standards. The matter hinges on perceiving and comparing at the level of specific *particulars* so as to expand one's awareness of the possibilities which are opened in terms of judgement. Openness and a willingness to follow, as it were, *where the configuration leads*, are paramount.

Indeed, it is important to emphasize that whilst many publically accepted critical terms have developed in relation to taste (such as harmony, balance, and economy in formal matters) these cannot be applied as general rules. Their general meaning only becomes relevant when they are explored through comparison and contrasts between directly perceived phenomenal configurations.

Ideally, the example, and opinions of other people in matters of taste offer a basis for guidance. Indeed, the claim to universal validity's implicit 'ought' is not a demand for compliance but a confident willingness to have one's judgement put to comparative test. Kant himself remarks (in relation to rational pursuits in general) that

if every subject always had to begin entirely from the raw predisposition of his nature, [he] would not fall into mistaken attempts if others had not preceded him with their own, not in order to make their successors into mere imitators, but rather by means of their method to put others on the right path for seeking out the principles in themselves and thus for following their own, often better, course.[32]

This openness to development is precisely the strength of the judgement of taste. For, by remaining open it embodies a constant imperative for cultivation—a sense that matters can be 'taken further'; that human beings can *become* in ways that build constructively on what has gone

---

[31] This does conflict with the involuntary aspect of the judgement of taste. What is involved here is a change of belief based on evidence; and changes of belief are, of course, involuntary.

[32] Ibid. §32, 163–4 (Pluhar, 146; Meredith, 138).

before whilst always following a trajectory that is defined by what they are, intrinsically, *as human*.

Now, it might be argued that things here are still left too open. The judgement of taste's claim to universal validity must surely issue in something more than a few platitudes concerning the fact that it can be cultivated in a comparative critical context. For example, in exactly what sense can such judgements 'build' on what has gone before?

In answer to this in a visual context the questioner might be referred to such texts as John Ruskin's *Elements of Drawing*, or his *Modern Painters*, or to William Gilpin's many works on the picturesque.

Some writers on the arts are theorists and aestheticians, and clarify general questions alone. The works of Ruskin and Gilpin are written mainly as aids to pictorial representation, but they are by no means reducible to this. Rather, through their pointing out and explanations of relational factors, a wealth of *possibilities* for *informed* perceptual exploration of visual manifolds is opened up.

Kant himself is aware of this kind of potential through his comments that the 'critique of taste' involves

bringing under rules the reciprocal relation of the understanding and the imagination of each other in the given representation (without relation to an antecedent sensation or concept), and consequently their concord or discord, and of determining it with regard to its conditions. It is art if it shows this only in example.[33]

Now, in mentioning Ruskin and Gilpin I am *not* advocating them as supreme arbiters of taste. Rather, I mention them because they (and many other writers since their times) exemplify the example-orientated critique of taste as an 'art' which Kant is pointing towards. Their discussions of taste provide key examples and ways of addressing them which allow a fund of descriptive formal concepts and ideas to be absorbed, *refined*, and deployed on one's own terms—that is, without this involving a mere conformity to standards of a rigid kind.

The sustained perceptual embrace of the visual particular found in Ruskin's and Gilpin's works unlocks aesthetic energies which are especially resistant to contemporary global consumerist tendencies. They invite cultivation, rather than persuade consumption. Indeed, the community of taste achieved through a free exchange of judgements

---

[33] Ibid. §34, 166 (Pluhar, 150; Meredith, 142).

of taste is engagingly *incompatible* with the instrumental means–ends logic of the global consumerist order.

Interestingly, one of the most important technical supports of global consumerism—the internet—can play an important role in resistance through taste. As more texts of the kind which I have described become available online, this means that a body of criticism—hitherto of only specialist historical interest—can now become available to the non-specialist through simple internet searches and simple search terms.

An enormously diverse body of example-orientated writing with a capacity to stimulate more critical orientations towards taste is now available. What gives this the potential to refine and move taste forward is not only the power of rediscovering ideas, but in being able to retrieve and juxtapose ideas from different historical and geographical areas.

From a historical point of view, such juxtaposition runs the risk of dealing with material 'out of context' and 'ahistorically'. From the viewpoint of the critical 'art' of taste, however, such incongruities pose no threat and, indeed, are to be welcomed. Here we are not concerned with comprehending historically specific events or institutions but in looking for new ways to enable enjoyment of the aesthetic particular.

The only danger this poses is of unbridled eclecticism in matters of taste. To some degree a sensibility of this kind has, indeed, characterized the postmodern era in its first phase. The key task is to now base the openness involved in such eclecticism on a more critical turn. This means an appropriation and deployment of critical concepts and examples in depth, as well as a mere mixing of styles.

Given this development of the comparative aspects of the claim to universal validity, the following summary is in order. The judgement of taste's universality makes it special. But, it is the possibility of cultivation which allows the judgement of taste to aspire to universal validity *as a methodological principle or ideal*.

To judge something as beautiful is to place it, at least tacitly, in the public arena as something which others ought to regard as beautiful. And the fact that such judgements can be supported or disputed through formal evidence mean that taste is an active, developing cultural capacity, rather than a nostalgic lingering amongst established forms and critical idioms.

A pleasure with such a basis is genuinely 'higher' in terms of its grounds and educability.[34] Such status allows further connections to be made with Kant's moral version of the deduction.

PART 6

To show this, I will mention a factor which Kant does not raise explicitly. In his *Groundwork of the Metaphysic of Morals*, the importance of 'duties to oneself' is emphasized. Since the judgement of taste is a 'higher' and thence *improving* pleasure vis-à-vis our existence as free, rational, sensible beings, one presumes that it is a moral duty to oneself to practise it.

Now, when Kant introduces the *sensus communis* as an aspiration towards universal validity as an exemplary ideal it seems that we have the link to such self-improvement as a practice. But, Kant leaves matters at a very static level, and does not clarify what it means in *concrete terms* to try and bring one's judgement of taste into accord with those of one's fellow humans.

His notion of an 'interest in the beautiful' does not provide the requisite active element here. This is because it involves only a settled disposition for taste—a disposition which might amount to no more than responding in the appropriate way when the appropriate kind of configuration is encountered.

However, in my account, I have emphasized taste as an activity conducted in a context of shared comparisons. If taste is a duty to oneself, then this surely means that the role of universal validity as an exemplary ideal for judgement has to be *lived* in active terms. It must be *cultivated* in terms of the claim to universal validity, and the only criteria for cultivation in this respect are surely those involving the comparative dimension which I have just outlined.

Indeed, if our judgements of taste have this active comparative aspect, it is easy to see how they might settle into the sustained interest in the beautiful which Kant emphasizes. They do so, because they involve a refinement of taste achieved in a social context. This does not mean, of course, that they are just pleasures of sociability; rather,

---

[34] Interestingly, Béatrice Longuenesse arrives at a similar conclusion via a wholly different route in 'Kant's Leading Thread in the Analytic of the Beautiful' (repr. Kukla, *Aesthetics and Cognition in Kant's Critical Philosophy*), 194–219, esp. 219.

the social dimension clarifies and consolidates the quality of our own judgements of taste by offering the possibility of critique, improvement, and confirmation of success.

Now, in all this, there are some clear affinities between the judgement of taste and moral awareness. In Kantian (and other) conceptions of morality, impartiality is a key factor. Indeed, if one wishes to talk of *moral* codes, as opposed to simply shared rules for social co-existence in particular contexts, impartiality seems to be a fundamental notion. Universality is likewise entailed.

It might also be noted that whether a moral decision is genuinely moral or not (and is in fact the 'right' thing to do) is not just a case of following one's conscience. On matters of conscience, it often turns out that a mistake was made which mature reflection reveals to us retrospectively. In such cases, it is often a matter of regret that at the time one was not guided by wiser counsels.

These points suggest that in moral matters a willingness to frame decisions in a comparative context can be of the greatest help in making the authentic moral choice, even if, in the final analysis, what one chooses is one's own responsibility.

Impartiality and universality in moral judgement are analogous in formal terms to the disinterestedness and universality of the judgement of taste. The willingness to shape one's moral decisions in a comparative context—whilst taking final responsibility for one's choices—also parallels the active cultivation of taste which I have emphasized. In fact, our *concrete* moral life is full of the kind of decisions, revisions, and new initiatives which characterize that cultivation.

CONCLUSION

I have argued, then, that Kant's deduction of the judgement of taste's claim to universal validity can be established through revising his epistemological approach with input from his moral version of the deduction. The key element is the importance of taste pursued in a comparative, developing, critical context.

As a final point, it is worth reflecting on Kant's own special attentiveness to the moral import of taste. For reasons described at length, his view that taste and morality mutually reinforce one another necessarily is not acceptable. However, given that the judgement of taste is something which can be developed, and is 'higher' than ordinary pleasures of sense;

this would suggest an affinity between the two dimensions of experience which is not a merely passive one.

To wit, if a person actively pursues higher pleasures which are not driven by the means–ends instrumentalist logic of practical gain and accumulation, then it is reasonable to imagine that such a pursuit *might* dispose the agent to be more thoughtful and reflective in his or her dealings with other persons. There is, in other words, at least reason for *faith* in such a possibility, if not the certainty which Kant ascribes to it.

5

Adherent Beauty and the Scope of Perfection

INTRODUCTION

The most fundamental features of Kant's aesthetic theory have now been set out. However, there is much in the third *Critique* which does seem to go beyond or conflict with these fundamentals. The relation between beauty and perfection is a case in point. Through its combination of the cognitive and the sensuous, beauty was once thought to be a less distinct form of perfection. In the third *Critique*, however, Kant draws a very clear distinction between the two. Indeed, his characterization of beauty in terms of pleasure that is disinterested and free (through its grounding in the appreciation of formal qualities alone) is one which, in previous chapters, I have argued to be a definitive feature of pure aesthetic experience.

Where, then, does this leave the notion of perfection? Is it simply a concept that was once used as a crude model for comprehending aesthetic experience, but which is now outmoded; or, is the very fact that it could be used this way symptomatic of the fact that perfection actually *does* play a role in the aesthetic domain?

In this respect, it is interesting that whilst in the third *Critique* and its (subsequently shelved) First Introduction Kant is at great pains to separate judgements of beauty and perfection, he does, nevertheless, in §16 of the *Critique,* introduce a distinction between free and adherent beauty—the latter of which involves concepts of perfection. The significance of this distinction goes beyond internal issues in the third *Critique*. For, if a Kantian aesthetic is to do justice to the complexities of aesthetic phenomena in general terms, then it must be adaptable enough to encompass potentially problematic factors. The distinction between free and adherent beauty, in other words, enables us to make a first significant test of the *scope* of Kant's basic aesthetic theory.

In this chapter, therefore, I shall in Part I analyse the nature of Kant's distinction and will show that, whilst not compelling, his structure of argument is at least consistent and, indeed, contains two crucial insights that extend his basic position. These are, first, that considerations of perfection must sometimes take precedence over beauty, thus showing that beauty is of conditional rather than absolute value; and, second, that judgements of perfection can themselves be aesthetic in character.

After offering an argument in defence of this first claim, I will go on to suggest that there is a rather better way than Kant's of grounding the second claim. In Part II, accordingly, I will show this by arguing that the disinterestedness and freedom whereby Kant defines the pure aesthetic judgement can also hold, in a modified way, for some judgements of perfection. I will then suggest that Kant himself indirectly recognizes this fact through his account in §16 of how the experience of adherent beauty involves a harmony of reason and cognition.

PART 1

Kant introduces his distinction between free and adherent beauty respectively, in the following terms:

the first presupposes no concept of what the object ought to be; the second does presuppose such a concept and the perfections of the object in accordance with it. The first are called (self-subsisting) beauties of this or that thing; the latter, as adhering to a concept (conditioned beauty), are ascribed to objects that stand under the concept of a particular end.[1]

Kant goes on to develop this distinction through the use of examples. Specifically, we are told that flowers, some kinds of birds and crustacean, designs à la Greque, and musical fantasies are amongst those things which 'signify nothing by themselves: they do not represent anything, no object under a determinate concept, and are free beauties'.[2]

Now, as Donald Crawford has pointed out,[3] whilst Kant treats free beauty here as though it were a property of certain kinds of objects, it is clear from points elsewhere in §16 of the third *Critique* that, in

---

[1] Immanuel Kant, *The Critique of the Power of Judgment*, trans. Paul Guyer and Eric Matthews (Cambridge: Cambridge University Press, 2000), §16, p. 114 (Pluhar, 76; Meredith, 72).   [2] Ibid. (Pluhar, 77; Meredith, 72).

[3] Donald Crawford, *Kant's Aesthetic Theory* (Madison, Wis.: University of Wisconsin Press, 1974), 116.

principle, any object can be judged in terms of free beauty, so long as we 'make abstraction' from the 'concept of its end' (i.e., that set of phenomenal properties which defines the kind of thing it is). Why, then, does Kant conduct his exposition primarily in terms of examples?

The answer is, I would suggest, relatively straightforward—namely, that in some objects formal qualities are simply more manifest (and thence more accessible to pure aesthetic judgements) than in others. Most people, for example, would be inclined to enjoy the formal intricacy of a flower, or bird's plumage, for its own sake rather than because it shows the flower or bird to be perfect instances of their respective species. It is, in other words, just more natural to appreciate their formal qualities in subjective and aesthetic, rather than objective and intellectual, terms.

In the case of those examples of adherent beauty which Kant goes on to provide, however, the reverse is true. Such things as human beings, horses, or buildings, do not usually possess the luxuriant and intricate formal qualities which would dispose us to respond to them in fundamentally subjective terms. Indeed (in the case of these specific examples at least), such objects play an important and familiar role in the practical vicissitudes of everyday existence.

At this point, Kant's exposition becomes very problematic. In relation to the examples just mentioned, he informs us that their 'beauty' presupposes a concept of the end which defines what the thing has to be, and consequently 'a concept of its perfection'.[4] As Geoffrey Scarré, however, has forcefully observed,

After he has told us so insistently that judgments of beauty are determined by feeling and not by concepts, can he really be saying now that there is another kind of beauty whose recognition requires not feelings but concepts? If so, it is a remarkable *volte-face* and to all appearances a purposeless one, for it is obscure what Kant would want to say the two views have in common to justify to common label.[5]

Scarré's own solution to the problem is to claim that, for Kant, adherent beauty has no connection with the concept of perfection. It

---

[4] Kant, *Critique of Judgment*, §16, p. 114 (Pluhar, 77; Meredith, 73).
[5] Geoffrey Scarré, 'Kant on Free and Dependent Beauty', *British Journal of Aesthetics*, 21 (1981), 358. The inhibiting role of moral factors is scarcely dealt with by some commentators. Rather, they treat Kant's position as if it were based exclusively on perfection's role as a logical presupposition of a distinctive kind of aesthetic judgement. For an effective example, see Robert Wicks, 'Dependent Beauty as the Appreciation of Teleological Style', *Journal of Aesthetics and Art Criticism*, 55 (1997), 387–400.

is, rather, free beauty whose apprehension is restricted by a judgement as to whether it is decorous (i.e., morally appropriate) for the object in question to be freely beautiful.

In the case of paradigm free beauties, such as flowers and Crustacea, the question does not arise; in the case of humans, horses, and buildings, in contrast, it *does*, and, in so far as there is nothing indecorous about such objects being regarded as beautiful, they are, therefore, to be classed as adherently so.

The major problem with Scarré's interpretation is that whilst, say, it might be morally 'indecorous' to appreciate the beauty of tattoos on human skin, it is not immediately apparent as to why the appreciation of the beauty of a horse or house should be regarded in such terms. Indeed, not only does Kant himself make no mention of 'decorum' in his exposition but, indeed, he asserts the link between perfection and adherent beauty so often that it is scarcely conceivable that perfection should not play some role here. The question is *what* role?

The answer is, I would suggest, that whilst Kant's idea that adherent beauty 'presupposes' a concept of perfection suggestive of a relation of logical dependence (thus leading to the problem noted by Scarré) his intended meaning may involve a rather looser relation. This enables an alternative interpretation which not only fits in well with Kant's example-oriented approach at the start of §16 but which allows, also, the overall structure of argument in that section to read consistently.

It is instructive here first to consider a precedent in the *Groundwork of the Metaphysics of Morals* (1785). In this work, Kant suggests 'the dependence of a will not absolutely good on the principle of autonomy (that is, moral necessitation) is obligation'.[6] Now, in broad Kantian terms, will is a capacity for inaugurating rational activity. Whilst, however, a wholly rational being (i.e., an absolutely good, or, as Kant sometimes puts it, a 'holy will') can, by definition, do the rational thing as a matter of course, an imperfectly rational *finite* creature, in contrast, is beset by distracting sensuous impulses, and, in consequence, can only conceive rational or moral action in terms of obligation. That is, if I want x then I *ought* to do y, or, in the case of moral action (simply), I *ought* to do x.

The point to gather is that a will is made dependent (i.e., adherent) by the empirical fact that its rational being is combined with, and

---

[6] Kant, *Groundwork of the Metaphysics of Morals*, trans. H. Paton (London: Hutchinson & Co., 1955), 107.

inhibited by sensuous impulses. Hence, whilst having a rational will does not presuppose sensuous impulses, and whilst having sensuous impulses does not presuppose having a rational will, to be an adherent will involves the possession of both features.

Working from this model, something can be characterized as adherent if it consists of two logically independent elements which are empirically combined in a way that allows one of the elements to inhibit the operations of the other. This, I would suggest, is exactly the case with adherent beauty.

Consider the following contrast. In the case of a bird of paradise, we have an animal whose plumage is overwhelmingly striking and complex at a purely perceptual level, and which (unless one happens to be an ornithologist) is of little interest apart from this. Here, in other words, because of the nature of the object involved, our appreciation of its beauty is wholly free and unrestricted.

In the case of a horse, however, whilst we could, *in principle*, appreciate its beauty alone, we will find, in practice, that we are preoccupied by all sorts of other interests. What kind of horse is it? Is it old or young? Is it healthy? Can it pull a cart or clear a fence?

Here, because the animal strikes us primarily in terms of intellectual and practical considerations, reason demands, in consequence, that we give priority to judgements of how perfectly it satisfies such ends. Its beauty, in other words, is a secondary consideration, a kind of pleasing 'extra' whose appreciation, indeed, will tend to be inhibited by our interest in the object's perfection.

This interpretation of adherent beauty is given striking general viability by the fact that all the terms which Kant uses to describe the adherent relation—'attached to', 'appendant', and 'conditioned by'—are ones which connote empirical conjunction, or secondariness, or both. Indeed, immediately after introducing his first examples of adherent beauty, Kant goes on to say:

Now just as the combination of the agreeable (of sensation) with beauty, which properly concerns only form, hindered the purity of the judgment of taste, so the combination of the good (that is, the way in which the manifold is good for the thing itself, in accordance with its end) with beauty does damage to its purity.[7]

---

[7] Kant, *Critique of Judgment*, §16, pp. 114–15 (Pluhar, 77; Meredith, 73).

Hence, as my interpretation would lead us to expect, Kant is suggesting that if a thing is such that it leads us to judge it in terms of its perfection, then we can expect our appreciation of its beauty to be inhibited. This, indeed, is why Kant further suggests, in a famous passage:

One would be able to add much to a building that would be pleasing in the intuition of it if only it were not supposed to be a church; a figure could be beautiful with all sorts of curlicues and light but regular lines, as the New Zealanders do with their tattooing, if only it were not a human being.[8]

In these cases, we are dealing with things whose significance for us is so predominantly intellectual or moral that any beautiful embellishments of the sort mentioned are entirely superfluous, in so far as our appreciation of them would be totally inhibited and spoilt.

Given, then, that Kant's distinction is not between two distinct kinds of beauty but between contrasting conditions (determined by the nature of the object involved) in which beauty is encountered, the question arises as to why we should need a term such as 'adherent beauty' at all.

One can, of course, understand why in his moral philosophy Kant needs the notion of a dependent will—in so far as, with human beings, rational intention and sensuous impulse are always and inescapably conjoined. But, surely the conjunction between perfection and beauty is not of *this* inescapable empirical order. Indeed, does not Kant himself admit that we can abstract away from an object's end and appreciate its beauty alone? Why, then, do we need a special term to pick out the conjunction of perfection and beauty?

It is perhaps salutary in this respect to consider the example of gunpowder. Here we have a mixture of different chemicals, all of which we value individually for reasons other than their role in gunpowder. Their relation is simply one of tight conjunction rather than the unity of a chemical compound.

We need 'gunpowder' as a term, however, because, in combination, its constituents have an effect that is useful, and which cannot be attained from them individually. It is considerations similar to these—in terms of the conjunction of beauty and intellectual response—which, in the second half of §16, Kant uses to justify the notion of adherent beauty. '[T]aste gains by this combination of aesthetic satisfaction with the intellectual in that it becomes fixed and . . . can have rules prescribed to

---

[8] Ibid.

it in regard to certain purposively determined objects'.[9] Kant then goes on to offer a rather difficult description of how this comes about:

strictly speaking, however, perfection does not gain by beauty, nor does beauty gain by perfection; rather, since in comparing the representation by which an object is given to us with the object (with regard to what it ought to be) we cannot avoid at the same time holding it together with the subject, the entire faculty of the powers of representation gains if both states of mind are in agreement.[10]

Now, as I interpret him here, whilst Kant holds that a perfect object is not made more perfect by being beautiful (or vice versa), there is, nevertheless, a strong empirical tendency to move from judging an object's perfection to judging its beauty (i.e., simply estimating it on the basis of sensations of pleasure or displeasure). Indeed, if an object should have both qualities it will produce a complex state of mind that combines intellect and sensation in a manner conducive to the whole province of mental activity. Kant's reasoning here is based on the fact that, for him, mental activity comprises both *reason* (i.e., judging and/or acting in relation to the concept of an end or ideas of totality) and cognition (whose formal conditions involve the co-operation of imagination and understanding).

As we have seen at great length in earlier chapters, Kant has already argued that beauty in its pure aesthetic sense is grounded on a harmony of imagination and understanding, recognized only through a sensation[11] of pleasure in the judging subject. Hence, if we combine a judgement of perfection (which involves appraising an object in relation to the end which defines what kind of thing it is) with a judgement of beauty (where a sensation of pleasure shows our cognitive faculties to be in accord) then we are, psychologically speaking, harmonizing reason and cognition—the two definitive features of our mental life. Indeed, the very fact that a rational judgement is accompanied by aesthetic pleasure will be conducive to further such intellectual endeavours on our part.

This is why Kant talks of taste becoming 'fixed' and subject to rules. Whereas the pure experience of beauty is free and governed only by

---

[9] Kant, *Critique of Judgment*, §16, pp. 114–15 (Pluhar, 77; Meredith, 73).   [10] Ibid.
[11] Of course, Kant generally uses the term 'feeling' rather than 'sensation' in relation to our pleasure in the beautiful. There are, however, precedents in the third *Critique* for him opting for the latter usage. For example, ibid. §9, p. 104 (Pluhar, 63; Meredith, 60), where he suggests that the 'subjective unity of the relation [between the cognitive powers] can make itself known only through sensation'.

an 'inherent causality'[12] that tends to prolong and reproduce itself for its own sake, the experience of beauty in the context of perfection, in contrast, fixes it in a secondary role, but one which enables it to function as a means or incentive to the higher ends of reason, as *well* as something that can be enjoyed for its own sake.

I am arguing, then, that for Kant adherent beauty is essentially beauty experienced in the wake of perfection, and that whilst Kant regards this as a restriction of aesthetic experience he eventually shows it to have some positive consequences.

There are some interesting points, both particular and general, which must be raised about the scope of this theory. For example, in what way, if any, does it apply in the case of fine art? In this context, Kant tells us that, as a product of human artifice, the fine artwork must be created in accordance with the concept of an end, and, 'since the agreement of the manifold in a thing with its inner determination as an end is the perfection of the thing, in the judgment of beauty of art the perfection of the thing will also have to be taken into account'.[13]

Whilst the obvious inference to be drawn from this is that fine art is most appropriately regarded as adherently beautiful, Kant, interestingly, never does *explicitly* describe it in such terms. The reason for this, I would suggest, is his claim that, through its grounding in genius, the fine artwork does not look like the product of rule-governed artifice, but has, rather, the uncontrived and spontaneous appearance of an object of nature.[14] (I will explore this at much greater length in the next chapter.)

This means, of course, that in the case of the successful artwork, it is so easy and natural to make abstraction from its artefactual origins that (like some other artefacts, such as wallpaper and designs à la Greque) it can be appropriately regarded as a free beauty.

However, as I have argued elsewhere,[15] the very fact that this approach does place fine art in such insipid company is a good reason to stay

---

[12] Ibid. §12, p. 107 (Pluhar, 67; Meredith, 64).

[13] Ibid. §48, p. 190 (Pluhar, 179; Meredith, 173).

[14] Ibid. §46, pp. 186–7 (Pluhar, 175; Meredith, 168–9).

[15] In Part 2 of my 'Fundamental Ontology and Transcendent Beauty: An Approach to Kant's Aesthetics,' *Kant-Studien*, 76 (1985), 55–71. It should be noted that whilst in that paper I offer a somewhat different interpretation of beauty from the one offered in the present study its main points of argument are, nevertheless, substantially unaffected by my revised position. Similar considerations hold in respect of my 'Kant and Greenberg's Varieties of Aesthetic Formalism', *Journal of Aesthetics and Art Criticism*, 42 (1984), 442–5.

clear of it. Indeed, there is an altogether more viable reason why we should think twice about regarding the fine artwork as simply adherently beautiful. It consists in the following.

The experience of adherent beauty involves a combination of judgements of perfection and judgements of beauty which, whilst logically distinct, are phenomenologically combined and bring about a psychological harmony of reason and cognition. Now, since in the case of fine art Kant informs us that its definitive end is the production of an aesthetically delightful 'beautiful presentation',[16] it follows that to judge its perfection involves judging how beautiful it is, and to judge its beauty is (*implicitly*) to judge its perfection.

Here, in other words, we have not only a psychological harmony of reason and cognition but also a *logical* connection between perfection and beauty. I would suggest, therefore, that the beauty of art is properly regarded as, *sui generis*, fact, which Kant himself *tacitly* acknowledges through his subsequent attempts to articulate artistic meaning in terms of the distinctive notion of the 'aesthetic idea'.[17] (Again, this will be explored in more detail in the following chapter.)

Let me return, then, to some of the more general points concerning the scope of Kant's theory of adherent beauty. First, whilst it is clear that for Kant some things are most appropriately regarded as adherent beauties and others as free beauties, his position allows, nevertheless, for some flexibility in the way these terms are applied.

For example, Kant's claim that judgements of perfection tend to invite judgements of beauty does not commit him to the view that *all* perfect objects are always adherently beautiful. The reason for this (a fact not noted by Kant, but one which is consistent with his overall position) is that it is always possible that the judgement of beauty which trails in the wake of our estimating an object as perfect might issue in wholly negative results. In this case, of course, our pleasure would be purely intellectual, and not at all aesthetic.

It is also worth pointing out (though, again, Kant does not do so himself) that even if an object strikes us primarily in terms of its free beauty Kant can quite consistently hold that this need not always be the case. The object may be such that, *on occasion*, we are disposed to make abstraction from its free beauty and appraise it in purely intellectual terms as a perfection; or, alternatively, to combine this intellectual

---

[16] See Kant, *Critique of Judgment*, §48, p. 189 (Pluhar, 179; Meredith, 172).
[17] See ibid. §49, pp. 191–5 (Pluhar, 181–8; Meredith, 175–82).

appreciation with that of its aesthetic qualities, thus treating it as an adherent item.

Having, then, outlined the substance and scope of Kant's theory of adherent beauty, I shall now briefly summarize and review it. His argument is constructed on the basis of the following four points: (i) with some objects, reason demands that judgements of perfection must take precedence over judgements of beauty; (ii) the fact that this is so means that our experience of beauty in such objects will be psychologically inhibited; (iii) despite this, however, there is an empirical tendency to move from making judgements of perfection into making judgements of beauty; (iv) indeed, when an object is judged to possess both perfection and beauty the combination of the two will produce a positive experience wherein reason and cognition are in harmony. This is adherent beauty.

Now, whilst these points provide a consistent (though hardly compelling) *structure* of an argument, I shall not consider points (ii) and (iii) since, if true, they express at best contingent facts about the psychological context in which judgements of beauty sometimes arise.

Point (i) and point (iv), however, are of considerable further philosophical interest in their own right. Through (i), for example, Kant is indirectly claiming that whilst beauty is a logically distinct form of value, and pursuable for its own sake, it is, nevertheless, not of absolute and unconditional worth. In relation to *some* objects, our need for intellectual and practical perfection—the demands of reason in its broadest sense—must take precedence over aesthetic considerations.

Kant asserts rather than argues his claims, but his position can be defended on the following (though not particularly Kantian) grounds. In our everyday lives, the need for perfection (in the broadest sense) is intrinsic to our goal-orientated and practical activities. Indeed, the pursuit and achievement of such excellence enriches our general cognitive stock in a way that both equips us for, and impels us towards, the search for an even greater perfection still.

Let us suppose, however, that the craving for beauty overtook perfection as the focus of such goal-orientated activity—that is, that aesthetic considerations (however small) were *always* given precedence over perfection.

Now, if this were the case, the world would, initially, be transformed; things that were hitherto only of mundane significance might now appear in a wholly new light. And yet, the very fact that aesthetic contemplation had become the norm rather than the exception would eventually make beauty all-pervasive, and the source of merely routine and commonplace pleasure. Rather than liberating us from the mundane, beauty would itself become an expression of mundanity.

Indeed, should the pre-eminence of aesthetic attitude lead us to neglect our interest in cognitive and practical perfection, and thence denude our general cognitive stock, then it may be expected that our capacity for searching out and discriminating the higher, or more subtle and elusive, forms of beauty, would likewise be coarsened. We would eventually be satisfied by the merely pretty.

This position has also some important contemporary implications. It is commonly observed, for example, that the postmodern era involves a widespread 'aestheticization' of everyday life. This takes the form of an obsession with how consumer items are packaged as well as with their practical applications. Indeed, this attitude can extend even to the items themselves.

In this respect, for example, think of the extraordinary regard in which people hold the appearance of such things as cars, or the look of such things as mobile phones and computers. Such 'style' factors are often ranked on a par with or even more important than actual practical function. Here, the relation of beauty to 'perfection' has the potential to inhibit the proper appreciation of both aspects. In the case of beauty, this involves (amongst other considerations) the rendering of it *commonplace*.

There is an even greater danger. In the world of politics, for example, how a politician is presented in terms of appearance and rhetoric is often much more powerful in persuading than the actual substance of his or her policies. In areas of societal organization (such as educational policy), there is a tendency to standardization on the grounds of 'quality assurance' and other factors that putatively involve criteria of efficiency. All too often, however, this amounts to little more than management pursued as an end in itself—of *how things are made to appear* rather than how they cash-out in practice. Appropriate packaging overwhelms the practical content.

All these examples describe a kind of *aestheticization* of phenomena and/or procedures which are end-orientated, but where, as it were, the perfection of the end as a practical means of dealing with a problem is overwhelmed by the presentational means which are supposed to 'deliver' it.

On these terms, Kant's wariness about the relation between beauty and perfection is especially timely. As we have seen, free beauty is a pleasure taken in phenomenal appearance exclusively. To allow anything even remotely like this criterion to be applied in practical contexts means that the practical ends in question can all too easily be distorted. It follows that we must be especially critical in terms of the scope of application which is allowed to the aesthetic. We must—following Kant's criteria—ask whether a pleasure in appearance is *really* appropriate in relation to such and such a practically relevant phenomenon or activity.

This being said, Kant's point (iv) concerning a state of mind wherein reason and cognition are in harmony suggests that perfection may, *at least sometimes*, have genuine application, and amount to much more than the processes of aestheticization just described. In certain contexts, our experience of perfection may have something of the aesthetic about it.

Unfortunately, Kant separates the logical grounds of perfection and beauty *so* rigidly that the only way he can account for this link with the aesthetic is by positing adherent beauty as a logical hybrid involving both judgements of perfection and judgements of beauty. The problem with this, however, is the question of how these judgements are phenomenologically 'combined'.

Kant, unfortunately, is not only ambiguous on this issue but, indeed, the two alternative approaches which constitute the ambiguity are both unacceptable. On the one hand, if Kant is saying that, in the experience of adherent beauty, regard for perfection and regard for beauty are coextensive in the very *same* act of judgement, then his claim is incoherent, since (as *he* presents them) the logical grounds of judgements of perfection and beauty are wholly exclusive of one another.

On the other hand, if he is simply saying that a judgement of beauty immediately *following on* a judgement of perfection is the mode of combination involved, then it is left unexplained as to why this mutual proximity should not (as in the case of the tattooed Maori) be a source of conflict and incongruity rather than one of harmony.

Despite these problems, I would suggest that Kant is not only right to posit a connection between perfection and the aesthetic but that he is also, broadly speaking, right to characterize it in terms of a harmony of reason and cognition.

To establish this, I shall abandon Kant's logically hybrid notion of adherent beauty and will show instead that some judgements of perfection are logically akin to judgements of beauty through their embodying (in a modified way) the disinterestedness and freedom, in terms of which Kant defines the pure aesthetic judgement. It is to this task I now turn, in Part 2 of this chapter.

PART 2

Let me start with the notion of disinterestedness. First, it will be remembered that, for Kant, judgements of perfection are judgements of an object's 'goodness' in relation to the concept of its end. Now, when pleasure arises from judgements of the good, Kant claims that such delight is 'determined not merely through the representation of the object but at the same time through the represented connection of the subject with the existence of the object'.[18]

As we saw in previous chapters, Kant's reasoning here is complex, but he *at least* means that if an object's goodness (in whatever respect) causes us pleasure, then the grounds of our pleasure logically presuppose that the object is real. If it turned out, for example, that the object was an optical illusion of some sort, then its goodness would also be illusory, and we would have, therefore, no grounds for taking pleasure in it.

In the case of our aesthetic pleasure in the beautiful, however, matters are entirely different. Here our appreciation is focused exclusively upon the object's formal qualities—that is, upon its mere structure in the way it appears to the senses. This means, of course, that from the viewpoint of the pure aesthetic judgement it simply does not matter whether the object is real or illusory. Our judgement, in other words, is wholly disinterested as to questions of real existence.

Now, it is clear that at least one kind of judgement of perfection can satisfy criteria of absolute disinterest, in so far as to take pleasure in an object's simply *looking* how a perfect object of that kind should look is to appreciate it at the level of appearance alone. In this case (as in that of the pure aesthetic judgement), the object's ontological status as real or illusory has absolutely no logical bearing on the grounds of our pleasure.

This narrow mode of appreciation is, of course, very much the exception rather than the rule, in so far as, normally, when we call an object perfect we expect it to possess all the definitive dispositional properties of its kind, as well as the strictly phenomenal ones.

---

[18] See Kant, *Critique of Judgment*, §5, pp. 94–5 (Pluhar, 51; Meredith, 48).

In this respect, the discovery, say, that an oak tree initially judged as perfect is, in fact, rotten to the core, would, of course, oblige us to revise our original judgement. There are, nevertheless, two senses in which judgements of more than simple phenomenal perfection can count as *relatively* disinterested.

For example, whilst perfection in roses and quartz crystals is a property which could (through its respective selling power and theoretical signif- icance) give special practical pleasure to the florist and mineralogist, in the case of most people such perfection will tend to please *for its own sake*. In the latter case, therefore, our pleasure could be characterized as, at least, *relatively disinterested*.

Indeed, this line of approach can even be extended to encompass (in a modified way) objects that are of intrinsic instrumental significance. For example, suppose we take pleasure in a Bauhaus chair's perfect combination of form and function. In the case of most artefacts, our pleasure in their perfection arises from our actually using them, or, if we have not had the opportunity to do so yet, from the anticipation of optimum performance.

Yet, whilst our pleasure in the Bauhaus chair presupposes reference to a context of potential use—that is, someone must be able, in principle, to sit on the chair—it does not presuppose reference to a context of actual use—that is, the anticipation that we or some other person *will*, in practice, sit on the chair. (Indeed, if the chair is in a museum, it is very likely that no one will ever sit on it again—but this in no way diminishes our pleasure in its perfection.) In cases such as these, therefore, our pleasure might be characterized as relatively disinterested.

Having, then, suggested that pure aesthetic judgements and judge- ments of perfection have affinity as different idioms of disinterested pleasure, the question now arises as to how such pleasure is possible. Answers to this have been provided in preceding chapters. The approach can be put in summary terms as follows. In relation to the pure aesthetic judgement of free beauty, Kant informs us that

The powers of cognition that are set into play by this representation are hereby in a free play, since no determinate concept restricts them to a particular rule of cognition. Thus the state of mind in this representation must be that of a feeling of the free play of the powers of representation in a given representation for a cognition in general.[19]

---

[19] Ibid. §9, p. 102 (Pluhar, 62; Meredith, 58). Robert Wicks takes an interesting approach with similarities to the one that I am about to develop. He argues that 'Dependent

On these terms, to experience an object's formal qualities does not involve objective determination—that is, reference to what kind of thing the object actually is. Rather, we are free to explore perceptually the relation between its formal qualities in different ways.

One might, for example, attend to the overall balance of phenomenal masses in the object or to the structural effect created by the way its colours 'sit' upon one another; one might, alternatively, trace the development of individual linear elements, or note the changing effects produced by the light source upon the total configuration.

To explore perceptually the object in this unrestricted way means that our two basic cognitive capacities—imagination and understanding—are in a harmonious and leisurely relation that issues in, and is recognized through, a feeling of pleasure. For Kant, in other words, the aesthetic character of the experience of beauty lies not simply in the fact that we feel pleasure but in the fact that our pleasure is subjectively determined—through a free exercise of our capacity for concept application.

The question which must now be asked is whether there is anything in common between this experience and our application of the concept 'perfection'. The answer is a qualified 'yes'. For, whilst our judging an object to be perfect is objectively determined in the sense of logically presupposing reference to what *kind* (using 'kind' here in a very broad sense) of thing the object is, such simple objective determination is, nevertheless, not a sufficient condition of our judgement.

It is implied, in addition, that the object manifests the properties which define the kind of thing it is in an *exemplary* way—that is, more completely than most other instances of the kind. This, of course, means that a comparative critical dimension is brought in, in so far as questions of 'more completely than' are not intelligible without it.

Now, 'more completely' entails, I would suggest, the satisfaction of two further comparative conditions. First, the object must be free from

beauty . . . amounts to an appreciation of an object's teleological style. The kind of pleasure involved here is based on the free play which occurs in our imagination when we reflect upon the various ways to realize any given purpose, i.e., the purpose typical of imagining how to realize any plan' ('Dependent Beauty', 393). Rachel Zuckert also moves in a similar direction but, like Wicks, she underplays the relation to morality and, in common with Wicks again, devotes great energy to tracing possible links between adherent beauty and fine art. I do not find these connections to be persuasive. Indeed, the level of attention devoted to such possibilities has tended to distract from proper consideration of those key factors that are essential to fine art—namely, 'originality' and 'exemplariness'. See Zuckert, *Kant on Beauty and Biology* (Cambridge: Cambridge University Press, 2007) 202–9.

both distracting blemishes and impurities due to the presence of foreign elements and any inessential properties which might be unrepresentative of the kind. For example, we would not usually judge something to be a perfect rose if it showed evidence of being diseased or crossed with another species; or if it was of inordinate size or coloured in a hue extremely uncharacteristic of roses generally.

Second, the perfect object should not simply embody all the definitive properties of its kind, but should do so in a well-balanced way. The perfect elephant, for example, doubtless needs a trunk, but not one that is exaggeratedly large or small in relation to the rest of its frame.

The interesting question arises as to how these very general criteria are applied in comparative practice? Perhaps, in two ways. First, suppose we describe a quartz crystal as perfect, on the grounds that spectroscopic analysis shows it to be free from impurities, statistics show it to be of average (and thence representative) size, and that comparison with visual data in a textbook shows that its facets are of the right geometric shapes, distributed at exactly the right angles, and in exactly the right ratios of proportion. In this case, we would be applying our criteria of perfection in a *technical* sense, in so far as the presence or absence of relevant properties could be determined by measurement.

In practice, of course, judgements of perfection are rarely made in this exact manner. Not only, in most situations, do we simply lack the relevant data, procedures, and technical competence, but indeed many kinds of things (especially artefacts) have definitive properties or functions which admit of such immense variety in their instantiations that purely technical standards of judgement are entirely out of the question.[20] We rely, rather, on standards constructed from both general knowledge and personal acquaintance with the kind of object in question.

[20] Interestingly, in his book *Kant and the Claims of Taste* (Cambridge, Mass. and London: Harvard University Press, 1979), Paul Guyer 'speculatively' conjectures that it may be (somewhat like) this very fact which underlies Kant's theory of adherent beauty. In relation to a certain kind of object, such as churches, 'The concept of purpose imposes *some* constraint on the freedom of imagination with respect to the appearance of a church, but still leaves that faculty such latitude within this constraint that pleasure may yet be produced by its free harmony with the understanding's demand for unity' (pp. 246–7.) However, whilst an approach on *broadly* these lines is (as I am at present trying to show) a viable basis for linking perfection and the aesthetic, it should not be taken as reflecting Kant's actual strategy in §16. As Guyer himself admits, it might not do justice to the stipulation that adherent beauty *presupposes* a concept of the object's end. Neither, it should be noted, would it do justice to Kant's characterization of such beauty as secondary (i.e., 'appendent') or his very extensive discussion of it as a *combination* of the 'good' and the beautiful (i.e., as a logical hybrid).

It is crucial to note that this introduces a significant element of freedom into our judgements of perfection. For, whilst an object's possession of minor impurities, slightly unrepresentative inessential properties, or slight disproportion amongst its essential features may disqualify it from strictly technical perfection, these may not be so striking as to disappoint our personal expectations of what a perfect object of that kind should be like.

On these terms, then, the practical applications of our technical criteria of perfection will tend to involve a crucial element of subjective determination. Now, it is important to note that this subjective dimension to judgements of technical perfection is of a provisional and empirical nature only. For example, it is logically possible that computer modelling will enable us to measure with objective precision whether *any* given object is a technically perfect instance of its kind. We are simply waiting, as it were, for the right computer program to come along.

Let us suppose, then, that the said program is available, and reveals that the rose which is scanned in relation to the model is, in fact, a technically perfect specimen. Let us suppose also that whilst the rose in question strikes us as an admittedly good specimen it seems something of a stereotype, and not really what we would want to call 'perfect'. Is our unease justified? Or is it just a foolish refusal of technological inevitability?

The answer is, I would suggest, the former, in so far as what I shall call judgements of *phenomenological* perfection have a subjective element that is logically irreducible. One might argue this as follows. Technical computer-modelled standards can certainly do justice to the definitive properties of kinds, but, in the final analysis, such properties are always embodied, naturally, in the kind's particular instances. Any natural kind is subject to the exigencies of its origins in natural causality, and its instances will always have *some* impurities, inessential properties, and disproportion amongst its essential features. *Contingency, in other words, is a distinctive feature of kinds at the level of their natural being.*

Similar considerations hold in relation to the production of artefacts. We do not demand that *every* phenomenal and dispositional property of a specific instance of some kind of artefact must play an essential role in fulfilling the function or functions which are definitive of artefacts of that kind; neither, indeed, are we capable of producing artefacts of such a superhuman order of efficiency. There will, in other words, always be some phenomenal and/or dispositional property which is wholly contingent: neither facilitating nor inhibiting the artefact's function.

Given these considerations, then, I would suggest that, *phenomenologically speaking*, contingent features are just as essential to a kind in its *totality of being*, as are its definitive properties. It is, therefore, reasonable to demand that if an object is to be a perfect instance of its kind in the fullest sense—that is, concretely as well as abstractly—it must manifest this contingent dimension in a positive way.

Now, this does not contradict the general criteria of perfection noted earlier, because, on the one hand, not all impurities necessarily distract us from essential properties and not all inessential properties are unrepresentative of the kind; on the other hand, being well-balanced does not necessarily entail strictly proportionate individual phenomenal parts.

In relation to the first of these, for example, the specific shape of a particular rose's petals, or a certain alignment of impurities in a quartz crystal, may be such as to give added phenomenal definition to their respective essential structural features. Similarly, inessential properties such as the varying intensity of redness of a rose, or the above-average size of a quartz crystal, might serve to make essential structural features more accessible to cognition.

In the case of being 'well-balanced', matters are more interesting still. Suppose, for example, that our computer program tells us that a certain man we know would have bodily parts in perfect proportion with one another (for a man of his age and ethnic origins), were it not for a slightly over-pronounced forehead. It may be that for us, however, this very disproportion is highly affecting, in that it powerfully suggests a definitive property of human kind—namely, its rationality.

Similarly, a particular oak tree may have a trunk that is slightly too broad in relation to the size of its branches but which, by its very girth, suggests the oak's general qualities of strength and sturdiness.

Now if in such cases there were also evidence to suggest that the thing actually *did* possess the essential and highly desirable properties it looks to have, then the total effect would rightly incline us to regard it as a fuller, more-complete instance of its kind than a merely technically perfect specimen. The contingent element of (slight) phenomenal disproportion, in other words, would be balanced out by the essential dispositional properties it served to disclose.

Similar considerations, indeed, can apply at the strictly phenomenal level. Whilst, for example, the pronounced forehead may be slightly disproportionate in relation to other bodily parts individually considered, the manner of its disproportion may, nevertheless, introduce an interesting complexity into the balance of the whole that leads us, in turn, to attend more closely and appreciatively to both individual parts and the way they relate to each other.

I am suggesting, then, that sometimes an object's contingent features are in a state of *disclosive harmony* with its essential properties, and that in such cases we have perfect exemplars of the kind in its totality of being. When we judge perfection on the basis of concept-guided personal experience, rather than concept-determined technical standards, we are embracing the phenomena in question at a much fuller level of their being.

True, we may be familiar with specimens which satisfy textbook criteria of technical perfection, but equally our judgements will be informed by experience of kinds in their natural setting—that is, will tend (even though we may not be explicitly aware of it) to take account of disclosive contingency.

When this sort of contingency does inform our judgement, we will have a mode of estimating perfection that fully justifies our reluctance to accept computer-based appraisals. The reason for this is that the *recognition* of whether or not some contingent feature of an object is in disclosive harmony with the properties that define what kind of thing it is is logically adherent upon a context of cultural and subjective interpretation.

In some cultures, for example, the particular shape of rose petals, or the size of quartz crystals and foreheads, may be of immense ritualistic significance in themselves, and would thus tend to distract from, rather than disclose, the essential properties of their bearers.

Again, at the personal level, if one lacks imagination or is interested in phenomenal perfection alone, the broadness of an oak tree's trunk might not suggest its sturdiness; and if one lacks perceptual sensitivity, a pronounced forehead will remain just that, and its possible contribution to the phenomenal and dispositional balance of the whole will remain unnoticed.

Indeed, whether or not a property counts as disclosive may even change during the life of a particular person and culture—on the basis of new knowledge, experience, and interests acquired, and old values discarded. On these terms, the only way a computer could cope with phenomenological perfection grounded upon total being would be to invest it with the total cultural values and personal identity of its owner, or to give it cultural values and a personal identity of its own. But then, of course, it would no longer be just a computer.

I am arguing, then, that judgements of perfection are of two sorts: the technical and the phenomenological. The first of these has both an objective element and (until the right computer program is applied) an empirical dimension of subjective determination. The second has, again, both these features, but this time with a subjective factor that is necessary and irreducible.

Although neither sort of judgement of perfection is wholly free in the way that pure aesthetic judgements are, the presence of subjective determination enables us to characterize them as *relatively free*, in so far as, through them, our capacity for concept application is exercised not simply by following a rule determined by the nature of the object but on the basis of standards constructed, in part, from personal experience. In the case of perfection, in other words, we are dealing with an objective or rational cognitive *content* whose conceptualization involves a harmonious interaction with (rather than rigid determination of) cognition's creative and subjective aspects.

If such a judgement is directed *only* towards perfection, as such, then our pleasure in it will be relatively disinterested. Our judgement, in other words, will be aptly characterized as aesthetic (and its object as adherently beautiful) in so far as, through it, the task of rational comprehension attains a zest and vitality *of its own*. Indeed, the very fact that our rational activity has such pleasurable consequences will tend to dispose us towards further activity of that kind.

This, I would suggest, is what Kant implicitly recognized and was trying to articulate through his account of how the experience of adherent beauty involves a harmony of reason and cognition that brings a gain 'to the entire faculty of our representative power'. The theory of adherent beauty contains, in other words, broadly, the right characterization of perfection's link with the aesthetic, but it arrives at that characterization by the wrong route.

The interpretation of the aesthetics of perfection on these terms can also provide criteria for resolving the problematics of postmodern aestheticization noted at the end of Part 1. For it allows us to distinguish between artefacts whose aesthetic significance involves a genuinely complementary relation between form and function, and those where function becomes little more than a bearer of style for its own sake.

CONCLUSION

Kant's claim (noted in Part I) that beauty must sometimes take second place to perfection still applies, even in relation to the aesthetics of perfection. If our judgements of perfection were *always* aesthetic and their instrumental and practical significance always played down, then the intensity of our aesthetic pleasure in perfection, and our capacity to discriminate its more subtle forms, might, in the long run, be expected to suffer.

However, the fact that perfection can be assimilated within the broad terms of the Kantian aesthetic is evidence of the extraordinarily powerful scope of his approach. The realm of the aesthetic has beauty as its absolutely disinterested logical extreme. But, there is a wealth of other relatively disinterested idioms of cognitively engaging with sensible phenomena that engage those capacities which are fundamental to cognition.

In addition to perfection, Kant's notion of the dynamical sublime might be one such idiom. And the experience of the picturesque, and those more complex 'realizations' described by Ronald Hepburn, might also figure in such terms. However, the most important object of relatively disinterested pleasure is *fine art*. Having touched already on some of its aspects, I shall now consider it in much greater detail.

6

From Aesthetic Ideas
to the Avant-Garde: The Scope
of Fine Art

INTRODUCTION

Kant's theory of fine art has not been given anything like its due. This is probably because the aesthetic criteria established in the course of his discussion of beauty are of fundamental significance. Hence it may appear that fine art can be dealt with as a mere extension of this.

However, the relation between Kant's general aesthetic and his account of fine art is very complex, and the latter can be developed into an especially viable and comprehensive theory that goes far beyond the simple aesthetic criteria of taste. In what follows I shall first expound the theory in a way which identifies its basic logical structure and will revise and extend it, so as to be workable.

This requires an account that frequently departs from Kant's own order of exposition. Part 1 addresses the notion of fine art as an embodiment of 'aesthetic ideas' since it is this ontological factor which is the basis of fine art's broader characteristics of genius and originality. In Part 2, focusing on the importance of artistic style, I examine Kant's treatment of these characteristics and identify some difficulties.

These are explained in more detail in a critical review of Kant's position that is offered in Part 3. It is argued, in particular, that he needs to ground 'originality' and 'exemplariness' on a comparative critical dimension rooted in relations between artworks, rather than in the psychological process of creation. Part 4 offers a detailed presentation of what this might amount to based on the role of style in painting. In Part 5, the approach is shown to encompass radical avant-garde tendencies also—albeit in a qualified way. I conclude with a summary of my approach and a further extension of it based on the relative disinterestedness of our experience of fine art.

PART 1

In Chapters 3 and 4, it was shown how the pure aesthetic judgement involves a stimulated interaction of imagination and understanding. The interaction is 'free', in that both these capacities explore the manifold in harmony but without culminating in a simple act of recognition or classification. It involves an emergent judgement of reflection that does not converge on a 'definite' concept of the object.

Now, it is clear that fine art must differ from this in at least one key respect. In §48, for example, Kant observes that

if the object is given as a product of art, and is as such supposed to be declared to be beautiful, then since art always presupposes an end in the cause (and its causality), a concept must first be the ground of what the thing is supposed to be, and since the agreement of the manifold in a thing with its inner determination as an end is the perfection of the thing, in the judging of the beauty of art the perfection of the thing will also have to be taken into account.[1]

As I suggested in the previous chapter, the relation between specifically artistic beauty and artistic perfection is a logical one. Kant notes that 'A beauty of nature is a beautiful thing; the beauty of art is a beautiful representation of a thing'.[2] This means that art's perfection consists in a capacity to represent its subject-matter in a beautiful way. The artist exercises 'taste' in a process of trial and error attempting to create a form which will embody such beauty. This form must be adequate to the artist's idea, but also express 'a free swing of the mental powers'.[3] The decisive factor here is whether the form successfully embodies 'aesthetic ideas'. Kant introduces this important notion as follows.

by an aesthetic idea . . . I mean that representation of the imagination that occasions much thinking though without it being possible for any determinate thought—that is, concept, to be adequate to it, which, consequently, no language fully attains or can make intelligible.[4]

[1] Kant, *Critique of the Power of Judgment*, trans. Eric Matthews and Paul Guyer (Cambridge: Cambridge University Press, 1999), §48, p. 190 (Pluhar, 179; Meredith, 173).
[2] Ibid. §48, p. 189 (Pluhar, 179; Meredith, 172).
[3] Ibid. §48, p. 191 (Pluhar, 180; Meredith, 174).
[4] Ibid. §49, p. 192 (Pluhar, 182; Meredith, 175–6).

The term 'idea' is warranted according to Kant because the artwork presents sensible intuitions which exceed what is given in nature. On the one hand, the artist can render items or states of affairs which are not present in the phenomenal world—such as 'invisible beings, the kingdom of the blessed, the kingdom of hell, eternity, creation, etc.'[5] On the other hand, and more importantly,

[he ventures] to make that of which there are example in experience, e.g., death, envy, and all sorts of vices, as well as love, fame, etc. sensible beyond the limits of experience, with a completeness that goes beyond anything of which there is an example in nature, by means of an imitation that emulates the precedent of reason in attaining to a maximum.[6]

Kant does not provide a complete criterion of 'a maximum' in this context. This is unfortunate for it is clearly the factor which is basic to art's embodiment of aesthetic ideas. He does suggest further that

Those forms which do not constitute the presentation of a given concept itself, but, as supplementary representations of the imagination, express only the implications connected with it and its affinity with others, are called (aesthetic) attributes of an object whose concept, as an idea of reason, cannot be adequately presented.[7]

This passage is important in that it shows the kind of cognitive connections—namely, implication and kinship between concepts—which are involved in aesthetic ideas. In this way we have an at least partial criterion of 'a maximum'. The aesthetic idea presents its conceptual core in a way which opens up innumerable avenues of implication and affinities of meaning embedded in the avenues of further imagining prompted by the idea.

The passage shows also that since, in aesthetic ideas, we are dealing with a play of connections between concepts and imaginative associations, this gives our experience a rather different aesthetic character from that of free beauty—where mere possibilities of finding unity in the manifold are explored. Through the aesthetic idea, in other words, fine art is given a distinctive phenomenological characterization.

However, we still need an explanation of what it is which enables the aesthetic idea to have this distinctive effect in the first place. Our criterion of 'a maximum' must be clarified in terms of *the object whose form embodies it*, as well as through its effects on the subject.

---

[5] Ibid. (Pluhar, 183; Meredith, 176).   [6] Ibid.   [7] Ibid.

As it happens, this is the most complex aspect of Kant's theory, and has a number of different aspects. An important clue to one of them is the earlier claim that aesthetic ideas involve 'a maximum' that exceeds what nature can offer. This surely involves some feature of the object's form as well as the aesthetic elucidation achieved in the subject's experience of it.

An obvious contender for this feature is the *'Ideal'* — that is, a form which exemplifies some kind of thing in terms of its definitive phenomenal characteristics, and which removes those physical and (where appropriate) moral blemishes and other manifestations of ugliness which accompany its usual presentations. This, in effect, represents the defining traits of the kind of thing in question more fully than any individual phenomenally given instances of it.

There are good historical reasons for reading the aesthetic idea's maximality in terms of the Ideal. It was the major official *rationale* for the visual arts and literature of Kant's own time (and, indeed, for some hundreds of years before that). Such works were taken to offer edifying representations with the capacity to lift us above the mundanities and limitations of commonplace natural and social existence.

In this respect, it is significant that in §17 Kant himself offers an account of the 'ideal of beauty'. For present purposes, its most important element is that of the 'aesthetic normal idea', which Kant understands as ideal in a similar sense to that outlined above—namely, 'the image which has as it were intentionally grounded the technique of nature, to which only the species as a whole but not any separate individual is adequate'.[8]

However, whilst Kant himself probably thinks of aesthetic ideas in terms of the Ideal, this is somewhat restrictive in terms of his theory's broader viability. The Ideal is an aesthetic concept whose primacy has long been challenged, and overthrown. Hence, if the theory were felt to depend on it, we would have to regard it as, in large part, superseded, in historical terms. Indeed, it would be difficult to see how it might function in relation to such things as music, abstract art and avant-garde works, and the applied arts. However, the conceptual basis of Kant's position is actually much broader than the Ideal. In fact, the Ideal itself should be seen as one aspect of a general concept which is integral to art at its objective level.

---

[8] Ibid. §17, p. 118 (Pluhar, 81; Meredith, 77).

Curiously enough, whilst Kant negotiates the major features of this concept, he does so between the lines. It is something which is implicit, mainly, in his further key notions (namely, genius, 'originality', and 'exemplariness'), which I will deal with in the next section. The linking notion which Kant needs here is that of *'artistic style'*. Sometimes this is understood as a mainly collective phenomenon—as when we talk of the style of a specific artistic school or movement. However, there is a more fundamental sense of artistic style which is basic to Kant's approach. If an artist renders a subject-matter, he or she does not mechanically reproduce it, but rather adapts it to the demands of the specific medium in which he or she is working. This involves selection, omission, exaggeration, and understatement in relation to which of the subject-matter's aspects are rendered in the work. A key consequence of this is that it is possible for the artist's interpretation to embody a distinctive *individual* style—a factor to which I will return, at length, further on.

The Ideal should be understood in relation to this. It is just one of many general stylistic emphases which are available to artists. But, for those who are orientated towards it, *it can be realized in many different and sometimes highly individual ways, even when embodied in the same kind of subject-matter.*

In this respect, for example, Michelangelo and Rubens idealize the female nude through a shared emphasis of its fleshy corporeality. But, they do so with radically different inflections vis-à-vis such things as musculature, facial expression, and gesture.

Given these points, one might say that it is artistic style which gives the represented subject a maximality at the level of objective appearance, which goes beyond nature. Style *acts* upon the subject-matter so that, in the artwork, it appears in a form defined by what the artist takes to be its most aesthetically significant aspects, rather than by its normal features.

This approach encompasses language also. Here, the way in which narratives are constructed (in terms of choice of words and subject-matter and idioms of phrasing) can give even ordinary descriptive language some inflections which manifest a dimension of individual style. When this is expressed through formal structures which are not common in everyday discourse (such as rhyme and metre or fictional narrative), the focus of linguistic meaning shifts. The emphasis falls not merely on *what* is said, but the quite particular way *in which* it is said. Style and structure transform the factual content.

Reading the maximization of meaning in terms of stylistic transformation fits in well with Kant's next important characterization of the
aesthetic idea. He holds that

if we add to a concept a representation of the imagination that belongs to
its presentation, but which by itself stimulates so much thinking that it can
never be grasped in a determinate concept, hence which aesthetically enlarges
the concept itself in an unbounded way, then in this case the imagination is
creative, and sets the faculty of intellectual ideas (reason) into motion.[9]

To show what is at issue here, the example of *Romeo and Juliet* is
instructive. This is a dramatic narrative whose content hinges on the
concepts of intense love in adverse social circumstances, driven by deadly
confrontations and unfortunate contingencies. However, Shakespeare's
style of characterizing the deeds and words of his protagonists, and the
exact content and order of their unfolding, makes the basic concepts
into features which engage us in terms of feeling and imagination to the
most powerful degree. And this is not *just* an imaginative involvement.
It raises questions of responsibility, blame, commitment, group identity,
and loyalty which have implications far beyond the confines of the play
itself.

However, it must be emphasized that these are not *purely* rational
questions, for the terms in which they address us are constantly mediated by the specific existential depth and insight which is distinctive
to Shakespeare's rendering of the narrative. Even though the play constellates around general factors in the human condition, we constantly
return to the *individual* tragedy of Romeo's and Juliet's experiences of
them.

On these terms, then, the aesthetic idea involves themes and concepts
whose style of presentation brings rational and imaginative factors
into a reciprocally enhancing relationship. It is in this sense that
the determinate concepts involved are given an 'unlimited' aesthetic
expansion.

Several objections might be raised to my approach so far. First, it
might be pointed out that the foregoing approach has emphasized how,
in the aesthetic idea, the artist's style interprets some recognizable idea
or related content. But, in general philosophical terms, this notion
may appear to fall at the first hurdle, in so far as, if Kant's theory
is to be viable and comprehensive as a theory of art, it must surely

---

[9] Ibid. §49, 193 (Pluhar, 183; Meredith, 177).

encompass such things as music, abstract and avant-garde work, and the applied arts. These, however, do not appear to involve any concept or representational content which might give the 'aesthetic idea as stylized-interpretation' approach some purchase.

However, I have argued at the greatest length elsewhere that these supposedly problematic idioms do, in fact, have a basic image character, wherein the artist's style, in effect, presents an interpreted content or subject-matter.[10] In outline, the basis of the claim is as follows.

In the case of music, we are dealing with tonal and atonal harmonic and melodic structures which involve different kinds and ranges of culturally established emotional and gestural content, to which the composer's individual style gives a specific narrative characterization. Music has the character of *virtual expression*.

Abstract visual artworks involve formal configurations which are not simply 'there' as physical visual properties. By following or varying the culturally established presentational formats of representational visual art, we look to discover something which they are 'about'. There is a level of meaning that is *emergent* from physical visual level (even in such things as minimal sculpture, where the absence of textural or gestural detail allows the work to exemplify presence qua presence). This involves reading abstract works as individual disclosures of specific aspects of a '*contextual space*' composed of (usually unnoticed or disregarded) configurations of colour, pattern, shape, and other relations which subtend and give structure to the recognizable everyday visual field. (For example, in the case of Mondrian, we find a distinctive stylized presentation of a factor which is basic to our perception of visual reality—namely, the scope of perpendicularity. Jackson Pollock's action paintings evoke processes of growth and decay that might take place at microscopic surface levels of visual reality.)

Extending the theory further still, avant-garde works often involve the artist making use of artefacts that are not actually made by him or her in the first place. The significance of the work then resides in

---

[10] See, for example, my extended discussion of music and abstract and avant-garde works in chaps 7 and 4 respectively of my *Defining Art, Creating the Canon: Artistic Value in an Era of Doubt* (Oxford: Clarendon Press, 2007). The nature of meaning in abstract and avant-garde works is discussed at even greater length in Part 3 of my *The Transhistorical Image: Philosophizing Art and its History* (Cambridge: Cambridge University Press, 2002) and in the most complete terms of all in chaps 6 and 7 of my *Phenomenology of the Visual Arts (Even the Frame)* (Stanford, Calif.: Stanford University Press, 2009). Chap. 10 of this last work also contains a lengthy discussion of architecture as an art form.

aesthetic ideas and associations provoked by the relation between the kind of artefact made use of, and how the artist recontextualizes or modifies it (i.e., the stylistic dimension).

The applied arts can also be negotiated in terms of the stylistic treatment of 'content'. This is because, by definition, they involve artefacts which serve *specific kinds of function*. Most such artefacts are consumed in this function—we do not engage with them in any other terms. However, some of them exceed this. The way in which they are made—their style—makes us aware of them as, in effect, interpretations of this function, and evokes ranges of idea and association which exceed what the artefact amounts to in purely functional terms.

A second putative objection to my approach concerns the fact that, whilst Kant himself emphasizes the 'idea' aspect, this aspect might appear to be wholly omitted through my emphasis on artistic style

Such an objection does not hold. This is because those 'striving for a maximum' mental effects, which for Kant warrant the term 'idea', do not *just* happen. They centre on the relation between how the work is presented and the kind of thing which it presents—a dimension of style. If this were not the logically decisive feature, we would have to distinguish fine art from mechanical and agreeable art (concepts which I shall address further on) by reference to subject-matter alone. However, a decision by means of concepts is, in itself, totally at odds with everything which Kant says about the aesthetic, and is false in more general terms—in so far as kitsch works (instances of 'agreeable art') are sometimes banal presentations of important concepts, and fine art can sometimes present the most mundane concepts (for example, simple still lives) in the most profoundly engaging way. Style is the decisive factor.

Having emphasized this, it should not be supposed that I am importing a notion which Kant does not address himself. He does address artistic style, but in an indirect way, through a sustained analysis of the major factors which determine it and which distinguish art from other forms of meaning. It is to these I now turn.

PART 2

As a first step in this task, I shall address the way in which Kant distinguishes fine art from other idioms of representation. We are told that

If art, adequate for the cognition of a possible object, merely performs the actions requisite to make it actual, it is mechanical; but if it has the feeling of pleasure as its immediate aim, then it is called aesthetic art. This is either agreeable or beautiful art. It is the former if its end is that pleasure accompany the representations as mere sensations, the latter if its end is that it accompany these kinds of cognition.[11]

The notion of 'mechanical' art here is obscurely put by Kant. However, it is probably meant to encompass those representations which are constructed so as to provide *information* about the items or states of affairs to which they refer; or instruction in how they are to be constructed. Such things would include, for example, the images and texts found in travel books, or such things as architectural and draughtsman's plans, instruction manuals, and the like.

'Agreeable' art is also expressed by Kant in rather awkward terms. He goes on to describe it in terms of amusing stories at parties, background music, and games played just to pass the time. However, there is surely much more scope to this than Kant himself realizes. In particular, 'agreeable' art seems well suited to the notion of kitsch. This consists of artefacts which are produced with the sole purpose of pleasing the eye, or evoking familiar (often sentimental) emotions through well-tried and straightforward written or musical idioms. Such works are orientated solely towards 'looking nice' or making us feel good in a comfortable way. Obviously, some recognitional element is involved in this, but our pleasure is, in effect, simply a relaxing sensation brought about by cognitively unchallenging material.

In contrast to all this, fine art involves pleasurable ways of *cognizing* the object. This is why I started my account of Kant's position with his notion of aesthetic ideas and their reciprocity of imagination and reason. It is this reciprocity which allows the work's subject-matter to be expressed in a cognitively enhanced form.

I also emphasized the importance of style as the key factor in this cognitive enhancement. Whilst Kant does not himself address the notion in sufficiently direct terms, he leads us towards what is at issue in it through an important analogy between fine art and nature.

In a product of art one must be aware that it is art, and not nature; yet the purposiveness in its form must still seem to be as free from all constraint by arbitrary rules as if it were a mere product of nature. On this feeling of freedom in the play of our cognitive powers, which must yet at the same time be purposive, rests that pleasure which is alone universally communicable though

---

[11] Kant, *Critique of Judgment*, §44, p. 184 (Pluhar, 172; Meredith, 165).

without being grounded on concepts. Nature was beautiful, if at the same time it looked like art; and art can only be called beautiful if we are aware that it is art and yet it looks to us like nature.[12]

The point is that if a work's style appears laboured, or a mere result of copying, then this holds no perceptual or imaginative interest for us. It will seem no more than a representation of such and such a kind, referring to such and such a subject-matter.

One assumes that mechanical and agreeable art are of this order also. The former involves representations which are sufficiently understood as bearers of information. The latter (in its kitsch idioms, at least,) reassures and pleases through the very fact that it has a familiar and formulaic character. In both cases here, the representation is, as it were, consumed by its crude communicative function. It involves a rather formulaic following of rules in such a way that the rule-based character of the work is always manifest. There is no imaginative surplus to engage us aesthetically in deeper terms.

Fine art has such a surplus, which is expressed through it 'looking like' nature. In what does this consist? Kant's last-quoted comments seem to link the appearance of fine art to that of natural beauty, in so far as both involve a 'free' and heightened interaction of key cognitive capacities. But, of course, the capacities in question are not the same in both cases. Specifically, in fine art, imagination and reason are the players, whilst, in natural beauty, it is imagination and understanding.[13]

This means that we might expect fine art and free beauty to differ very much in terms of appearance. Whatever, the naturalness of fine art consists in, it will go beyond 'looking like' nature in literal terms.

---

[12] Kant, *Critique of Judgment*, §45, p. 185 (Pluhar, 173–4; Meredith, 166–7).

[13] Kant is inconsistent on this. In §45, he tries to present the harmony as one based on understanding and imagination. Outside the ambiguities of Kant's architectonics, there is no real problem here. All aesthetic experience depends on a relation between imagination and the understanding—defining the latter as a capacity for following cognitive rules in general. On these terms, reason should be regarded as a special employment of the understanding which holds in aesthetic experiences other than that of free beauty. One might put the contrast in terms of my notion of the emergent judgement of reflection. In beauty, such judgements are arrested in the act of cognitive discrimination and do not converge upon or culminate in a determinate concept. In aesthetic ideas, such judgements constellate around a concept bound up with the artist's stylistic presentation of a subject-matter, but this does not culminate in a simple recognitional act. Rather, the guiding concept act is sensibly embodied in a way which occasions imaginative associations and kindred ideas.

Rather, it involves the artwork having a *spontaneous* appearance which is, at the same time, instructive for other practitioners of the artistic idiom in question.

Such a criterion of naturalness in fine art runs very deep indeed, encompassing both cognitive and historical factors. These meet in Kant's account of genius. In his words,

> Genius is the talent (natural gift) that gives the rule of art. Since the talent, as an inborn productive faculty of the artist, itself belongs to nature, this could also be expressed thus: *Genius* is the inborn predisposition of the mind (*ingenium*) *through which* nature gives the rule to art.[14]

Kant does not explain the natural basis of genius in a detailed way, but a few simple points can do what is needed. First, human beings are by definition material bodies and, as such, cannot inhabit the exact same spatio-temporal coordinates as other such bodies. They have species characteristics in common with one another, but also many individual physical differences at both the perceptual and genetic levels. No matter how much a person shares an environment with others, he or she will not perceive the world in experiential terms which are exactly congruent with those others. He or she will have a different experiential life-narrative.

In human society, there is enough kinship to learn how to do things in a shared context—to learn to follow rules concerning the realization of ends. However, the differences just noted means that there will be always be levels of contrasting individual aptitude involved, no matter how simple the rules.

I am stressing these rather obvious points because they are the natural basis of the Kantian notion of genius. It is all too easy to think of this notion as no more than an outmoded Romantic concept, but Kant's version is clearly based on the physically grounded differential origins just described rather than anything mysterious or mystical or specifically Romantic. In the present context, it is a natural aptitude for artistic creativity which cannot simply be learned.

Kant links the major factors involved in this as follows. Genius

(1) is a talent for producing that for which no determinate rule can be given, not a predisposition of skill for that which can be learned in accordance with some rule, consequently . . . originality must be its primary characteristic.

---

[14] Kant, *Critique of Judgment*, §46, p. 186 (Pluhar, 174; Meredith, 168).

(2) . . . since there can also be original nonsense, its products must at the same time be models—that is, exemplary, hence, while not themselves the result of imitation, they must yet serve others in that way—that is, as a standard of a rule for judging.

(3) . . . it cannot itself describe or indicate scientifically how it brings its product into being, but rather that it gives the rule as nature.[15]

Overlooking some overlaps of exposition in the foregoing remarks, it is clear that, for Kant, innate talent, 'originality', and 'exemplariness' are the three factors which are basic to artistic style—that is, which determine *how* aesthetic ideas are embodied in a medium.

In terms of innate natural talent, we have already seen that such genius is naturally based. Kant now goes on to characterize it further through an example that is rather more complex than he realizes. He notes that it is possible to learn everything which Newton has propounded in terms of his scientific theories, but that it is not possible to learn how to write inspired poetry simply by following rules, or copying models.

This is because the connections which led Newton from 'the first elements of geometry' to the subsequent ones can be shown—to himself or others—in a clear 'intuitive' way, thus allowing others to follow. But, a poet such as Homer or Wieland cannot, in the same way, show how his creative ideas 'arise and meet' in the mind.

Unfortunately, Kant's treatment of this example obscures some fundamental points of contrast. In the case of Newton, he is describing how the logical structure of a scientific theory can be explained so as to allow this structure to be comprehended sufficiently. This is because the individual steps in its formulation are logically connected to its preceding ones.

But, this is not on a par with his example of the poets, for there Kant addresses the inspiration which leads them to create their work, rather than the structure of the work itself. The requisite contrasts cannot, therefore, be made. For example, the inspiration which led Newton to formulate his ideas may be just as inexplicable as that which informs poetic creation, and whilst the structure of an artwork may not be built on inferential and deductive steps it almost always has distinct and clearly connected parts (or networks thereof) which allow its general structural characteristics to be communicated in sufficient descriptive

[15] Kant, *Critique of Judgment*, §46, pp. 186–7 (Pluhar 175; Meredith, 168–9).

terms to anyone who wishes to know what it involves—at a basic communicative level, if not an aesthetic one.

Kant does, however, make another point which moves in a more viable direction. We are told that 'In the scientific sphere ... the greatest discoverer differs only in degree from the most hard working imitator and apprentice, whereas he differs in kind from someone who is gifted by nature for beautiful art'.[16]

Kant takes these points to follow from his previous ones. However, they move in a rather different direction which I shall now develop. Science in all its guises involves general theories and bodies of observation which are often organized around quantifiable factors. This means that the kind of knowledge embodied in the sciences can, *in principle*, be 'discovered' by someone other than the person who actually does so. Fine art, in contrast, involves irreducible particulars.

A fundamental logical contrast is implied by this. In the case of the sciences (and perhaps philosophical truth also), the individual identity and experiences of the theorist qua individual are not necessary to the meaning of the theories themselves. These meanings concern general structural characteristics of the world. In contrast, the artwork qua sensible or imaginatively intended particular, involves a particular way of expressing a subject-matter on the basis of the artist's own individual handling of a medium. Here the personal identity of the creator has a *necessary* bearing on the meaning of what is created.

It should not be thought that this entails recognition of some 'intention' embedded in the work. Rather, the meaning of art is grounded in the artist's style—perceived in a comparative horizon on the basis of similarities to, and differences from, the work of other artists.

That Kant does not develop these points explicitly is unfortunate. This is because—as we shall see in due course—they give the most direct accentuation to the importance of his other two major fine art concepts—namely, *'originality'* and *'exemplariness'*. Indeed, it is these two notions (in conjunction with that of the 'aesthetic idea') which give Kant's theory its enduring, if largely unappreciated, strength. Again, however, Kant's exposition of these is relatively thin.[17] Consider, for

---

[16] Ibid. §47, p. 188 (Pluhar, 177; Meredith, 170).

[17] The secondary literature is equally bare. 'Originality' is not even cited in the index of Allison's *Kant's Theory of Taste* (Cambridge: Cambridge University Press, 2001) and discussions of it in the body of his text are 'in passing'—despite Kant's explicit affirmation that it is the 'primary characteristic' of genius. Allison prefers rather to follow the fascinating but interminable intricacies of the theory of genius in its psychological setting, without any

example, his treatment of originality. His most substantial comments on what it might involve are as follows.

a certain boldness in expression and in general some deviation from the common rule is well suited to [the genius], but is by no means worthy of imitation, but always remains in itself a defect which one must seek to remove, but for which the genius is as it were privileged, since what is inimitable in the impetus of his spirit would suffer from anxious caution.[18]

Once the original step has been taken, it becomes a challenge to the talents of other geniuses. This is the dimension of the exemplary. As Kant says

the product of a genius (in respect of that in it which is to be ascribed to genius, not to possible learning or schooling) is an example, not for imitation (for then that which is genius in it and constitutes the spirit of the work would be lost), but for emulation by another genius, who is thereby awakened to the feeling of his own originality, to exercise freedom from coercion in his art in such a way that the latter thereby itself acquires a new rule, by which the talent shows itself as exemplary.[19]

Kant's position in these passages is somewhat awkward. For example, whilst (by definition) 'originality' must involve some deviation from a rule, in the first passage just cited, Kant appears to invest this with a provisional worth only—as a defect which must be tolerated in order to give momentum to creativity.

However, in the second passage, it is clear that the product of such activity is basic to inspiring other geniuses to follow the spirit of the

sustained analysis of works in which it is embodied. This has the additional misfortune of not foregrounding real points of contrast between fine art and scientific meaning that emerge when Kant's position is subjected to appropriate critical scrutiny. The problem is also present in Paul Guyer's important paper 'Kant's Conception of Fine Art', *Journal of Aesthetics and Art Criticism*, 52 (1994), 275–85. He rightly emphasizes the broad scope of Kant's theory but, as far as I can see, never even mentions 'originality' or 'exemplariness', let alone discusses them. He is content rather to describe the historical and broader context into which Kant's theory of fine art fits, the subjective dimension of genius, and especially the relation between 'aesthetic ideas' and 'powers of the mind'. Unfortunately, none of this material is linked cogently to those phenomenological characteristics of the artwork which give it genuine inter-subjective intelligibility. A scholar who does address this is Salim Kemal in his *Kant and Fine Art* (Oxford: Oxford University Press, 1987), 40–9. Indeed, to his great credit, Kemal actually clarifies the nature of 'originality' and 'exemplariness' by means of a sensitive analysis of specific works of visual fine art. However, this promising approach is quickly subsumed within a much broader concern with Kant's approach to culture in general. The immense potential of the theory of fine art per se is, thereby, left undeveloped.

18 Kant, *Critique of Judgment*, §49, p. 196 (Pluhar, 187; Meredith, 181).   19 Ibid.

work, so as to achieve their own inspiration rather than simply to imitate. By doing this, the second genius establishes a new way of doing things which lesser talents will imitate and other geniuses will inflect with their own originality.

It may be that the awkwardness here can be avoided, if we read Kant's comments in the first passage as referring to the process of creativity instead of its end-product. On these terms, the 'boldness of expression' is a feature of the work-in-progress which helps drive the creative process forwards, but in the end is toned down and 'polished' according to the demands of taste.

In this respect, indeed, Kant devotes considerable effort to emphasizing the importance of taste as a constraint upon the excesses of genius. In his words, 'by introducing clarity and order into the abundance of thoughts it makes the ideas tenable, capable of an enduring and universal approval, of enjoying a posterity among others and in an ever progressing culture'.[20]

On these terms, whilst 'originality' is a necessary condition of fine art, it is not a sufficient one. It must depart from established rules, but so as to enable the possibility of new rules being created. If, in contrast, 'originality' is pursued for its own sake, then it runs the risk of being 'mannered' (in a negative sense) or of being mere nonsense.

It should also be noted that Kant introduces another candidate for the role of constraining influence upon genius—namely, 'something academically correct'.[21] However, this does not sit easily with the notion of 'taste' just described, and I will return to the problematics of this in the next section.

Kant's theory of fine art can be summarized, then, in terms of the following logical progression of argument. Fine art is the embodiment of aesthetic ideas which, in the 'originality' of their presentation have a natural and spontaneous look to them—even whilst being products of rule-governed artifice. This 'originality' and natural look is possible because fine art is produced by genius—that is, a natural talent which cannot be acquired by simply learning rules.

Now, whilst appearing free from rules in a rigid sense, fine art must maintain some standard—which Kant equates with tasteful refinement or with academic correctness (at the expense of excessive boldness). Through this combination of 'originality' and constraining factors, fine

---

[20] Ibid. §50, 197 (Pluhar, 188; Meredith, 183).
[21] Ibid. §47, 188 (Pluhar, 178; Meredith, 171).

art becomes exemplary. It furnishes works which other geniuses can develop so as to open up new rules for artistic creation.

All in all, fine art is a sensible and/or imaginative idiom of representation where—in contrast to the sciences and other forms of knowledge—the identity of the creator (through his or her individual artistic style) becomes inseparable from the meaning of the work.

I shall now offer a critical review and development of Kant's position.

PART 3

First, the notion of the 'aesthetic idea' is an extremely viable one—as long as we acknowledge the importance of individual artistic style as the key factor in how it is embodied in the individual work of fine art.

However, before these points can be further developed, we should consider the weaknesses in Kant's position.

Generally speaking, his theory of fine art puts far too much emphasis on the subjective dimension of artistic creativity and aesthetic response. That Kant does this is understandable. The burden of emphasis in his general account of the aesthetic falls upon the interaction of the key cognitive capacities of understanding and imagination. Hence, if his theory of fine art is to harmonize with this, it must be shown to involve similarly accentuated cognitive interactions.

We have already seen that this raises some confusion as to whether a relation between understanding and imagination, or with reason and imagination (or some hybrid of these) is involved. However, the confusion created by Kant's subjective orientation is more serious still when it comes to comprehending the 'originality' of fine art.

The problem here is that his account of 'originality' per se is asserted rather than argued. And, whilst it has a logical connection to genius understood as a natural talent which cannot be learned by following rules, this connection in itself provides no immediately apparent criteria for 'originality' in art.

In the absence of this, his points concerning constraints on 'originality' are equally insufficient. Kant argues this connection mainly on the role of 'academic correctness' or the effect of 'taste' in regulating 'originality' and making it accessible for assimilation in a shared context. But, this approach is problematic in its own right. 'Academic correctness' and 'taste' are surely very different from one another. The former centres on the following of rules whilst the latter centres on a dimension of freedom in its creative refinements.

This means that the complementary relation between 'originality' and its constraining factors is here analysed through the components of the latter being *separated off from one another*. Hence, in the course of his exposition Kant sometimes emphasizes the one, and sometimes the other. However, whilst the aspects of something can be considered as logically independent of one another for some analytic purposes, it must be remembered that ontologically—in concrete experience—they are not so separated.

Kant's subjective emphasis is unfortunately not equipped to deal with this. The relation between 'originality' and its constraints is left in mainly negative terms—as a case of clear restraint or slightly more relaxed control exerted on originality.

This results in a major difficulty from which others follow. It consists in the fact that the relation between 'originality' and its constraints described by Kant offers no clear criterion of 'exemplariness'. For, whilst the 'toning down' of possible individual excess may make an artist's work more intelligible to others, this, in itself, provides no reason why the work should inspire other artists to anything other than trying to do something different.

But, as Kant himself clearly recognizes, 'exemplariness' involves the making of works which can create 'new rules' for artistic creation. Merely doing something different is not a sufficient characterization of this. The constraining factors on 'originality' must be shown to have relevance to issues which are, in some sense, fundamental to artistic creativity in the medium in question.

It should also be emphasized that Kant's own sense of fine art is very much an eighteenth-century one. However, the scope of art is now understood in a much broader sense than his. This means that as well as being insufficient within the terms of his own theory the constraining role of 'academic correctness' and 'taste' are not at all adequate for dealing with the more avant-garde developments in art since Kant. If his theory is to be comprehensive, it must be adaptable to criteria of constraints upon 'originality' which are not unduly restrictive on art's expanded scope.

The insufficiency of Kant's account of originality, constraint, and 'exemplariness' also threatens a broader point of his—namely, the contrast between fine art and scientific understanding. As I showed earlier, Kant tries to base this on—in effect—the contrasting psychologies of learning involved in these two spheres of cognitive endeavour. But, I suggested that the real point of substance rather exceeds this, and that, clearly, the individuality of the creator and the particularity of the fine artwork are central to its meaning, in a way that they are not at all relevant to the meaning of scientific explanation qua scientific explanation.

This means that, again, we need more exact criteria of 'originality' and its relation to 'exemplariness', so that we can apply these to the work which is produced as well as to the psychological process of their creation. We must be able to contrast their spheres of meaning at the *objective* level.

I am arguing, then, that Kant is right about the role of aesthetic ideas, and the centrality of 'originality' and 'exemplariness'. But, he does not articulate the latter two factors and their relation in a philosophically adequate way. Interestingly, in the final analysis, his arguments here fall at the same kind of hurdle which I noted in relation to his arguments for the universal validity of the judgement of taste. There, we will recall, I argued that what Kant lacked was an adequate sense of the comparative dimension which necessarily informs any such claim to validity.

It is a failure to do full justice to comparative factors which restricts Kant's theory of fine art also. Instead of grounding 'originality' on genius as a central concern, he would have been better advised to make this secondary to an approach based on the fine artwork itself. His points about the natural-looking quality of such work is a gesture in this direction, but no more than a gesture—and one which demands significant qualification in its own right.

Now, it will be recalled that in order to show how aesthetic ideas go beyond nature, I introduced the notion of individual artistic style. Kant does not make this an explicit factor in his account but it is at least implicit, and needs to be made much more of. By doing this, it is possible not only to make the notion of the aesthetic idea fully functional, but also to overcome the problems with 'originality' and 'exemplariness' just described.

However, this requires, in addition, reference to a factor which Kant does not explicitly consider. For individual artistic style is not merely a subjective aspect of artistic creation achieved *in abstracto*. We can only identify individual style through patterns of objectively recognizable sameness or difference in relation to other styles—that is, on comparisons between the perceptible or imaginatively intended properties of artworks, viewed in a *critical/historical horizon*. This means that the burden of stylistic meaning falls on how a work characterizes its content through *engaging with a specific medium and tradition of artistic creation*, be it painting and sculpture, literature, music, or whatever. Unfortunately, the most that Kant has to say about different art media are a few speculative thoughts on the effects which are appropriate to them individually considered, and to their supposed hierarchical relations.[22]

But, if 'originality' and 'exemplariness' are to be understood in terms adequate to the demands which Kant places on them, and to the more general viability of his theory, they must be made specific to horizons of critical comparison operative within individual media.

To show this comprehensively would involve, of course, a sustained and detailed study in itself.[23] However, I can, at least, offer a 'case history' based on the role of style in painting. To this end, I will first clarify the notion of individual artistic style per se. Then detailed consideration will be given to its comparative relational significance. This latter strategy will provide adequate criteria for 'originality' and 'exemplariness' in the case of painting as a fine art.

PART 4

Artistic style concerns that which gives an artefact its distinctive character as the expression of an individual person. It may seem an outdated notion, given the interest in 'intertextuality'—an approach which suggests, often, that individual artistic expression is little more than a function of the various different textual idioms which the artist mixes in making an individual statement.

However, in contrast to literature, painting has complex meaning at the level of immediate visual perception. It is important to get a purchase on this, so that we can comprehend *what* is stylized in art, over and above those concepts of pictorial subject-matter (mentioned at various points earlier).

Of great use here are some ideas from Roger Fry. For him, there are two basic idioms of pictorial unity—a unified idiom where the

---

[22] See, for example, ibid. §§51–3, pp. 197–207 (Pluhar, 189–201; Meredith, 183–93).

[23] I have offered this in a recent work on general aesthetics entitled *Defining Art, Creating the Canon: Artistic Value in an Era of Doubt* (Oxford: Clarendon Press, 2007). The work contains substantial individual chapters on distinctive characteristics of pictorial art, literature, and music.

relation between the parts of a work are comprehended simultaneously, and a successive unity, where they are comprehended successively. Though Fry links these to different idioms of visual art, it is surely the case that they are aspects of our general orientation to any work. To enjoy a visual artwork aesthetically is to explore the different vectors of order opened up by such orientations, or by their over-lapping.

Fry identifies five more 'design' elements which give pictorial order its 'emotional' significance:

(1) The rhythm of linear forms—which record the artist's physical gestures, as modified by his or her feeling.
(2) Mass—'when an object is so presented that we recognize it as having inertia, we feel its power of resisting movement, or communicating its own movement to other bodies, and our imaginative reaction to such an image is governed by our experience of mass in actual life'.[24]
(3) Space—in the sense of forms which present contrasting scale and variations of magnitude in relation to normal perception.
(4) Light and shade—where variations of density and magnitude offer to contextualize objects in ways which profoundly affect their emotional significance for us.
(5) A speculative further element—namely, 'the inclination to the eye of a plane, whether it is impending over or leaning away from us'.[25]

Fry remarks also on the broader significance of such factors:

nearly all these emotional elements of design are connected with essential conditions of our physical existence: rhythm appeals to all the sensations which accompany muscular activity; mass to all the infinite adaptations to the force of gravity which we are forced to make; the spatial judgment is equally profound and universal in its application to life; our feeling about inclined planes is connected with our necessary judgment about the conformation of the Earth itself; light, again, is so necessary a condition of our existence that we become intensely sensitive to changes in its intensity. Colour is the only one of our elements which is not of critical or universal importance to life, and its emotional effect is neither so deep nor so clearly determined as the others.[26]

[24] Roger Fry, *Vision and Design* (Mineola, Tex. and New York: Dover Publications, 1998), 24.   [25] Ibid.
[26] Ibid.

I have set out Fry's ideas here for a number of reasons. First, he is an artist of great distinction, as well as an important 'formalist' theorist. However, what is striking about the ideas just presented is that they take aesthetic appreciation of form to involve rather more than a few 'harmonies' of lines and colour. They centre on *a creative exploration of cognitive features which are fundamental to our objective knowledge of world*. Some of the Kantian categories and transcendental schemata (such as those of relation and quantity, and variations of magnitude, respectively) are implicit in this account, and others could doubtless be related to it.

A rather interesting supplement to Fry's approach, in this respect, is provided by the significance of the modal categories. In painting a picture, each brushstroke is contingent, individually considered. It is one of an indefinite range of possibilities from which the artist chooses. As the work progresses, the individual brushstrokes accumulate—placed by the artist in accordance with the demands of the developing pictorial whole.

When the work is complete, an interesting transformation has taken place. All the brushstrokes which are contingent, individually considered, are now necessary vis-à-vis the identity of the finished artwork qua phenomenal particular. Remove any one of them, and the character of the work would be changed in qualitative terms. It would be a different existent.

This modal transformation might be claimed to have a broader symbolic significance. It centres on a felt dialectic between the sense of necessity just described, and the play of contingencies in how the work is actually created. The transformation of contingency into necessity vis-à-vis the completed work offers a dimension of existential resolution which compensates, in part, for the irredeemable flux of human experience. In another work, I have described this in more detail as follows.

All human beings die; but works of art need not. They preserve and declare ways of experiencing the world. This is not just a case of experience being translated into a more enduring form. Rather, it is at the same time, an overcoming of contingency by finite means. Each brushstroke, each stone, each word, each note (together with the symbolic content which they bear) has its necessary place in the symbolic and necessary relation vis-à-vis the finished product of artistic labour. They are gathered up and redeemed. The individual artwork entails the existence of its unique creator, with his or her personal history. More than this, it presents that experience in a form which is directly accessible to other human beings. The artist's audience *inhabits* the work. It finds there the echo of its own existential problems, and ways of elucidating—and thence dealing with—these. By engaging with the artwork the audience is lifted—imaginatively and emotionally—out of the immediate continuum of personal existence into one informed by a more universal dimension of aeonic becoming. This is far enough from everydayness to be *release* but near enough to be *real*. It is our secular immortality and redemption.[27]

At the heart of effects such as these and the emergent judgements of reflection that embody them, is the importance of the artist's style viewed in the comparative context of 'originality' and 'exemplariness'. We should also be mindful of how this embodies and refines a factor which is intrinsic to imagination. It will be recalled that in Chapter 2 I emphasized the stylized and selective character of schemata, and suggested further that this is a phenomenological characteristic of mental imagery per se—especially that involved in memory. Stylization in such imagery is an integral subjective feature of imagination's complex functions in relation to both knowledge of world and knowledge of self.

To understand style in painting, therefore, we must understand how the cognitive basis of perceptual exploration embodied in the rules and techniques of the medium and the stylizing tendency of imagination per se find mutual expression in painting.

There are four different key factors involved. In what follows, I will distinguish them as logical components, but it must be emphasized at the same time that in artistic practice they are inseparably combined.

The first key aspect of style concerns *choice of a medium and choice concerning the kind of subject-matter which is to be represented*. Initiation into the techniques of different media and their uses is the kind of expertise which an artist acquires, characteristically, through early training. However, in undertaking work thereafter, he or she will often be able to choose a medium which is best suited to a certain choice of subject-matter or to choose a subject which is amenable to the artist's preferred medium of expression.

Choices in both these directions are manifestations of the artist's style of negotiating the medium in question. This can be taken even further in terms of which aspects of a certain kind of subject-matter the artist chooses to represent (a notion which is paralleled in abstract art by the choice of an idiom such as geometrical form and relations,

---

[27] In my *Art and Embodiment: From Aesthetics to Self-Consciousness* (Oxford: Clarendon Press, 1993), 177.

or biomorphic form, or painterly masses and shapes per se). And, these chosen aspects will overlap very closely with the second major aspect of style—namely, an artist's way of articulating the medium.

In the case of painting, the specific way in which the medium is handled is perhaps constitutive of style in its most central sense. It involves choices concerning how pictorial space is structured (e.g., through perspective or looser visual syntax, or through abstract structures) and the basic means whereby its contents are represented (e.g., by outline, fundamentally, or by the placing of coloured marks on a surface, or—more often—by complex combinations of both).

Of special importance for style is the fact that through these idioms of handling the artist will focus on aspects of subject-matter or kinds of visual form which are of most interest to him or her. This may involve complex processes of idealization or, at the other extreme, the exaggeration of specific features. Alternatively (or, in some cases, additionally), it may involve selective processes which tend to diminish or even omit some of the subject's key visual features.

A third aspect of style is that of composition. This involves the linking of narrative and basic pictorial structures so as to enable the subject-matter and its formal expression to cohere as a unity (within the constraints of the artist's own style of handling). In terms of painting as a practice with standards of value and excellence this is an especially important aspect.

However, it is not by any means a sufficient criterion of artistic value. The three aspects of style just described are what might be called its *intrinsic* aspects. When a painter paints, he or she must of necessity negotiate these in quite explicit terms. They are the basic horizon of painting as a creative activity.

But, there is a fourth—somewhat more difficult—*relational* aspect to style. It is difficult because it concerns the broader context of diachronic history in which individual artistic practice is situated. In doing a painting, the artist internalizes a critical or more passive relation to ongoing history which he or she may or may not be aware of. At the very least, it means that the presence of the painter qua individual not only consists in what the immediate internal stylistic fabric of the work reveals, but also in its relation to a much broader context—of artists living, but mainly artists dead, or yet unborn.

This is precisely the aspect which must be focused on so as to give substance to the importance which Kant assigns to 'originality' and 'exemplariness'.

At the most basic level of artistic creation, an artist may be content to follow tried and tested models in order to make a satisfying image. This will be the case especially when dealing with a commission where the patron has exact expectations/specifications concerning the finished work. It will be even more the case in those cultures which place a premium on the unmodified transmission and repetition of specific stylistic features.

Works of these various kinds embody what I shall call *neutral historical difference*, in relational stylistic terms. Literally, they are the products of one individual rather than another, but this difference between individual painters is not manifest as a recognizable stylistic feature of the works in question. Works of this kind will often amount to no more than what Kant calls 'agreeable' art. They have no critical edge.

There are, however, many works which are recognizable as the product of a specific artist or artistic ensemble. Here we have the first glimmerings of 'originality' in a substantive sense. The most basic example of this I shall call *normal historical difference*.

Consider, for example, the Victorian artist Alfred William Hunt. His works from the mid-1850s are intense in their striking attentiveness to perceptual detail, fleeting light effects, and nuances of colour. These interests inform also the work of painters contemporary with Hunt (such as John Brett), but Hunt anchors them in a rich—even 'buttery'—handling of paint which gives his works a highly individual character. One can recognize the individuality of his intrinsic style in relational terms through its difference from the work of other artists.

The specialized western practice of visual *fine art* is closely bound up with the achievement of such individual style. It is the *difference* to which most artists aspire, and is *critical* in that it does not simply accept and reproduce what has gone before.

Now, the achievement of style in this basic sense is of interest to other artists, and they may be led to adapt certain aspects of it in their own work, to a limited degree. However, there is *much* more to the relational aspect of style.

The next major difference arises when an artist not only achieves individuality, but does so in a way which opens up significant possibilities for other artists. In this respect, the examples of Poussin and Rubens are highly instructive.

Poussin establishes a style with an insistently linear plastic emphasis, and which interprets pictorial space in highly structured terms. This structuring involves distinct phases of spatial recession (constructed on the basis of planes running parallel to the picture plane itself). Rubens' style, in contrast, achieves its plastic values through an emphasis on vivid colour, loose contours, and the building of mass from graduated and diffuse effects of tone and shadow. His pictorial space tends to present action which cuts across the picture plane obliquely, and appears to continue beyond the edges of the picture. Recession towards the distance occurs in more indeterminate planar phases than in Poussin.

Now, these intrinsic stylistic features have a broader significance. Consider, in this respect, the distinction between the linear and painterly emphasis in pictorial style. The former emphasizes outline and clearly defined plastic contours whilst the latter blurs edges and is orientated instead towards broad masses and foreshortening achieved by graduated effects of tone and shadow.

These two dimensions of style are not only factors which determine Poussin's and Rubens' individuality respectively: they open up creative possibilities for other artists. Of course, even a 'normal' individual style such as Hunt's can engage the interest of other painters. It is something which can be learned from, or even copied. But Poussin's and Rubens' innovations engage with *pictorial fundamentals* in a more extensive way. Occurring when they did, they offer critical emphases which refine some basic conditions of pictoriality itself.

This is because linear and painterly emphases manifest the two basic gestural extremes between which making an image on a plane surface takes place. On the one hand, it can be achieved by defining forms through *outline* (drawn, painted, or inscribed upon the physical surface of the plane); on the other hand, it can be achieved by *generating masses* from marks *placed upon* the surface. All painters operate at varying points along a continuum defined by these two opposite gestural possibilities.

The innovations of Poussin and Rubens focus on and declare the possibilities of these opposites with an insistency and perspicacity that was not present in painting before them. And this radicalization extends to the structure of pictorial space also. For, again, two basic polar possibilities are thematized. These consist, on the one hand, of organizing pictorial space parallel to the structure of the picture plane and within strict vectors determined by its boundaries; or, on the other hand, by projecting forms obliquely to the plane, and suggesting the continuation of narrative action beyond the plane's boundaries. Once more, it must be stressed that this is a problem which all painters must negotiate, but in Poussin and Rubens it becomes an intense and declared *issue*.

It is for these reasons that their innovations are more than normal historical difference. They should be described, rather, as *effective historical difference*, in so far as here individual style accentuates radical new possibilities for painting as a practice.

Other examples are also instructive. Consider the problem of light. If something is pictured, it must be visible, and this entails that it is illuminated in some way. Again, all artists must negotiate the conditions of illumination, but whether or not these conditions become a manifest source of pictorial interest per se depends on the intrinsic stylistic features in the individual artist.

In this respect, Caravaggio and Rembrandt are of special interest. In their work, the radical contrast of highlights and shadows becomes a major factor in unifying the total contents of pictorial space. What was previously one factor in the phenomenon of illuminating the visible becomes a major vehicle of meaning in its own right.

The work of artists such as Turner and Monet (in their later phases, especially) develops the problem of light in a different but equally fundamental direction. Their painting emphasizes the role of transient effects in such a radical way as to challenge accepted criteria of what a 'finished' painting should look like. The presence of the brushstroke qua brushstroke is no longer concealed. In this way, the shifting character of the visible in moment to moment terms is made accessible through painting.

This is by no means rendered absolutely, of course, because painting is an art of spatial rather than temporal realization. However, the diminution of 'finish' in Turner and Monet means that the dimension of change in the visible—and the implicit presence of a mobile observer—is *suggested* in a way that the imagination can develop in the requisite dynamic terms.

Of decisive significance in all these examples is chronological position vis-à-vis diachronic history. The *achievement* of difference—whether normal or effective is dependent on the painter having done something which has not been done before in just those terms. Such 'originality' can involve a telling refinement of pre-existent idioms, or various levels of innovation. Whatever the case, the vital point is that this is done in the arena of public intercourse and transmission before others have done it in such terms.

In the case of effective historical difference, this achievement has large-scale knock-on effects in relation to the development of painting as a medium.

Now, it should be clear that normal and—much more so—effective historical difference give substance to what Kant means by 'originality' and 'exemplariness'. 'Originality' in an artist's individual style opens up specific new possibilities of creative practice in relation to how work in that medium is realized.

This is not a case of 'originality' being constrained by Kant's demands of 'academic correctness' or 'taste', but rather through its becoming exemplary through its comparative position in relation to the ongoing tradition of practice within a medium. In those cases where they are appropriate at all, academic correctness and taste are entirely secondary to this.

Interestingly, there is a further, and even more important, relational dimension to artistic style. It involves the culmination or instigation of *revolution* in the medium.

As an example of the first of these aspects we might consider Masaccio's *Trinity*. This work is the culmination of a long development which might be summarized as follows.

In Giotto's work the foreshortening of three-dimensional figures and their linkage in a three-dimensional space becomes much more systematic than in previous painting. The distinction between above and behind in terms of figures in pictorial space is made manifest—even if it is not systematically calibrated, in every respect.

Over the next hundred years in Italian painting—by intent or chance—this principle of spatial organization is gradually developed in even more-systematic terms. Masaccio's *Trinity* is the culmination of this. It renders perspectival space in exact mathematical terms. This enables the systematic connection of visible items in a three-dimensional space to be projected with equal systematicity in pictorial terms. The revolutionary character of this is shown by the way in which it is taken up (in Italy and beyond) to become the basic way of articulating pictorial space for the next four hundred or so years.[28]

It is important to emphasize that the significance of perspective here is not that of a scientific discovery. Rather, it is one which opens

---

[28] The reasons for this are bound up with perspective's privileged status as the mode of pictorial representation which is most consistent with the systematic character of relations between visible items in three-dimensional space per se—an issue which I have explored at great length in 'The Objective Significance of Perspective: Panofsky with Cassirer', chap. 3 of my *The Transhistorical Image: Philosophizing Art and its History* (Cambridge: Cambridge University Press, 2002), 36–66.

up new stylistic opportunities for articulating the complexity of visual phenomena and their relation to one another.

Masaccio's individual achievement of mathematical perspective, then, is of the profoundest artistic significance in terms of the relational stylistic opportunities that it creates for pictorial art in general. It has the character of *paradigmatic historical difference* in so far as it is an achievement which, in bringing a path of stylistic exploration to a culmination, determines the entire course of painting thereafter. Of course, the character of mathematical perspective is such that, even if Masaccio had not lived, someone else could have 'completed' it. But, in the event, the achievement is his. And, more importantly, the particular style in which he achieves this is one that makes the perspectival aspect into an embodiment of artistic meaning, rather than a merely scientific accomplishment.

Paradigmatic historical difference also occurs later, in a more complex way. In this respect, one must consider Cezanne, Picasso, and Braque.

Cezanne's work in the late 1880s and 1890s achieves an extraordinary visual effect. It emphasizes the three-dimensional plastic qualities of visible things whilst, paradoxically, at the same time affirming the two-dimensional nature of the picture plane itself. This opens up new representational possibilities of the type developed in Picasso and Braque's Cubism between 1908 and 1912. Here the stuff and fabric of the visible is reconfigured to harmonize with the two-dimensionality of the medium.

One consequence of this (though by no means intended by Picasso and Braque themselves) is the possibility of non-figurative modes of visual representation which embody entirely new semantic/syntactic principles of pictorial organization and effects. The innovations of Cezanne, Picasso, and Braque enable the development of new paradigms for painters to operate within. Their individual styles have, accordingly, the relational character of *paradigmatic historical difference*.

On these terms, then, I have given substance to the notion of individual artistic style by first clarifying what is involved in style per se and then its relational and comparative significance, vis-à-vis 'originality' and 'exemplariness'. This development, however, has one more hurdle to negotiate before I return to the general significance of Kant's theory of fine art. It is that of the special status of radical avant-garde works—that is, ones which seem to challenge the whole notion of 'fine art' itself.

PART 5

'Avant-garde' as a term is often associated with artists who subscribe to extreme politics (usually of the left but sometimes also of the far right). However, not all avant-garde artists have been thus politically engaged, and not all radically politicized artists are necessarily 'avant-garde'. The epithet is applied best to those works where accepted idioms of art practice are challenged in ways that contain broader implications of social critique.

There is an important sense in which almost all 'modernist' art, in its first emergence, is avant-garde in these terms. Such works lack technical 'finish' and incline towards mundane and worldly subject-matters, rather than elevated or morally edifying ones.

The critical social implications of this are shown in the widespread public ridicule which accompanied Impressionist and post-Impressionist painting in its first emergence. Likewise, the advent of abstract work was greeted with similar public scepticism—a scepticism which remains present even now in some quarters.

However, within the world of painting as a professional practice, the tendencies just described have normalized themselves. They become established as exemplary procedures which artists can negotiate as they will. Indeed, it is now widely accepted that traditional notions of 'finish' and, indeed, the need for advanced technical skill in terms of naturalistic representation, are no longer necessary to artistic achievement.

Given more space, it would be possible to show the way in which even abstract tendencies have their own originating geniuses who establish exemplary procedures in terms of idioms and subjects (e.g., geometric abstraction, biomorphic imagery, 'all-over' field-painting) which open up cognate creative possibilities for other artists. (Individuals such as Mondrian, Miró, and Pollock, are decisive here). The Kantian notion of 'fine art' can, therefore, be applied to the realm of abstract art with little modification.

However, much more complex issues are raised by the legacy of Marcel Duchamp and his 'unassisted' 'readymades'. These are avant-garde in a much more radical sense through their use of 'found objects' and other material not created by the artist. This seems to call into question the entire aesthetic and social separation of art from the realm of non-art.

Since Duchamp, the use of found material has become commonplace. Indeed, the boundaries of art have been stretched to such a point that, with some 'Conceptual' works, there is sometimes no need to use an object at all. Surely, then, the notion of 'fine art' is entirely inappropriate here?

The matter is, however, rather more complex than might at first appear. It requires that we clarify what kind of meaning is exemplified in the readymades and cognate works, and then explore such works in relation to the all-important notion of aesthetic ideas. If it is possible to link aspects of Duchamp's legacy to these ideas (with an emphasis on their aesthetic character) then the link to fine art may hold, even in this unlikely avant-garde context.

As an initial guide to the readymade, some observations from Kant prove of unexpected interest. They occur in the course of his discussion of pleasures arising from the 'play of thought'.[29] What he is referring to here is pleasure in games of chance, music, and wit. Of these, it is the final one which is pertinent. Kant observes that this 'arises merely from the change in the representations, in the faculty of judgment, by means of which, to be sure, no thought that involves any sort of interest in general, but the mind is nevertheless animated'.[30] He remarks further that

Along with what is cheerful, closely related to the gratification from laughter, and part of the talent for beautiful art, there may also be reckoned the capricious manner. Caprice in the good sense signifies the talent of being able to transpose oneself at will into a certain mental disposition in which everything is judged quite differently from what is usual (even completely reversed), and yet in accordance with certain principles of reason in such a mental disposition.[31]

In describing these pleasures of caprice, Kant emphasizes their subjective role in stimulating the mind (and even, in some of his more unlikely claims, certain physiological functions also). These points can be developed further in relation to aspects of Conceptual art.

Duchamp's 'unassisted' readymades, such as *In Advance of a Broken Arm*, are best understood along these lines. This work consists of a snow shovel leaning against a wall. What is manifestly *not* an artwork is presented as if it were one, and through the manifest incongruity of the juxtaposition, and the comic implications of the title in relation to the

[29] Kant, *Critique of Judgment*, §54, pp. 207–12 (Pluhar, 201–7; Meredith, 196–203).

[30] Ibid. §54, p. 208 (Pluhar, 202; Meredith, 198).

[31] Ibid. §54, p. 211 (Pluhar, 206–7; Meredith, 203).

work, we are led to ponder on the scope of what counts as art, and be amused at its wit.

Consider also Robert Barry's work in the late 1960s and early 1970s. This often consists of mere statements typed on paper. In relation to him, Daniel Marzona remarks that

Works such as SOMETHING WHICH IS UNKNOWN TO ME BUT WORKS UPON ME and SOMETHING WHICH IS VERY NEAR IN PLACE AND TIME BUT NOT YET KNOWN TO ME can no longer be unambiguously defined, and must on principle mean something different to every recipient. In their open linguistic form, these works by Barry resign themselves to the loss of concrete reference in order to set in motion mental processes in their recipients.[32]

If Duchamp's readymades make fun of the boundaries between fine art and mundane objects, Barry's works are whimsical explorations of the boundaries between art and mental engagement per se. What we are dealing with in both examples here is not fine art but witty jokes or games played at a mentally stimulating, but mainly theoretical, level.

The question arises, then, as to whether there are criteria which might—in relation to other works using 'found' material—enable us to regard the play of thought which they give rise to as an expression of specifically *aesthetic* ideas.

Two possible (and related) criteria present themselves. The first concerns paraphrasability. Consider such works as Gillian Wearing's *60 Minutes of Silence* (1996) or Martin Creed's *Work No. 227: The Lights Going On and Off* (2000). The former consists of a group of twenty-six actors dressed as policemen and policewomen, standing or seated in rows, captured for a continuous sixty minutes on video. It would be possible to describe this work in more detail, but the gist has already been sufficiently communicated. Matters fare similarly with Creed's work. In fact, the title in itself is just about sufficient for grasping the nature of the piece. The point is, in other words, that with some Conceptual works descriptions are all we need. Seeing the work itself makes no great addition. Indeed, it came as some embarrassment to the organizers of the Turner Prize (which Creed won with the aforementioned work) that exactly the same thematic had been used in a work in the Venice Biennale nearly thirty years earlier.

If a work is sufficiently paraphrasable, in descriptive terms, this is indicative that its significance is, at best, that of wit and theory rather

---

[32] Quot. Daniel Marzona, *Conceptual Art* (Cologne: Taschen, 2005), 17.

than of fine art. In fact, with many Conceptual works it is hard even to find a dimension of wit. Rather, their meanings are assigned mainly on the basis of what can be read into them by friendly critics, curators, and other members of the art management and business world. (The works by Wearing and Creed are excellent examples of this.)

Of course, it might be insisted that something extra is *always* involved when such works are seen directly. This might be true in a literal sense in terms of accessibility to visual detail, but visual detail is not a sufficient condition of *aesthetic* meaning. If a work is not visually *interesting* in some respect then it has no entitlement to claim aesthetic significance.

This leads to a second criterion for determining a Conceptual work's status as art. Its particular idiom of visuality qua phenomenal configuration must be aesthetically relevant to its meaning. It must present aesthetic ideas rather than ideas which are merely, as it were, pointed towards by a visual object or configuration. If the work's visual specificity is not integral to its meaning then there are no immediately apparent grounds as to why it should be regarded as a visual artwork.

In the case of the Wearing and Creed works this is the very problem. Their visual specificity is not an essential part of their meaning, aesthetically. In the case of the former work, another arrangement of different actors dressed as police officers would have worked just as well. In the case of the latter work, any room with lights timed to go on and off would have made the same visual point.

The works by Robert Barry discussed earlier are also of this order, but in a more complex way. As we have seen, his statements may be imaginatively interesting in the thoughts which they give rise to, but this level of meaning is not a function of their visual specificity. They may be presented in a visual context, but they work through being *read* rather than through being seen. Oddly enough, this visual presentation inhibits them from functioning as aesthetic ideas of a poetic kind, whilst their written character inhibits them from working as aesthetic ideas of a visual kind.

Duchamp's case is rather more ambiguous. For example, the bottle rack which he selected for the unassisted readymade *Bottle Rack* (1914) is actually quite interesting in its appearance, and this imports an aesthetic dimension which *In Advance of a Broken Arm* lacks. In fact, his 'assisted' readymades—where the found object is actually modified by the artist—are often of great aesthetic interest in their own right, precisely by virtue of the specifics of their visual configuration.

I have argued, then, that radically avant-garde works in the Du-champian tradition require a critical Kantian approach. Such works are not always entitled to the artistic status which is assigned to them. However, if it can be shown that their visual specificity resists sufficient descriptive paraphrasing, and is aesthetically essential to their meaning, then such works do embody aesthetic ideas of a visual kind.

Kant himself, of course, suggests that such ideas involve an aesthetic 'expansion' of their conceptual components. In the case of some Con-ceptual works, and installation and assemblage art, recognition of their found components in terms of what they are—mundane 'real' objects or artefacts—acts as a springboard for, as it were, almost magical aesthetic visual transformations which work precisely through their transcendence of the mundane in the direction of complex plays of understanding and imagination.

Indeed, the key Kantian relational factors of 'originality' and 'ex-emplariness' can be linked also to Duchamp's innovations. In this respect, his assisted readymades are not only original in themselves but have become exemplary for other artists. Installation and assemblage art, for example, are tendencies which have now established them-selves but which derive ultimately from their smaller-scale beginnings in Duchamp's work. And within these tendencies we find works (such as those by David Mach and Cornelia Parker) which are exemplary in their use of found materials to make representations, and artists (such as Erwin Redl) who use such material to create magnificent abstract evocations of the sublime.

CONCLUSION

In this chapter, I have expounded and developed Kant's theory of fine art. I have shown how it focuses on the notion of the embodiment of aesthetic ideas, and that individual artistic style should be seen as central to this. It is style which *characterizes* the work's conceptual content in a way that transforms its bare cognitive significance, and gives it varying degrees of critical edge vis-à-vis works that preceded it and works that come after it.

It was further argued that whilst Kant is right to link fine art to genius (as a natural talent) and 'originality' and 'exemplariness', his emphasis on genius and the subjective dimension of artistic creativity means that his treatment of 'originality' and 'exemplariness' is insufficient. What is lacking is an artwork-based account of the importance of critical comparative factors. Such factors involve an inseparable combination of historical and technical issues which are specific to the individual art media.

These points were then made more concrete by a detailed considera-tion of the role of style in the specific case of painting as an art practice. It was shown further that the Kantian approach can even be extended to radical avant-garde idioms.

Before underlining finally the decisive significance of Kant's approach to fine art, an objection and an omission need to be addressed. The objection is pointed towards by a remark from Paul Guyer. He notes that 'concern with such matters as the novelty, rarity, or value of works of art all too often overshadows genuinely aesthetic appreciation of objects'.[33] Does this not suggest, therefore, that the emphasis which I have placed on 'originality' and 'exemplariness' imports considerations which are extra-aesthetic and thence inhibiting factors. The answer is 'no'. An art historian might make technical comparative judgements concerning the 'originality' and 'exemplariness' of a work which amounted to no more than that. However, 'originality' and 'exemplariness' can also act as conditions of a judgement, rather than as its content per se. For example, if our orientation towards a work by Turner is informed by knowledge that it is indeed from his hand, and we know also the broader exemplary significance of his innovations, this means that we negotiate the work in an aesthetically enriched way. The form of the work and the aesthetic ideas which it occasions are ones which involve the work's structure of appearance being mediated to a higher level of aesthetic experience (though Kant would not himself, of course, regard this as 'higher').

If this broader knowledge did not mediate our judgement we would negotiate the work only as a 'free beauty'—a level which, in broad aesthetic terms, would be a gross travesty of the work's aesthetic significance.

However, this brings us to the key omission from my account so far. The interaction of reason and imagination which is central to fine art gives it a clear connection to Kant's general *cognitive* grounding of the aesthetic. But, what of his other main aesthetic criterion—namely, '*disinterestedness*'?

---

[33] Guyer, *Kant and the Claims of Taste* (Cambridge, Mass. and London: Harvard University Press, 1979), 202.

At no point does Kant link this to fine art. And, indeed, he cannot, because with the work of fine art we must clearly have an interest in the 'real existence' of the object. Indeed, the knowledge of the fact that the artwork is created by a fellow human being is of the most vital significance in our response to it.

In fact, it is possible to go beyond what Kant says, but in a way which allows his general approach to be usefully developed. This involves the argument that our experience of fine art is at least *relatively disinterested* in its own distinctive way. For, whilst we know that the work was made by someone, we do not need to have any further factual knowledge of the creator's biography or the specific circumstances of the work's creation. We may have such knowledge, and it may enhance our enjoyment of the work, but we do not have to have such knowledge in order to appreciate it aesthetically.

Indeed, it is the possibility of this distinctive relative disinterestedness which enables art to engage us *so* deeply. When another person describes how he or she sees the world, we may learn things from this, but the presence of that person always pressures us to respond in a certain psychological way. We may agree with them so as not to hurt their feelings. We may very much like what we are being told, but the person's immediate presence may make it difficult to assimilate what they are saying on our own personal terms. Their 'real existence' is of the most immediate import in how we negotiate them.

However, with the work of fine art, things are very different. For, even whilst we have an interest in its 'originality' and 'exemplariness', as a condition of our aesthetic experience of them in other key respects there is a dimension of relative disinterestedness involved. The work is physically detached from its creator, who may be long dead. The fact that it is encountered without the specific circumstances of its creation being attached to it as a commentary means that we are free to identify with, or reject, what it shows us, in a way we are not in direct personal encounters.

The artist's individual style, in other words, illuminates its subject-matter at a level of sensible or imaginatively intended immediacy, *but without interference from the creator*. The relative disinterestedness of our experience of the work, therefore, is a liberating one. We become close to another person's *way of viewing* things, but can assimilate it on our own terms in a way that is difficult in more-direct personal interactions. We experience the artist's aesthetic idea in the fullest terms—as experiential possibility rather than as mere recognition of conceptual content.

Ultimately, what Kant's theory of fine art shows is this. There is a form of meaning which is embodied in sensible or imaginatively intended artefacts. This meaning depends on how individual style is embodied in its creation in a way that other forms of meaning are not. It centres on a cognitive elucidation of subject-matter and material that is achieved through the (original and exemplary) stylistic embodiment of aesthetic ideas.

We need a name for this distinctive form of meaning. 'Fine art' does the job.

7

The Kantian Sublime Revisited

INTRODUCTION

In this chapter, I will complete my reappraisal of the Kantian aesthetic by exploring the main topic left outstanding—namely, Kant's (at times, formidably difficult) approach to 'the sublime'.

There is much about this approach which is 'out of synch' with the dominant body of the Kantian aesthetic, orientated as it is towards the judgement of taste. However, Kant's approach has extremely rich potential in relation to general problems in aesthetics. I have explored major aspects of this, at length, in my book *The Kantian Sublime: From Morality to Art*. I now take the opportunity to deepen and extend the account offered there.

Part 1 expounds Kant's theory of the mathematical sublime. In Part 2, I argue that his rather baroque argumentation raises considerable problems, not least of which is the very entitlement of judgements of the sublime to be even regarded as aesthetic, on Kant's own terms. In particular, I argue that the necessary role which he assigns to infinity is, in fact, at best a contingent one.

The arguments in Part 3, however, go on to identify a more austere line of argument which is embedded in Kant's baroque approach. I argue that this is consistent with Kant's most important concepts, and then go on to deepen my previous account of it by paying special attention to those 'perceptual cues' which allow us to distinguish judgements of the mathematical sublime from those concerning vast phenomena which are imaginatively overwhelming in a non-aesthetic way. In the course of this, I clarify also the sense in which the rational idea of phenomenal totality which is basic to Kant's approach can be made sense of in relation to vast phenomena per se, rather on the basis of reference to infinity.

In Part 4, I expound and criticize Kant's theory of the dynamical sublime. It is argued that Kant's approach is wholly counter-intuitive and is, again, in clear contradiction with the sublime's claim to aesthetic status. I show, further, that the austere approach adopted in relation to the mathematical sublime can be applied in this context also, and results in a more unified and generally viable theory.

Part 5 goes beyond what Kant himself attempts by exploring the Kantian approach in the context of fine art. It is argued that we can, with justification, use the term 'sublime' descriptively in relation to a genre of art that ranges from romantic idioms through to avant-garde and postmodern tendencies. More importantly, a case is put for there being a *distinctively artistic* mode of the sublime, where the role of the rational idea of totality is replaced by a sense of the comprehensive power of creative rational *artifice*.

By way of conclusion, I summarize, briefly, the salient points made in the course of the chapter.

PART 1

Kant observes that 'The beautiful in nature concerns the form of the object, which consists in limitation; the sublime, by contrast, is to be found in a formless object in so far as limitlessness is represented in it, or at its instance, and yet it is also thought as totality'.[1]

Beauty is final in relation to the capacity for cognition, through stimulating the interaction of imagination and understanding. The sublime is final in relation to reason and the higher ends of morality. This means that moral dimension is much more to the fore than in beauty—a factor which, as we shall see, complicates the aesthetic status of judgements of the sublime.

Now, since judgements of the sublime are of the reflective kind, it would be logical to expect that Kant's analysis would be conducted in terms of those same four 'Moments' which were involved in the judgement of the beautiful. However, Kant's use of the Moments takes a rather different form. This is because judgements of the sublime are of two different varieties—based on two different ways in which natural phenomena can be found overwhelming. On the one hand, this can arise through their sheer *vastness*—the '*mathematical sublime*'—or

---

[1] Immanuel Kant, *The Critique of the Power of Judgment*, trans. Paul Guyer and Eric Matthews (Cambridge: Cambridge University Press, 2000), §23, p. 128 (Pluhar, 98; Meredith, 90).

through their overwhelming or threatening power—the '*dynamical sublime*'.

His most sustained treatment is of the first of these—the mathematical sublime. In §25, it is established that the 'greatness' of phenomenal items is always dependent on a comparative context, and thence can never be determined in absolutely conclusive terms. Likewise, no phenomenal item can be absolutely great. There is always the possibility that somewhere there may be something which is bigger than it. However, Kant observes that

> just because there is in our imagination a striving to advance to the infinite, while in our reason there lies a claim to absolute totality, as to a real idea, the very inadequacy of our faculty for estimating the magnitude of the things of the sensible world awakens the feeling of a supersensible faculty in us; and the use that the power of judgment naturally makes in behalf of the latter (feeling), though not the object of the senses, is absolutely great, while in contrast to it any other use is small.[2]

When presented with a vast phenomenon, reason demands that we comprehend its phenomenal totality. Such a totality, however, exceeds our power of imaginative representation, and, in so doing, suggests the idea of infinite continuation. Now, whilst such an idea exceeds what can be imagined, it can, at least, be thought as a rational idea. In this way, imagination's inability to represent a phenomenal totality makes us aware of the superior cognitive scope of our rational, 'supersensible' aspect. It is this being which is sublime, in so far as, in judgements of the sublime, even the vastest forms of nature are put to use in its service.

This outline position is filled in—often with puzzling detail—in §26. For Kant, mathematical notions provide rules of progression in relation to the measurement of phenomena. However, these only allow us to assign determinate magnitude to such phenomena in so far as, at some point, they adopt a 'fundamental' measure based on what is given in intuition. This is why, in the 'last resort', all estimates of magnitude are aesthetic in character. Rules for multiplying and dividing are all very well, but in order to determine magnitude through these rules basic units of measure based on sensibilia (such as metres, centimetres, and the like) are necessary. All measurement, in the final analysis, involves the use of units derived from such 'aesthetic estimates'.

---

[2] Ibid. §25, p. 134 (Pluhar, 106; Meredith, 97).

Mathematical operations based on these can continue ad infinitum. But, with the aesthetic estimate which yields the basic unit of measure matters are very different. Presented with a vast phenomenon Kant holds that reason's demand for the comprehension of its total phenomenal magnitude involves, in the first instance, an attempt to find an appropriate sensible measure for it. Indeed, the challenge is such that this takes the form of an 'absolute' or 'fundamental aesthetic measure', which will allow the total magnitude to be determined in the most complete terms.

Now, of course, in judging magnitude one can do so either by calculating how many times the relevant unit of measure will fit into the object measured, or by taking a measure which is greater than the measured item and judging how many times the item would fit into it.

Kant assumes (without explanation) that it is the latter strategy which holds in the case of vast phenomena. This leads him to one of the most important and productively ambiguous passages in the whole of his discussion of the mathematical sublime. I shall quote it at length.

> To take up a quantum in the imagination intuitively, in order to be able to use it as a measure or a unit for the estimation of magnitude by means of numbers, involves two actions of this faculty: apprehension (*apprehensio*) and comprehension (*comprehensio aesthetica*). There is no difficulty with apprehension, because it can go on to infinity; but comprehension becomes ever more difficult the further apprehension advances, and soon reaches its maximum, namely, the aesthetically greatest basic measures for the estimation of magnitude. For when apprehension has gone so far that the partial representations of the intuition of the senses that were apprehended first already begin to fade in the imagination as the latter proceeds on to the apprehension of further ones, than it loses on the one side as much as it gains on the other, and there is in the comprehension a greatest point beyond which it cannot go.[3]

The process just described is what arises when we attempt to search out an appropriate measure for the vast phenomenon. Imagination is tested to the full. In the course of this,

> the mind hears in itself the voice of reason, which requires totality for all given magnitudes, even for those that can never be entirely apprehended although they are (in the sensible representation) judged as entirely given,

---

[3] Ibid. §26, p. 135 (Pluhar,108; Meredith, 99).

hence comprehension in one intuition, and it demands a presentation for all members of a progressively increasing numerical series, and does not exempt from this requirement even the infinite (space and past time), but rather makes it unavoidable for us to think of it (in the judgment of reason) as given entirely (in its totality).[4]

As I understand it, Kant's major points here are that in searching out an appropriate measure for the phenomenon, the imagination is led to increasingly vast measures—even down to the infinite itself. All of this must issue in (as demanded by reason) a measure embodied in a single intuition.

This process leads to the overwhelming of imagination described in the lengthy passage quoted before last. However, whilst imagination cannot present the infinite, rational thought can comprehend it as an idea. This has an important consequence. As Kant says,

But even to be able to think the given infinite without contradiction requires a faculty in the human mind that is itself supersensible. For it is only by means of this and its idea of a 'noumenon', which itself admits of no intuition though it is presupposed as the substratum of the intuition of the world as mere appearance, the infinite of the sensible world is completely comprehended in the pure intellectual estimation of magnitude under a concept, even though it can never be completely thought in the mathematical estimation of magnitude through numerical concepts.[5]

The point is, as *The Critique of Pure Reason* has shown, that if infinity as a whole is to be thought of coherently and completely this presupposes a 'noumenal' substrate which limits the infinite (in metaphysical rather than spatio-temporal terms). This substrate is the seat of our rational (and moral) being. Kant holds, therefore, that imagination's inadequacy to present the infinite draws attention to the superiority of our rational being.

It must be emphasized that this is more than a simple act of intellectual recognition. For through it our capacity for feeling is affected: it is this which constitutes the judgement of the sublime. In Kant's words,

The feeling of the sublime is thus a feeling of displeasure from the inadequacy of the imagination in the aesthetic estimation of magnitude for the estimation by means of reason, and a pleasure that is thereby aroused at the same time from the correspondence of this very judgment of the inadequacy of the greatest

[4] Ibid. §26, p. 138 (Pluhar, 111; Meredith, 102).   [5] Ibid.

sensible faculty in comparison with ideas of reason, in so far as striving for them is nevertheless a law for us.[6]

It is clear, then, that judgements of the mathematical sublime involve a complex series of 'mental movements' at several levels. In cognitive terms, there is a felt recognition of the inadequacy of imagination to satisfy what reason directs it to do (vis-à-vis the presentation of infinity as an absolute measure). However, this involves not only a recognition of the superiority of reason per se but a felt pleasure also in the knowledge that imagination's present inadequacy in relation to it is in accord with the higher ends of reason—that is, the realization of our moral vocation. This accordance is based on the fact that such realization involves, as a central factor, decisions based on the rational overcoming of sensible impulses and other obstacles.

The accord in question here is why Kant describes the feeling of the sublime as one of 'respect'—the very term used in the *Critique of Practical Reason* to describe the feeling arising from the moral law's determination of the will. This linkage, in itself, should make us wary of the mathematical sublime's status as a mode of aesthetic judgement. Its full ramifications can be brought out by a review of Kant's main arguments so far.

PART 2

First, the idea that vast objects present a challenge to cognition is perfectly intelligible on lines suggested by Kant. As phenomenal items, they are finite, and thence we know that their size—no matter how great—is relative to that of other items. For any great phenomenon, there is always, in principle, the possibility that somewhere there is one which is greater than it. We also know that, as finite items, vast formless phenomena have the unity of an object or an event (or of a series of either of these) and form totalities which occupy a determinate amount of space and time. However, it is one thing to understand that something has determinate total magnitude, and another thing entirely to comprehend this in perceptual or imaginative terms.

Now, whilst this latter comprehension is clearly a challenge, Kant fails to explain why it is that not all vast phenomena stimulate us to

---

[6] Ibid. §27, p. 141 (Pluhar, 114–15; Meredith, 106).

meet it, and why it is that when such a challenge *is* met not every such challenging phenomenon is actually found sublime. Or is it that *all* vast phenomena are sublime? This would surely be counter-intuitive. We encounter such phenomena in some (lack of) shape and form almost every day, but it is, surely, only exceptionally that we find them sublime. Kant, in other words, offers no criterion for distinguishing the merely overwhelming from the sublime.

Problems build up when we look at the phenomenology of the sublime in more detail. Two related problems arise immediately. The first is why the attempt to comprehend a vast item's phenomenal magnitude should involve searching out a measure which is larger than it; and the second is why the notion of infinity as a whole should be arrived at as the only appropriate measure.

In relation to the first of these, it may be that we could calculate how many times the unit could fit into the vast object, but Kant's point is that we have to comprehend this fit in a single intuition, rather than through a concept. However, what he does not realize is that a small unit such as an inch or millimetre would function just as well as infinity in this context. To try and make sense of a mountain range by attempting to comprehend every inch or millimetre of its total extent in a single intuition (rather than applying these through a rule of understanding) is something which defeats imagination.

And, even if we tried to comprehend total phenomenal magnitude by searching for a measure which is bigger than the object, why *must* this involve some kind of progression towards infinity? The very fact that we are looking for a measure for the vast phenomenon means that its magnitude has *already* been found overwhelming. Hence, for each larger measure into which it might fit, then we would totally overwhelm the imagination yet again.

It may be that Kant's reasoning here is based on the assumption that a vast phenomenon challenges us to comprehend its phenomenal totality in *absolute* terms. Hence, in so far as all estimation of magnitude is relative, the only absolute measure for this will be the phenomenal world as a whole—that is, an infinite series. However, this again invites the question of *why* it is in any sense necessary that we should be driven to comprehend the vastness of the object in absolute terms, when our immediate perceptual encounter with it has already suggested that its magnitude cannot be comprehended adequately in imagination at all.

On these terms, then, there is no reason why infinity should play any necessary role in the experience of the sublime. There are other problems also. For example, we saw how in the pure aesthetic judgement we are dealing with cognitive activity of a playful complexity which is recognized mainly through the feeling of pleasure which it occasions. In the case of the sublime, in contrast, whilst Kant's account of searching for an aesthetic measure may introduce some vague parallel to this play, it also involves some quite *definite* concepts.

In this respect, for example, we not only have to recognize the superiority of reason over imagination, but also to know that this is in accordance with the broader demands of reason. Our pleasure arises, we will recall, 'from the correspondence of this very judgement of the inadequacy of the greatest sensible faculty in comparison with ideas of reason, in so far as striving for them is nevertheless a law for us.'[7] This means that, in Kant's main exposition, the sublime hinges on quite specific (morally significant) concepts concerning *the scope and significance of reason*. This determinate conceptual content, of course, raises problems concerning the sublime's aesthetic status. There is a case for seeing it as no more than feeling based on quasi-moral insights, provoked by certain natural phenomena.

I shall not take these criticisms further at this point, as there is a far more constructive possibility: whilst the rather *baroque* line of argument just assessed is his main approach, there is the hint also of a more *austere* and viable one.

PART 3

An important clue to this more viable approach is found in the lengthy and 'ambiguous' passage quoted earlier.[8] In it, Kant claims to be describing what is involved, phenomenologically, in the search for an aesthetic measure. In the broadest terms, the more parts of a phenomenon are apprehended, the less easy is it to reproduce them in imagination. We are gradually overwhelmed by the sheer profusion of parts.

Now, whilst Kant describes this initially in relation to the search for a measure, he goes on to illustrate it with examples based on the perceptual apprehension of vast artefacts—namely, the Great Pyramid and St Peter's in Rome. There is much about his choice of examples which is puzzling. But, the very fact that he uses them shows that the

---

[7] Ibid.   [8] Ibid. §26, p. 135 (Pluhar, 108; Meredith, 99).

imagination can be overwhelmed by individual vast phenomena, as well as by the search for a measure for them.

This means that what Kant is attempting to do can be achieved in much more economical terms. We could argue that the very attempt to comprehend the total phenomenal magnitude of a vast object in a single imaginative intuition is bound to fail. But, reason can comprehend, without remainder, the *idea* of such a totality. In this context, the felt limitations of sensibility are challenged and transcended by the scope of rational ideas. *Imagination's inadequacy makes the liberating scope of reason vivid at the level of sensibility itself*.

In this respect, consider the following passage.

> And who would want to call sublime shapeless mountain masses towering above one another in wild disorder with their pyramids of ice, or the dark and raging sea, etc.? But the mind feels itself elevated in its own judging if, in the consideration of such things, without regard to their form, abandoning itself to the imagination and to a reason which, although it is associated with it entirely without any determinate end merely extends it, it nevertheless finds the entire power of the imagination inadequate to its ideas.[9]

This passage (considered in itself) is a perfect statement of the austere approach.[10] It avoids all the contortions of the infinity-as-a-measure

---

[9] Ibid. §26, pp. 139–40 (Pluhar, 113; Meredith, 104–5).

[10] This interpretation has not recommended itself to Prof. Allison. In *Kant's Theory of Taste* (Cambridge: Cambridge University Press, 2001), 396–7 n. 22 he argues that because, for Kant, the mathematical sublime is 'final' in relation to theoretical reason he must use a relevant theoretical notion—such as infinity. But, whilst this may be a requirement of the baroque architectonics of Kant's philosophical system, it is one which actively weakens the philosophical viability of his explanation of the sublime. The austere interpretation does not. Allison's major worry, however, centres on another aspect of Kant's architectonics: 'If we take seriously the initial conception of the mathematical sublime as the absolutely great . . . the reference to infinity is clearly essential to the Kantian account, for reason's demand on the imagination follows directly from the latter's endeavour to provide an intuitive representation of something fitting that description. Moreover Crowther's version of reason's demand suffers from a complete failure to distinguish between the totality required by the understanding, that is "Allness" [*Allheit*], defined as "plurality considered as a unity" (B 111), which like all the categories, expresses a condition of the unity of apperception (or the understanding), and the absolute totality or unconditioned required by reason. Consequently "reason's demand" on Crowther's austere reading, which he claims is all that is required by the Kantian mathematical sublime, is not even a demand of reason, and it is one which the imagination can easily meet' (p. 397). Allison's points here are confused in several respects. It is, for example, difficult to know what sense to make of his claim that reason's demand on imagination 'follows directly' from the imagination's 'intuitive' attempt to represent the infinite. Is Allison saying that when apprehending a vast phenomenon the imagination first tries to represent the infinite and then attempts—this time directed by reason—to find (unsuccessfully) an absolute aesthetic measure based on the infinite which it has already failed to present? Apart from the oddness

of these dynamics, why should imagination even attempt to negotiate the vast phenomenon in terms of infinity in the first place? Why should overwhelmingly large phenomena demand to be comprehended absolutely? In positing such negotiation, Allison is probably following a similar point made by Patricia Matthews in 'Kant's Sublime: A Form of Pure Aesthetic Reflective Judgment', *Journal of Aesthetics and Criticism*, 54 (1996), 165–80 (see esp. 170–1). It holds that the vast phenomenon *appears* to be infinite, and it is imagination's inability to present this rational idea in a whole of intuition that leads to our sense of the superiority of reason. But, contra Matthews, a phenomenon can surely be experienced as *overwhelming* per se without appearing to be infinite. Indeed, if one person insists that the infinite must be involved, then another, with equal validity, can claim that this is not the case, in so far as they can find no introspective evidence that it figures in their own experience of the sublime. It should be emphasized also that if the overwhelming of imagination involves the phenomenon *seeming infinite* then this is, of course, a *recognitional* act involving a quite definite concept. This adds further difficulty to the aesthetic status of the judgement. The logic of Allison's and Matthew's positions, then, is confused and adds yet another strange 'mental movement' to the already overburdened 'baroque' approach. Allison's confusion here is closely connected to a quite specific error. He suggests that I fail to distinguish between totality understood as a concept of understanding ('allness') and as a demand of reason. This is relevant because, according to Allison, totality understood in relation to a single whole of intuition involves an *understanding* of 'allness'; and not—as I hold—a demand of reason. He claims, further, that phenomenal totality of this sort presents no problem for comprehension through the imagination. Now, for Kant, understanding is the capacity to follow cognitive rules, whilst the 'interest of reason' is a special use of this. Understanding centres on recognition per se whilst the interest of reason drives the understanding to seek unconditional knowledge in relation to its object. In the first *Critique*, Kant emphasizes the role of reason or 'rational ideas' in relation to the comprehension of infinite phenomenal series, and it is this legacy which clearly determines Allison's approach. On these terms, if a demand of reason is operative in relation to vast phenomena, this can *only* be intelligible in so far as it involves infinity as a factor generated in the course of this encounter. For Allison, in other words, the demand is exercised not in relation to the object itself, but rather in relation to finding a measure for it. This baroque reasoning, however, is strikingly at odds with an important point made by Kant in a passage actually quoted by Allison himself. We are told that the 'voice of reason' 'requires totality for all given magnitudes, even for those that can never be entirely apprehended although they are (in the sensible representation) judged as entirely given, hence comprehension in *one* intuition, and it demands a *presentation* for all members of a progressively increasing numerical series, and does not exempt from this requirement even the infinite' (Kant, *Critique of Judgment*, §26, p. 138 (Pluhar, 111; Meredith, 102)). Contra Allison, in these remarks, Kant *implies*—even if he does not develop the insight in such terms—that reason's demand for comprehension must be operative in relation to *any* phenomenal manifold. Given such a configuration, reason demands that its phenomenal totality be comprehensible absolutely in a whole of intuitions. Infinity is 'not exempt' from this demand. But, the fact that Kant presents infinity's role as an exception which is not allowed suggests that it is encompassed by a more general demand of reason exerted in the comprehension of large-scale phenomenal totalities per se. The term 'comprehension' here should, of course, be understood in the sense used by Kant in the 'ambiguous lengthy passage' quoted earlier. It concerns the imagination's attempt to retain the parts of an apprehended phenomenon in a single complete representation or representational sequence. Clearly, what Kant is talking about here is not the mere understanding of 'allness' which Allison regards as a sufficient explanation of our cognitive relation to a completely given phenomenon. It is, rather, the exercise of a demand of reason wherein we try to comprehend a phenomenal totality in absolute terms through a single representation of the imagination. (I shall explain what this involves, and the circumstances under which it might arise, in much 'baroque' alternative. It avoids also the contra-aesthetic involvement of 'definite concepts',[11] in so far as we are dealing here with an exhilaratingly felt, intuitive illumination of the scope of reason, rather than a pleasure based on *the recognition that* reason's overcoming of sensible factors is in accord with that which is a general 'law' for us.[12]

Having outlined the basis of the austere interpretation of Kant's approach to the mathematical sublime,[13] I can now fill in some important details which develop it further.

more detail in the next section.) This demand for complete comprehension is, of course, the starting-point of my austere interpretation of Kant's theory of the mathematical sublime. The interpretation goes on to hold that the very fact that imagination cannot present the rational idea of totality is enough, *in itself*, to make the remarkable cognitive scope of reason vivid at the level of the phenomenal. With this interpretation available, the main baroque approach must fall victim to Occam's Razor several times over. Allison's mistakes are, nevertheless, instructive in a number of ways. He is clearly anxious to ensure that Kant's main baroque approach holds right of way in the understanding of the sublime and attempts to disqualify my alternative on the grounds of a technicality. As we have seen, the technical objection does not hold, but even if it had this would have been irrelevant in terms of general philosophical validity. For, I could have argued simply that even if the austere approach were not implicit in Kant's position it at least shows the most economical way in which that position would have to be revised in order to be made philosophically credible. The fact that Allison clings to such an untenable aspect of Kant's theory is a clear sign of the dangers of that 'interminablist' approach which I noted in the Introduction to this book. The more Kant's arguments and historical contexts are explored for their own sake, and in terms of rigid internal consistency on the basis of a *narrow interpretation* of his own operative concepts, the greater is the temptation to neglect his work's potential for solving general philosophical problems. In the present case, Allison's (mistaken) emphasis of a technical difficulty, and an oversensitivity to precedents from the first *Critique*, leads him to reject an approach which is consistent with Kant's basic position and which would make it viable in favour of a more 'official' line of argument which is contradictory in terms of Kant's own aesthetic, which falls foul of Occam's Razor, and which (in the light of post-Wittgensteinian philosophy of mind) seems almost bizarre. Kant as an object of *interminable* technical exploration is preferred to Kant the problem solver.

[11] Malcolm Budd has also recognized the philosophical untenability of Kant's linkage of the sublime and infinity. In his 'Delight in the Natural World: Kant on the Aesthetic Appreciation of Nature, Part III: The Sublime in Nature', *British Journal of Aesthetics*, 38 (1998), 233–58 he offers an excellent critical analysis of the problems involved (see p. 238, in particular).

[12] It should be emphasized, of course, that the recognition of something being a 'law' for us not only involves the mediation of definite concepts but would amount, in practice, to a veritable *chain of reasoning* concerning the nature of morality and the demands it places upon the human subject.

[13] Sarah Gibbons discusses the sublime in *Kant's Theory of Imagination: Bridging Gaps in Judgement and Experience* (Oxford: Clarendon Press, 1994), 124–39. She argues that 'Crowther's claim that explaining imagination as "overwhelmed" by attempting to present "reason's idea of the object as a whole" is less complex than referring to infinity, as an absolute measure simply avoids telling us how it is that imagination becomes aware of its inadequacy and in what that inadequacy consists' (p. 136). I do not think that this is true, but the amplification of my position in the next section should eliminate any ambiguities.

PART 3

Let us start with a key difficulty which Kant does *not* address. It is that of the criterion for distinguishing between vast overwhelming phenomena per se, and those which are overwhelming in a sublime way. By following this up, the austere approach to the mathematical sublime can be deepened. I shall approach the problem by clarifying first the nature of the 'overwhelming' in this context, and then the correlated features which enable this to have a sublime character.

As we have seen, the austere interpretation does not involve the search for an aesthetic measure of magnitude. But, in the absence of a relevant measure, how can we judge a phenomenon to be overwhelming? The answer is—because the size of the human body itself is a *pre-given measure* in relation to which we gauge the size of things (mediated by our distance from, or the nature of, our perceptual orientation towards them). Things which are small in relation to the human body are phenomenal totalities whose magnitude we can grasp imaginatively without much effort, under normal perceptual circumstances. Larger-size objects into which the body could fit (in terms of its size) begin to present more obstacles. We can imagine the phenomenal totality of a car, but that of a building in excess of hut size begins to be difficult. In the case of large buildings, hills, panoramic landscapes, mountain ranges, ocean views, and the like, the problems are expanded even further.

However, we now reach the decisive point. If one encounters a vast phenomenon at a distance, one can easily comprehend its phenomenal totality. This is because viewed in *this* perceptual context the phenomenon's scale in relation to the body can be simply understood in terms of the understanding. It is simply a 'damned sight bigger' than we are. But, on some occasions, vast phenomena perceived at a distance are found sublime. How is this possible?

Clearly, there must be something about such phenomena—over and above mere recognition of their size in relation to us—which leads us to find them imaginatively overwhelming. Our sense of their size in relation to the body must be emphasized through some further feature of the object. There must be some *perceptual cue* in the object which leads us to differentiate the whole into its multitudinous parts rather than simply take them as given. It is reasonable to suppose that when such differentiation occurs our awareness of the phenomenon's overwhelming size is energized, even though we may be perceiving it from a great distance.

Kant himself provides a vital clue to what this might amount to through his frequent characterizations of the mathematical sublime as 'counter-purposive'. In this respect, we will recall that individual natural forms are purposive in relation to an 'end'. The 'end' consists of those kind-instantiating features which define the natural form in question.

On these terms, a form might be counter-purposive if there is something about its particular sensible manifold which overcomes our merely recognitional sense of what kind of thing it is. I would argue, further, that this should be broadened to encompass contexts in which the form is encountered, as well as its internal manifold. This yields the following major possibilities.

Insistent Repetition

This occurs when a phenomenal item or series thereof sets up perceptual rhythms of possible continuation, or a succession of elements which continue beyond the limits of the perceptual field, literally. In both cases, even if this involves individual items which are purposive in relation to the end which defines them (e.g., the stones from which the Great Pyramid is made), their repetition diminishes this individual identity in favour of a sense of their accumulation *parte-extra-parte*. The insistent repetitiveness of their configuration challenges us to comprehend this accumulation in an imagined whole wherein all these elements are presented *as individual parts* simultaneously. But, of course, this overwhelms our imaginative capacity.

Insistent and/or Complex Irregularity or Asymmetry

The very contrast between such features and the kind-defining characteristics of the form in question may make us attentive to the accumulation of individual parts which constitute its manifold, but without us being able to form an imaginative representation where all these parts characterized individually. We may, for example, have seen many mountains. But some of them may be so configured as to make us attentive to the foregoing features in a way that most examples do not. Here, we are not content merely to recognize the whole but are compelled, rather, to negotiate the parts.

Animation or the Suggestion of it

Vast phenomenal items are usually stationary. If, however, they are in motion—as is the case with a stormy day at sea or the wind blowing through a forest—we become attentive to the individual elements of the manifold set in motion, and their overlaps and potential for further motion. And, even in the case of absolutely static items such as mountains, individual forms or ranges of these may suggest visual rhythms which occasion the imaginative responses described above. In all these cases we want imaginatively to comprehend the animated or apparently animated whole in terms of the parts which are involved; but we cannot. They are imaginatively overwhelming as a sequence of individual elements.

Exaggerated Size

If something is much, much bigger than is normal for things of that size, and if this involves it being many times larger than a human being, then we are again challenged to comprehend the part-based structure of this form in individual terms, with the results described already.

Suggestive Concealment

Many large things are not striking in the aforementioned ways, but if they are partially concealed (by, say, mist or shadow) this leads us to imagine all the parts which might be hidden. The more interesting and suggestive the concealment, the keener we are to imagine what these parts are like, and how they link with one another.

Given these points, I would restate the austere interpretation of Kant's theory as follows. Vast items are judged overwhelming in relation to the human body as a measure. Now, with most vast phenomena we will be content simply to *understand* their vastness in bare recognitional terms. They form wholes which we can recognize simply as overwhelming in terms of their scale in relation to us.

However, under certain circumstances, understanding in excess of mere recognition is involved. We form an idea of the object's phenomenal totality; that is, we are made aware that its vastness is not simply there—a recognizable 'allness'—but is a function of multiple individual parts or elements connecting or overlapping in complex ways so as to constitute, *parte-extra-parte*, the item's phenomenal totality. This *idea* cognitively represents the phenomenon in its fullest or absolute state of being—in terms of all the factors which constitute the completeness of the whole. It is an idea of reason rather than a mere concept of understanding.

An idea of this sort forms the basis of our cognitive orientation when the vast phenomenon presents perceptual cues of the kind just described. *Our curiosity is engaged.* We want the imagination to satisfy our rational idea of the object's phenomenal *parte-extra-parte* totality by providing an imaginative representation which will fill out the idea by presenting all the parts of the phenomenon individually considered.

The very failure of imagination to do this makes the extraordinary scope of human reason vivid at the sensory level. Through rational ideas we know the phenomenal character of things in more than mere recognitional terms. At the very outset we know that this vast phenomenal whole is composed of many, many parts. But this 'maximum' of knowledge cannot be matched by imagination and sensible being in terms of apprehension and comprehension of all the individual parts. In this way, the mathematical sublime centres on a felt rational transcendence of the limitations of embodiment. Thought encompasses in an instant what our sensible being cannot.

A few possible objections must now be considered. First, I have criticized Kant's main baroque approach on the grounds that it involves an unlikely superfluity of 'mental movements'. But, could not the same be said about the austere approach, which I have just developed. The answer is 'no'. The experience of the sublime which I have described centres on straightforward dialectic of appraisal based on sensible phenomena, wherein a positive factor exceeds and benefits from a negative one. This does not involve a mental movement from pain to pleasure; rather the feeling of the sublime—like many other feelings in life—is simply psychologically complex. In contrast to the baroque approach, it explains the feeling on a philosophically economical and sufficient basis.

A second objection is that the austere interpretation centres on the scope of reason being made vivid to the senses. Does this not—as the baroque thesis does—involve a determinate, and thence contra-aesthetic, conceptual content?

Again, the answer is 'no'. In this respect, we must recall the pure aesthetic judgement. Our pleasure in it arises from a felt enhancement of the interaction of imagination and understanding. But, we do not find it pleasurable *because* we recognize it as having this significance.

Similar considerations hold in relation to the feeling of the mathematical sublime. The scope of rational thought—as a transcendence
of the limits of sensibility—is made vivid through its relation to the
limits of imagination; but this transcendence is something which is felt
intuitively. In Kant's baroque articulation, the ground of our pleasure is
a recognition that the inadequacy of imagination in relation to reason
serves the purposes of higher ends, which are a 'law' for us. This kind
of awareness is not at all intuitive and bound up with intrinsic features
of the relation between cognitive capacities per se: it is something
much more definite, and centres on a 'higher-level' understanding of
philosophical matters.

This being said, it is true that whilst the judgement of beauty does
not presuppose the mediation of any definite concept in order to be
found beautiful, the mathematical sublime does require a sense of the
phenomenon as being a perceptually overwhelming totality. However,
we do not judge the configuration in relation to this concept per se;
rather, the concept functions intuitively as the mediating factor which
enables rational thought to transcend the limits of sensibility by means of
the vast phenomenon. On these terms, the judgement of mathematical
sublimity is not absolutely disinterested, but it is so in at least *relative*
terms—in so far as our pleasure in it arises from the interplay of
cognitive powers and not from a recognition of the phenomenon's
general theoretical or practical interest for us.

This relatively disinterested character is symptomatic of the austere
approach's restoration of the *aesthetic* character of judgements of the
mathematically sublime. In this approach, the feeling of the sublime
is tied to the direct perceptual experience of phenomena, in so far
as the scope of reason is made vivid to the senses at the level of the
phenomenal world itself. It has the singular character of a pure aesthetic
judgement.

Indeed, the perceptual cues which I described earlier mean that the
mathematical sublime has further common ground with judgements of
beauty. For, as we saw in previous chapters, whilst one can describe
forms as beautiful, the question of whether or not they are, in fact,
beautiful can only be decided through direct perceptual acquaintance
with them. This is also true of the mathematical sublime. The perceptual
cues which I outlined earlier might be used to describe a phenomenon
as sublime; the question of whether or not the perceptual cues *succeed* in
having this effect can only be decided if we have had direct perceptual
experience of the phenomenon in question.

One final issue needs to be clarified. I have argued that the idea of infinity need not be brought into the experience of the mathematical sublime. However, whilst it need not be brought in of necessity, it can, nevertheless, play nevertheless a significant *contingent* role. This does not involve the baroque idea of it being used as a 'measure', but rather the much less extravagant fact that when the imagination is overwhelmed by the vastness of a phenomenal totality the plethora of parts may well *suggest* the idea of infinite continuation. Infinity may, in other words, *sometimes* play an important role in enhancing rational thought's felt transcendence of the limits of sensibility, even if this role is not logically presupposed.

I turn now to Kant's treatment of the dynamical sublime.

PART 4

In contrast with his theory of the mathematical sublime, Kant's account of the dynamical mode is relatively straightforward. This mode is based upon *might* which has the power to overcome us, and which, in consequence, we have grounds to be fearful of. Now, whilst some phenomenon may be genuinely fearful in these terms, there are occasions when our relation to it takes on an aesthetic character. In such contexts our pleasure does not arise through the diminution of our fear. Rather, it is of a distinctively aesthetic kind. Kant observes that

the boundless ocean set into range, a lofty waterfall on a mighty river, etc., make our capacity to resist into an insignificant trifle in comparison with their power. But the sight of them only becomes all the more attractive the more fearful it is, as long as we find ourselves in safety[14]

Again, whilst we must be in a secure position in order to enjoy the dynamical sublime, it is not the sense of security involved in this which is the ground of our aesthetic pleasure. The factors involved are more complex. Kant sets them out, at length, as follows.

the irresistibility of its power certainly makes us, considered as natural beings, recognize our physical power less, but at the same time it reveals a capacity for judging ourselves as independent of it and superiority over nature on which is grounded a self-preservation of quite another kind ... it calls forth our power (which is not part of nature) to regard those things about which we are

[14] Kant, *Critique of Judgment*, §28, p. 144 (Pluhar, 120; Meredith, 110–11).

concerned (goods, health and life) as trivial, and hence to regard its power . . . as not the sort of dominion over ourselves and our authority to which we would have to bow if it came down to our highest principles and their affirmation or abandonment. Thus nature is here called sublime merely because it raises the imagination to the point of presenting those cases in which the mind can make palpable to itself the sublimity of its own vocation even over nature.[15]

Kant's key point, then, is that when a fearful phenomenon is encountered from a position of safety it can provoke insights beyond such things as our possessive needs, or physical survival. We become aware of the dignity of our moral self. This involves the imagining of situations where our moral resolve in the face of dangerous natural forces is put to the test, successfully.

There is a famous passage from Pascal which encapsulates perfectly the insights which are at issue in Kant's account. It reads

Man is only a reed, the weakest thing in nature, but he is a thinking reed . . . if the universe were to crush him, man would be nobler than his destroyer, because he knows that he dies, and also the advantage that the universe has over him; but the universe knows nothing of this.[16]

In Kant's account, the fearfulness of the natural phenomenon provokes moral awareness and courage of this kind. Such a response is not far-fetched in itself, since (as we will recall), in his Introduction to the third *Critique*, Kant holds that the only basis on which the universe can be regarded as having purpose is as the ground which sustains human moral decisions and activity. In the dynamical sublime, the idea of this metaphysical superiority of our moral vocation over fearful natural phenomena is exemplified at the level of the senses. More specifically, we recognize that, in so far as this sense of our ultimate vocation is realized in an extreme natural context, then the relation is 'final' in relation to the higher ends of practical reason.

Whilst Kant's theory is quite easy to understand, it is extremely contentious in a number of ways. To pick up an objection used a little earlier (in relation to the supposed necessary role of the infinite in the mathematical sublime), whilst, in *some* people, it may be that the fearful phenomenon leads to those imaginings of moral defiance which Kant describes, in other people, it may well not. Indeed, the present author can confirm that his great propensity to find erupting volcanoes,

[15] Kant, *Critique of Judgment*, §28, 145 (Pluhar, 121; Meredith, 111).
[16] Pascal, *Pensées*, trans. J. Warrington (London: Dent, 1973), 110.

tidal waves, haunted-looking houses, and the like extremely sublime has rarely—if ever—involved the strange fantasies described by Kant.

Considerable problems arise also from the nature of the fantasies themselves. If these have an aesthetic significance this will surely be more an instance of subjective aesthetic ideas rather than a judgement of the sublime. But, even this may be conceding too much. For, unless they are embodied in an artwork, it is difficult to describe such ideas as anything other than *morally significant notions* whose emotional power happens to be strongly accentuated by the context in which they are experienced.

Indeed, if the dynamical sublime is to amount to anything more than this, it must involve some kind of relation of subjective finality. Kant holds that this is indeed the case in so far as the imagination's production of the relevant fantasies in the face of such phenomena is 'final' in relation to the higher ends of reason.

This, however, is *not* subjective finality. The occurrence of such moral defiance logically presupposes the involvement of concepts concerning the nature and implications of morality. It involves the positing of scenarios where we understand and are moved by the philosophical grounds of our higher vocation. We imagine ourselves facing the fearsome phenomena on the basis of the correct kind of moral motivation. Even though we may not be making a moral judgement per se, our judgement centres on the concept of moral ends.

All this is in *complete contrast* to the pure aesthetic judgement. In beauty and my austere interpretation of the mathematical sublime, subjective finality is *an achieved effect* of specific interactions between cognitive capacities. Our pleasures in these interactions can be wholly *intuitive*. They can be felt irrespective of whether or not we know the specific cognitive grounds which make them possible. In the case of Kant's account of the dynamical sublime, matters are entirely different. Here, the judgement hinges on both the positing of a morally significant scenario and the recognition that this serves the ends of our higher vocation. It is a pleasure in the *good*, broadly considered.

Clearly Kant is aware of these difficulties, even going so far as to raise the possibility that 'this principle seems far-fetched and subtle, hence excessive for an aesthetic judgement'.[17] However, rather than grappling with this problem in terms of the logic of pure aesthetic judgement, Kant drifts off into an entirely irrelevant set of bizarre empirical observations

---

[17] Kant, *Critique of Judgment*, §28, p. 146 (Pluhar, 121; Meredith, 112).

concerning how the kind of sentiments expressed in judgements of the dynamical sublime are ones admired even amongst savages.

In view of these difficulties I would propose a further austere interpretation which restores the aesthetic status of the dynamical sublime by reinterpreting it on lines analogous to my treatment of the mathematical mode. The key term here is *power* rather than fearfulness. On these terms, for example, we can recognize that many phenomena have the power to destroy us—even a single car or motorbike. An earthquake or a collapsing building has such power amplified many times over.

Now, in the case of the car, its destructive power is something whose potential consequences we can imagine and understand without difficulty. In fact, we rarely even trouble ourselves to think about them—except in bare terms, when crossing roads, and the like. But, in the case of the earthquakes, tidal waves, collapsing buildings, and the like, their power is such that it does evoke a sense of destructive potential whose consequences exceed what can be imagined.

The fascination, then, is in trying to imagine the totality of such consequences. We know that powerful phenomena have the power to destroy all the things in their path; we have, in other words, a *rational idea* of the immensity involved. But, imagination cannot present these consequences in a whole of intuition. What reason knows, and propels us to imagine, simply cannot be imagined in complete terms. This very inadequacy, accordingly, at the same time makes the scope of rational comprehension vivid at the sensory level. We have a genuine, *aesthetic* judgement of the dynamical sublime.

This model can also apply to smaller-scale phenomena. Suppose, for example, that we are fascinated by a haunted-looking house or a sinister-looking glade of trees. The 'look' of such phenomena suggests a destructive potential. This potential is not of a quantitatively vast kind, but it has a qualitative character *suggestive* of a destructive unknown force, entity, or entities dwelling beyond what we can perceive. Here, we may try to imagine what these factors may amount to, but their unknown (or uncanny) character means that we cannot imagine them with any certainty or completeness. Rationally, we posit the idea of a determinate power to destroy contained within the threatening phenomenon, but the exact character of this power and the scope of its potential effects, exceed, qualitatively, what can be presented in imaginatively determinate terms. (In this respect, think of the film, *The Blair Witch Project*, where the witch's destructive power is suggested, but never actually shown 'in action' and where the witch herself is never even seen.)

A contrast must be made, of course, between things which are merely frightening and those whose fearfulness is sublime. In the former case, the fearsome character grips us to the exclusion of anything else. The threat is taken to be *real*. But, in the case of the sublime, our rational comprehension centres on the mere *appearance* of fearful phenomena encountered from a position of security. Here, our power of rational comprehension is to the fore, and is rejuvenated through being tested by appearance.

I am arguing, in effect, that just as the mathematical sublime involves perceptual cues which make us regard it as sublime rather than merely overwhelming, similar broad considerations hold in relation to the dynamical mode. In order to be distinguished from the threatening and destructive per se, there must be something about such phenomena which evokes the scale of their potential destructiveness, or which—as the threatening *unknown*—makes the concealment of destructiveness into something which is found unusually threatening in its own right.

In terms of such evocations, the same perceptual cues described in relation to the mathematical mode are relevant here. These are insistent repetition of parts, insistent irregularity or asymmetry of parts, animation, exaggerated size, and suggestive concealment. Such factors emphasize our sense of something's destructive power in so far as whilst as properties of a vast spatial object they emphasize its overwhelming size, as properties of a dynamic phenomenon or force they connote a general *dissolution* into parts, the breakage or fracturing of forms, the destruction unleashed when power is manifestly in motion, the excess power of the gargantuan, and the horrors of the absolutely unknown. Perceptual factors such as these make the mighty phenomenon into something whose destructive power engages us imaginatively as well as in terms of simply recognition of it *as* mighty and fearful.

This austere interpretation departs radically from Kant's own treatment of the dynamical sublime.[18] However, it is highly consistent with

---

[18] This approach has not recommended itself to Prof. Allison. In the context of the dynamical sublime he suggests that 'The purely aesthetic nature of the feeling of the sublime, in contrast to the practically grounded nature of moral feeling, is either downplayed or neglected by critics, who tend to deny the aesthetic nature of judgments of the sublime' (*Kant's Theory of Taste*, 398). I am cited as one such critic. This is a *gross* distortion. In *The Kantian Sublime*, I take the greatest pains to clarify the aesthetic credentials of both the dynamical and mathematical modes. Indeed, my whole enterprise there—and even more so here—is geared towards establishing this aesthetic basis in a *viable* form. The key to Allison's confusion in relation to both Kant and me is found in his notion of the 'aesthetic'. For Kant, such a judgement is one whose 'determining ground' is constituted by feeling. Now, Allison

my reading of his theory of the mathematical mode, and thus yields a highly unified theory of the sublime, which is viable, also, in more general philosophical terms. It has a particular strength in being able to encompass a full range of destructive phenomena, without invoking those unlikely and entirely contingent imaginings which Kant emphasizes.[19] Even better, it makes the sublime per se into a genuinely aesthetic judgement—that is, one based on a pleasure arising from a specific interaction of cognitive capacities achieved through the perception of especially powerful and potentially destructive phenomena.

There is one final key question which must be answered in relation to the sublime in general. I have shown the perceptual cues which lead us to engage with phenomena in terms of the sublime, but have not yet explained why it is that not all phenomena which possess the relevant perceptual cues are actually found sublime.

and indeed Patricia Matthews ('Kant's Sublime', 175–8) attempt to show that the mental movement involved in Kant's notion of the dynamical sublime is different from that which characterizes the specifically moral feeling of respect. According to them, it has, therefore, aesthetic rather than moral significance. But, this conclusion is not justified. For, whilst feeling may be a determining ground of the aesthetic *it is not a sufficient one*. In order to distinguish pure aesthetic judgements from those of the agreeable or good, it is necessary to ground them also on specific idioms of interaction between cognitive faculties—interactions which are subjectively final in some respect. As we have seen, in the case of the dynamical sublime, the relation involved is not one of genuine subjective finality. It may be that moral defiance in confronting nature is the ground of a pain–pleasure feeling which is not the same as the moral law's determination of the will; but it is still, in the main, a morally significant idea which is found moving through being provoked by a fearsome context. This is not a 'pure aesthetic judgement'. And, even if it were argued that it is the relation between the fearsome phenomenon and the imagined moral resistance itself which is pleasurable (rather than the judging of it to be final in relation to our higher vocation), this would get us nowhere. For there would still be no grounds for describing the pleasure as anything more than a pleasing moral fantasy provoked by nature. Since it centres on the positing of explicitly morally motivated response to nature, it operates, accordingly, with the definite concept of an 'end', and thence cannot be aesthetic in Kant's own terms. Allison, however, never considers this decisive objection. His characterization of the dynamical sublime as aesthetic is, accordingly, wholly untenable. In fact, it again shows the great dangers of the 'interminablist' approach. His own discussion of the dynamical sublime centres on a scholarly comparison of it with Burke's theory and then a detailed investigation of some curious comments which Kant makes about the 'sublimity of warfare'. The key issue—namely, the blatantly counter-intuitive explanation offered by Kant himself—is not given the slightest critical scrutiny, and the gross contradictions which this (already unlikely) explanation raises in terms of aesthetic status are likewise overlooked. The irony of this latter point is, of course, that it indicts Allison on the very grounds which he uses—without warrant—to criticize others.

[19] Again, in his third paper on 'Delight in the Natural World' (pp. 242–4), Malcolm Budd offers arguments with strong similarities to my austere approach to the dynamic sublime—seeing, indeed, rather more direct intimations of it in Kant's own text than I do. He also recognizes the oddness of attempting to treat fantasies of moral resistance to overwhelming phenomena as though they were aesthetic judgements.

The answer to this is that the cues are activated when there is something perceptually attractive about the appearance of the phenomenon in question. If beauty involves phenomenal diversity which stimulates multiple possibilities for understanding the unity of the manifold, one might say that the sublime involves a unity which seems to emphasize the multiple diversity of the manifold.

This means that the unity in question (say, the particular character of the mountain range, or the particular appearance of a 'haunted' house) is striking or unusual in a way that draws attention to it, and thus activates the perceptual cues in a way that unexceptional mountain ranges, or mere old houses do not. Such a striking character need not involve explicit recognition. Rather, it emerges because the phenomenon stands out at an intuitive level from our customary experience of such things.

Having expounded and revised Kant's theory of the sublime, I shall now consider its artistic significance.

PART 5

Kant himself 'officially' must disqualify art from judgements of the sublime because, qua artefactual, they involve the concept of a definite end. He uses some examples of art in the context of the sublime, in passing, but mainly for secondary illustrative purposes concerning vast phenomena rather than to establish connections between art and the sublime. However, there are some very important connections which can be made on lines suggested by Kant's approach.

The most obvious one is in terms of artistic genre. Much romantic literature, painting, and music is commonly linked to the notion of the sublime. In painting, especially, John Martin and Caspar David Friedrich are figures who warrant the label. The former offers the most spectacular combinations of the mathematical and dynamical modes. *The Great Day of His Wrath* (1851–3) presents the Apocalypse on a grand visual scale, with mountain-size rocks being flung through the air. Friedrich's works are more restrained. Works such as *Abbey in the Oakwood* (1809–10) present a funeral procession before a ruined edifice, with the action ill-defined against a brooding backdrop of twilight clouds which are low in the sky. The merging of cloud and action and the shadowed edifice suggest the passage of age upon age, and the supreme mystery of that power which sustains life, death, and rebirth across the generations.

Even though, in physical terms, these paintings are not vast physical objects, the way they represent content is characterized, stylistically, on the basis of *perceptual cues* which provoke imaginings of its perceptually overwhelming profusion of individual spatial parts and relations. If an imaginative response of this kind is possible, then so is the rational idea of the overwhelming content's *parte-extra-parte* totality, or of its status as an intelligible force of ultimate totality, which is utterly incomprehensible in sensible terms. Hence, the imaginatively overwhelming and the rational idea of its totality can be presented *virtually* as well as in physical terms. The work can thence be the object of judgements of the sublime.

Similar considerations hold also in relation to some avant-garde Modernist and many postmodern visual artworks. Barnett Newman's canvases, for example, are often linked to the sublime, and the artist himself pushed interpretation in this direction through some of his writings and, indeed, through the titles of his works, as well as by their appearance.

Vir Heroicus Sublimis (1950–1) is a rectangular canvas measuring 242.2 × 541.7 cm. It consists of a largely undifferentiated red field divided at irregular intervals by five dominant vertical stripes, of different colour. The work is meant to be seen close up and the verticals energize the field—rendering it perceptually ambiguous as to whether they are behind the red ground or in front of it, optically speaking, or superimposed upon it physically. In this active relation of verticals and field there is a symbolic sense of individual human presence before an unstable and formless void. Here the relation of vertical and field is the basis of perceptual cues wherein emptiness is thematized so as to connote both endless space and ultimate transcendent power beyond the limits of form.

Similar effects can be found in the work of Mark Rothko and other 'colour-field' painters. The Rothko Chapel at Houston, in particular is a dedicated collection composed of a number of contrastingly articulated colour field works. These focus a deep sense of spirituality through the curious tension between the given spatial reality of the canvas and the instability—almost to the point of optical dissolution—of the colour field. There is an evocation of the overwhelming constancy of becoming, and its simultaneous comprehension through artistic expression.

Features of a 'sublime' kind characterize also a great deal of post-modern art.[20] Erwin Redl's *Matrix* series (begun in 2000) makes use of strings, and, in effect, curtains of small LED lights which are programmed to change colour over a period of hours. The series embodies a basic twofold structure. On the one hand, the individual installations disclose (or amplify) the *interior* physical space of the room in which they are staged by evoking a sense of it being constituted by various layers of atomic structure; on the other hand, they sometimes appear to extend the walls of the room outwards through the use of similar structures, but this time connoting stellar lights.

In all these avant-garde and postmodern works, we are dealing with artefacts containing perceptual cues suggestive of imaginatively overwhelming structures and/or forces, but expressed through works which comprehend and, in a sense, contain these forces.

Now, whilst these may evoke a sense of rational thought's transcendence of the limitations of sensibility *as such*, they can also suggest a more distinctively *artistic* variety of the sublime. For, in all these cases—from Friedrich to Redl—even as we comprehend the representation of unimaginable vastness and/or power, we know that this has been comprehended and expressed *in an artwork*. Those forces which are ultimate and/or destructive in physical terms can be comprehended and, in a sense, contained by the power of creative artifice as well as by that of rational thought.

Kant himself provides an excellent minor literary example of this in the form of that inscription concerning Mother Nature on the Temple of Isis. It states that 'I am all that is, that was, and that will be, and my veil no mortal has removed'.[21]

This simple poetic phrase is imaginatively overwhelming, as one reflects upon the profundity of its content. However, the stunning encapsulation of this in such lucid expression gives cause for wonder at the extraordinary scope of rational artifice. And it is this which surely characterizes, also, *any* work which *in the way it addresses* imaginatively overwhelming ultimates makes the creative scope of human achievement vivid to the senses. The void, the infinite, the unspeakable power beyond

---

[20] I have discussed this at great length in Part 2 of my *Critical Aesthetics and Postmodernism* (Oxford: Clarendon Press, 1993).

[21] Kant, *Critique of Judgment*, §49, p. 194 (Pluhar, 185; Meredith, 179).

all form, can be given expression and comprehended within the limits of the individual artwork. It can focus and clarify such overwhelming totalities in a way that defeats imagination alone. The physical edges of such works circumscribe the ultimate in symbolic terms; or, in the case of the Temple inscription, are brought to comprehension through even so slight a rational creation as a single phrase.

CONCLUSION

In this chapter, then, I have explored Kant's approach to the sublime. This has involved an exposition of the mathematical and dynamical modes, and a sustained critique of his explanations of them. In the course of this critique, I was able to indicate the basis of a more austere and much more viable argument embedded in his baroque, infinity-based account of the mathematical sublime. I was able to extend this also to the dynamical mode, and to develop the approach taken in my Kantian sublime book in much greater detail.

It is hoped, in particular, that my detailed attention to the importance of perceptual cues in activating the sublime, and the distinguishing of sublime phenomena from those which are merely overwhelming or fearful, will offer new tools for extending work in this area.

Finale

Throughout this work, I have tried to offer a sustained alternative to the 'interminablist' orientation in Kant interpretation. My approach is, I hope, one that proves truer to the spirit of Kant's own vocation as a philosopher seeking to solve general philosophical problems. The approach has involved following the logical thread of his arguments and substantive concepts, as far as possible. This has, however, sometimes centred on a willingness to see where Kant's arguments lead rather than a rigid observance to the letter of what he says.

The advantages of this strategy are manifold; not least among them is that it shows that the Kantian aesthetic is not merely one amongst others. It is a philosophy that allows us to solve some of the most fundamental problems in aesthetics, and in a way that does justice to the somewhat neglected *meta-aesthetic* dimension. This dimension concerns the broader experiential grounding of aesthetic phenomena. Kant shows that these phenomena involve not only distinctive forms of pleasure, but ones which are grounded in factors basic to knowledge and the unity of self-consciousness.

However, I also argued at length that the revised epistemological core of Kant's theory needed to be integrated with the notion of a horizon of critical comparison so as to do justice to the evaluative factors embedded in the judgement of taste's claim to universal validity, and fine art's 'originality' and 'exemplariness'. Fortunately, Kant himself was able to point us in the right directions here.

It is worth underlining the importance of all this. All too often, in postmodern times, one hears that patterns of taste in society and on the global scale have lost their critical edge. Everything is tolerated, pluralism is encouraged, and taste really is just 'a matter of taste'. Indeed, in questions of contemporary sensibility, the *mere fact* of differences of taste in terms of the consumption of commodities and cultural and sensible phenomena seems to be all that counts. Issues of quality are determined by personal preference alone. 'Elitism' is something to be avoided at all costs. It is just not politically correct, for example, to say that some forms of positive cultural practice are better than others.

The cultural contradiction involved in this is particularly manifest in art. On the one hand, art continues to exist in all its 'highness'—to be exhibited at specialist galleries, to be sold to a select, moneyed, clientele, and to have its own distinctive critical media. But, at the same time, there is a widespread reluctance to affirm that art is indeed a kind of higher cultural activity with a justified special and specialized status.

This contradiction is to some extent repeated within those bodies of more avant-garde contemporary art practice which make extensive use of materials made by persons other than the artist, including—very often—mundane objects from mass culture. Here the artist seems to compensate for the privileged cultural status of his or her vocation by using banal materials that will hide 'elitism' beneath trendy 'street-cred' content. Even worse, he or she sometimes adopts sensationalist strategies of content and/or presentation that will attract popular as well as specialist media attention, thus gaining markets and mass culture 'celebrity' status.

However, whilst one might run, one cannot hide. The cultural contradiction referred to above consists in the fact that aesthetic preferences concerning beauty, perfection, and the sublime are not—despite prevalent attitudes—of the same order as consumer choices. Whatever cultural rubbish global consumerism may heap upon one's sensibility, there are some forms of pleasure—of an aesthetic kind—which can be shown to engage with and celebrate our basic cognitive relation to the world. They renew it and, in some respects, return us to the origins of cognition itself.

And, whilst the artist may be reduced to using the detritus of mass culture, he or she may be shown to be more than a mere 'celebrity' in so far as the detritus is organized so that—through its style of configuration—the content's trivial meaning is suspended or trans-formed or negated. Some artists may not achieve this. They may offer nothing more than vehicles for expressing vague theories (known only unto friendly critics) or for creating a furore. But, others—even without knowing it—may genuinely extend or innovate in ways that evokes the phenomenal world's taking on of form, and its emer-gence from an atmosphere of imagination (as well as from material presence).

In this context, the Kantian aesthetic presents both a promise and a challenge. The promise is its searching justification of higher cultural phenomena; the challenge is to think this through critically in relation to specific cultural practices so as to preserve and enhance that which is of enduring significance in them.

Bibliography

Allison, Henry, *Kant's Theory of Taste* (Cambridge: Cambridge University Press, 2001).
—— *Kant's Transcendental Idealism: An Interpretation and Defense* (New Haven, Conn. and London: Yale University Press, 2004).
Bourdieu, Pierre, *Distinction: A Social Critique of Taste*, trans. Richard Nice (London: Routledge, 1979).
Budd, Malcolm, 'Delight in the Natural World: Kant on the Aesthetic Appreciation of Nature', *British Journal of Aesthetics*, 38 (1998), 1–18.
—— 'Delight in the Natural World: Kant on the Aesthetic Appreciation of Nature, Part II: Natural Beauty and Morality', *British Journal of Aesthetics*, 38 (1998), 117–26.
—— 'Delight in the Natural World: Kant on the Aesthetic Appreciation of Nature, Part III: The Sublime in Nature', *British Journal of Aesthetics*, 38 (1998), 233–58.
—— 'The Pure Judgment of Taste as a Reflective Judgment', *British Journal of Aesthetics*, 41 (2001), 247–60.
Crawford, Donald, *Kant's Aesthetic Theory* (Madison, Wis.: University of Wisconsin Press, 1974).
Crowther, Paul, 'Kant and Greenberg's Varieties of Aesthetic Formalism', *Journal of Aesthetics and Art Criticism*, 42 (1984), 442–5.
—— 'Fundamental Ontology and Transcendent Beauty: An Approach to Kant's Aesthetics', *Kant-Studien*, 76 (1985), 55–71.
—— *The Kantian Sublime: From Morality to Art* (Oxford, Clarendon Press, 1989)
—— *Art and Embodiment: From Aesthetics to Self-Consciousness* (Oxford: Clarendon Press, 1993).
—— *Critical Aesthetics and Postmodernism* (Oxford: Clarendon Press, 1993).
—— *The Transhistorical Image: Philosophizing Art and its History* (Cambridge: Cambridge University Press, 2002).
—— *Philosophy After Postmodernism: Civilized Values and the Scope of Knowledge* (London: Routledge, 2003).
—— *Defining Art, Creating the Canon: Artistic Value in an Era of Doubt* (Oxford: Clarendon Press, 2007).
Damasio, A. R., *Descartes' Error: Emotion, Reason, and the Human Brain* (New York: Penguin Putnam, 1994).
de Duve, Thierry, *Kant After Duchamp* (Cambridge, Mass. and London: MIT Press, 1996).
Dickie, George, *Art and the Aesthetic* (Ithaca, NY and London: Cornell University Press, 1974).

Elliott, R. K., *Aesthetics, Imagination, and the Unity of Consciousness*, ed. Paul Crowther (Aldershot: Ashgate, 2006).

Evans, Gareth, *The Varieties of Reference* (Oxford: Clarendon Press, 1982).

Foster, Eckart (ed.), *Kant's Transcendental Deductions: The Three Critiques and the Opus Postumum* (Stanford, Calif.: Stanford University Press, 1989).

Fry, Roger, *Vision and Design* (Mineola, Tex. and New York: Dover Publications, 1998).

Gallagher, Shaun, *How Body Shapes the Mind* (Oxford: Clarendon Press, 2006).

Gibbons, Sarah, *Kant's Theory of Imagination: Bridging Gaps in Judgement and Experience* (Oxford: Clarendon Press, 1994).

Ginsborg, Hannah, *The Role of Taste in Kant's Theory of Cognition* (Cambridge, Mass. and London: Harvard University Press, 1990).

Guyer, Paul, *Kant and the Claims of Taste* (Cambridge, Mass. and London: Harvard University Press, 1979).

—— *The Cambridge Companion to Kant* (Cambridge: Cambridge University Press, 1992).

—— 'Kant's Conception of Fine Art', *Journal of Aesthetics and Art Criticism*, 52 (1994), 275–85.

—— 'The Harmony of the Faculties Revisited', in Rebecca Kukla (ed.), *Aesthetics and Cognition in Kant's Critical Philosophy* (Cambridge: Cambridge University Press, 2006).

Henrich, Dieter, 'The Proof-Structure of Kant's Transcendental Deduction', in R. C. S. Walker (ed.), *Kant on Pure Reason* (Oxford: Oxford University Press, 1982), 66–81.

Kant, Immanuel, *Groundwork of the Metaphysics of Morals*, trans. H. Paton (London: Hutchinson & Co., 1955).

—— *The Critique of Pure Reason*, trans. N. Kemp-Smith (London: Macmillan, 1973).

—— *Critique of the Power of Judgment*, trans. James Creed Meredith (New York: Oxford University Press, 1978).

—— *Critique of Judgment*, trans. Werner Pluhar (Hacket and Co.: New York, 1987).

—— *The Critique of Pure Reason*, trans. and ed. Paul Guyer and Allen Wood (Cambridge: Cambridge University Press, 1998).

—— *Critique of the Power of Judgment*, trans. Paul Guyer and Eric Matthews (Cambridge: Cambridge University Press, 2000).

Kemal, Salim, *Kant and Fine Art* (Oxford: Oxford University Press, 1987).

Kitcher, Patricia, *Kant's Transcendental Psychology* (New York: Oxford University Press, 1990).

Kneller, Jane, *Kant and the Power of Imagination* (Cambridge: Cambridge University Press, 2007).

Kukla, Rebecca (ed.), *Aesthetics and Cognition in Kant's Critical Philosophy* (Cambridge: Cambridge University Press, 2006).

Longuenesse, Béatrice, *Kant and the Capacity to Judge* (Princeton, NJ: Princeton University Press, 1998).
—— 'Kant's Leading Thread in the Analytic of the Beautiful', in Rebecca Kukla (ed.), *Aesthetics and Cognition in Kant's Critical Philosophy* (Cambridge: Cambridge University Press, 2006).
Lyotard, Jean-François, *Lessons on the Analytic of the Sublime*, trans. Elizabeth Rottenberg (Stanford, Calif.: Stanford University Press, 1994).
Makkreel, Rudolph, *Imagination and Interpretation in Kant: The Hermeneutic Import of Kant's Critique of Judgment* (Chicago and London: University of Chicago Press, 1990).
Marzona, Daniel, *Conceptual Art* (Cologne: Taschen, 2005).
Matthews, Patricia, 'Kant's Sublime: A Form of Pure Aesthetic Reflective Judgment', *Journal of Aesthetics and Criticism*, 54 (1996), 165–80.
O'Neill, Onora, 'Transcendental Synthesis and Developmental Psychology', *Kant-Studien*, 75 (1984), 149–67.
Pendlebury, Michael, 'Making Sense of Kant's Schematism', *Philosophy and Phenomenological Research*, LV, 4 (1995), 777–97.
—— 'The Role of Imagination in Perception', *South African Journal of Philosophy*, 15 (1996), 133–7.
Scarré, Geoffrey, 'Kant on Free and Dependent Beauty', *British Journal of Aesthetics*, 21 (1981), 351–62.
Schaper, Eva, *Studies in Kant's Aesthetics* (Edinburgh: Edinburgh University Press, 1979).
Sellars, Wilfrid, 'The Role of Imagination in Kant's Theory of Experience', in Henry W. Johnstone (ed.) *Categories: A Colloquium* (University Park, Pa.: Pennsylvania State University Press, 1978).
Slater, A. N., and G. Bremner (ed.), *Infant Development* (Hillsdale, NJ: Erlbaum, 1989).
Stern, Daniel L., *The Interpersonal World of the Infant: A View from Psychoanalysis and Developmental Psychology* (New York: Basic Books, 1985).
Walker, Ralph (ed.), *Kant on Pure Reason* (Oxford: Oxford University Press, 1982).
Wicks, Robert, 'Dependent Beauty as the Appreciation of Teleological Style', *Journal of Aesthetics and Art Criticism*, 55 (1997), 387–400.
Young, J. M., 'Kant's View of Imagination', *Kant-Studien*, 79 (1988), 140–64.
Zuckert, Rachel, *Kant on Beauty and Biology* (Cambridge: Cambridge University Press, 2007).

Index

tracking procedure 19
trans-ostensive (in concept application
and formation) 48–50, 52,
54–55, 59
Turner, J. M. W. 162, 167, 170

understanding 1, 3, 4, 5, 6, 9–10,
13–24, 26, 28, 32, 36–37, 42, 57,
59, 60–88, 92–96, 104, 106, 111,
122, 130, 138, 146, 152–53, 169,
174, 179, 181–84, 186–88, 195
see also imagination and
understanding

voluntary forms of possible
intuitions 74–75, 85

Walker, R. C. S. 11, 12, 35,
203
Wearing, Gillian 168
Wicks, Robert 1, 118, 129, 204

Young, J. M. 22, 204

Zuckert, Rachel 1, 2, 66, 74, 76, 130,
204